MR.
OCTOBER

MR. OCTOBER

The
REGGIE JACKSON STORY

by
MAURY ALLEN

Times
BOOKS

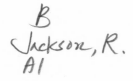

B
Jackson, R.
A1

Published by TIMES BOOKS, a division of
Quadrangle/The New York Times Book Co., Inc.
Three Park Avenue, New York, N.Y. 10016

Published simultaneously in Canada by
Fitzhenry & Whiteside, Ltd., Toronto

Library of Congress Cataloging in Publication Data

Allen, Maury, 1932–
Mr. October

1. Jackson, Reggie. 2. Baseball players—
United States—Biography. 3. New York (City).
Baseball Club (American League) I. Title.
GV865.J32A8   796.357′092′4 [B]   80–5774
ISBN 0–8129–0964–X

Designed by Sam Gantt

MANUFACTURED IN THE UNITED STATES OF AMERICA

FOR JANET, JENNIFER, AND TEDDY
My All-Star Team

IF YOU HEAR A SONG THAT THRILLS YOU,
    SUNG BY ANY CHILD OF SONG,
PRAISE IT. DO NOT LET THE SINGER
    WAIT DESERVED PRAISES LONG.
WHY SHOULD ONE WHO THRILLS YOUR HEART
LACK THE JOY YOU MAY IMPART?

                  —DANIEL WEBSTER HOYT

Acknowledgments

REGGIE JACKSON is an entertainer. His stage is the baseball field. His notices have been many and mixed. This work includes a fair sampling of the raves as well as the rips.

The critics were often past and present teammates of Jackson's—Catfish Hunter, Sal Bando, Joe Rudi, Rollie Fingers, Bill North, Vida Blue, Dave Duncan, Gene Tenace, heroic members all of those irreverent, irascible Oakland A's—and managers Bob Kennedy, Chuck Tanner, Dick Williams, and Hank Bauer. My thanks to all of them, as well as to manager Earl Weaver and teammates Jim Palmer and Ken Singleton in Baltimore for a look at Reggie's Baltimore season. To so many of the Yankees, to George Steinbrenner, sometimes wrong, never dull, to Dick Howser, Fran Healy, Bucky Dent, Jim Spencer, Lou Piniella, Paul Blair, Fred Stanley, Mike Torrez, Ken Holtzman, Mickey Rivers, and so many others there is much appreciation. As there is to so many other players, past and present, club officials, baseball executives, and fans who gave of their time that we might better understand this intriguing man.

No work of this kind can ever be attempted without the excellent reportage of daily sports journalists. Gratitude and thanks particularly to Ron Bergman and Herb Michaelson in the West and countless colleagues back East.

Gratefully accepted was the considerable help offered by Jennie Campos and Jovita Campos, without whom an important segment of Reggie's life would have remained unexplored.

This work gained illumination from other works on the subject, including *Reggie* by Reggie Jackson with Bill Libby (Playboy), *Charlie O. and the Angry A's* by Bill Libby (Doubleday), and *Reggie Jackson's Scrapbook* edited by Robert Kraus (Windmill). Also much insight was gained from *The Best Team Money Could Buy* by Steve Jacobson (Atheneum) and *The Yankees* by Dave Anderson, Murray Chass, Robert Creamer, and Harold Rosenthal (Random House).

Much thanks also to editor-in-chief of Times Books Ned Chase, for his confidence in this project; editor Bob Weil, for his constant faith and constructive advice; and agent Julian Bach, who always sees light at the end of the tunnel.

Lastly, so much is owed by this one man to so few, the troops at home. Nice going, gang.

MAURY ALLEN
Dobbs Ferry, New York

Contents

Illustrations follow page 106.

MR.
OCTOBER

The Black Babe Ruth

UPPITY.

That's how so many of his Yankee teammates in 1977 saw Reggie Jackson, a guy who drove to work in a $90,000 Rolls-Royce, a man who flashed $100 bills on the team bus, a black baseball player who openly romanced white women, drank fine white wine, and lived the sophisticated life of a successful white businessman.

"To them," he often said in his most sour moments, "I'm just an uppity nigger."

The strain of that emotional summer had begun to wear thin on his nerves. The tensions caused by the abrasive relationship with manager Billy Martin threatened his sanity. The silent treatment by his teammates, led by Thurman Munson, Graig Nettles, and Sparky Lyle, tore at his insides.

He would often sit alone on the patio of his nineteenth-floor Fifth Avenue apartment, once occupied by broadcaster Barry Gray, nurturing his houseplants, looking out across the deep green foliage of Central Park, aware that his struggles with his manager, his teammates, and his own fierce pride had gone too far, but not knowing how to achieve a peaceful compromise.

"We tried to talk things out," says Fran Healy, a bright, articulate man who was a backup Yankee catcher that summer and is now a Yankee broadcaster. "He had so many things he wanted to say. I don't know if I offered any advice. Mostly I offered an ear."

He had been publicly humiliated that summer in Boston by Martin and privately scorned by his teammates. He walked through the Yankee clubhouse, and players turned away from him, talked to each other past him, laughed often at inside jokes about him. His vanity and arrogance had become a well-known part of the baseball milieu.

When Jackson was with Oakland, a teammate named Darold Knowles, taking full note of Reggie's pomposity, once said, "There isn't enough mustard in all America to cover that hot dog."

The statement galled him and haunted him, following him everywhere he went, as a code word for his insatiable lust for attention. Latin players, boring in on Jackson's Spanish heritage, called him *perro caliente* ("hot dog") to his face.

He would spend quiet summer afternoons alone in his apartment, reading sections of the Bible, talking to friends across the country by telephone, checking with business associates about the latest growth of his properties. On some summer afternoons he would spend much time chatting in Spanish with Carlos, the doorman, in the small vestibule of his building or greeting the kids of apartment residents or sitting in the sun against the wall of the white brick building.

"I would walk by," says Marilyn Barrie, an attractive middle-aged woman separated from her husband, George, of the Fabergé family, "and he would give me the eye. I could only wonder what such a rich and famous baseball player was doing alone in the afternoon of a nice summer day."

"Reggie used to spend a lot of time with kids in hospitals," says Ray Negron, his twenty-two-year-old aide-de-camp, "but the demands were too much. Now I bring some autographed baseballs from him to the hospitals. Reggie's spare time before games is mostly taken up with business."

* * *

Jackson had awakened early on the morning of September 14, 1977. His competitive juices were bubbling. The anguish over his dealings with Martin, with his teammates, with the fans, with the press all had diminished now as his emotional drive toward excellence, spurred on by a pennant race, had come to the fore on the field.

"I love competition," he once said. "It motivates me, stimulates me, excites me. It is almost sexual. I just love to hit that baseball in a big game."

The Yankees were to play Boston that night in the second game of a three-game series. There were no bigger games. Boston versus New York, good versus evil. A rivalry tinged with tradition, bitterness, honest animosity. This was no baseball propaganda. This was the real thing. The Yankees had stolen Babe Ruth away from Boston. Boston had never forgotten. The Yankees had squeezed out pennant after pennant from the Red Sox, the most heartbreaking being the 1949 victory, when the Red Sox came to New York a game ahead with two games to go and Casey Stengel's Yankees won both. Joe DiMaggio was better than Ted Williams. Yankee pinstripes made the Red Sox choke. All New England was embarrassed at the Red Sox failures. Still, they believed, they prayed silently in Sunday church services, they hoped, they dreamed of sticking Yankee faces into Massachusetts mud.

Ron Guidry, a young left-hander from the bayou country of Louisiana, who spoke a patois of Cajun, had defeated Boston, 4–2, the night before. The Yankees led by two and a half games. Jackson was unhappy. He had gone hitless against Boston with three huge strikeouts. The fans had booed him. He had sulked when the game was over.

Yankee owner George Steinbrenner, knowing he needed Jackson in an upbeat mood for the next two big games, invited him out to P. J. Clarke's for a couple of drinks. Steinbrenner had stayed close to Jackson after signing him for nearly $3 million to a five-year Yankee contract. George wanted to be a buffer between Billy and Reggie.

They sat at a back table together as young Madison Avenue types stole peeks at them but left them alone. It was not chic to bother celebs at P. J. Clarke's, especially when one fancied oneself a celeb. The well-dressed young advertising executives were more interested, really, in bedding down the lovely blondes at the bar than in butting into Yankee business anyway.

"Don't let a game like this get you down, Reggie," Steinbrenner said.

"I had good pitches to hit. I let you down. I let the team down," Jackson said.

"You're in a good groove. Tomorrow night you'll win the game for us," Steinbrenner said.

At three-thirty that afternoon of September 14, Carlos called for Reggie's silver and blue Rolls Corniche from the parking garage in the next building. Jackson came out of the elevator, wearing a blue polo shirt, jeans, cowboy boots, and a leather jacket. He stopped to sign a couple of autographs for kids waiting outside his apartment who knew his ritualistic schedule as well as he did.

"Maybe I'll hit one for you," he said to one small black boy as he stepped into his car. He drove north on Third Avenue, past his favorite Manhattan restaurant, Oren & Aretsky's, just for luck, turned onto the East River Drive at Ninety-sixth Street, rolled north on the Major Deegan Expressway, and pulled into the parking lot across from Yankee Stadium. It was a couple of minutes before four o'clock.

Parking lot attendant John Addeo waved to him as he got out of his car. "How you doin', John?" asked Jackson, who always made it a point to learn the names of the people around the ball park. He found it important to maintain these ordinary contacts in light of his arrogant image.

He was in the clubhouse now, stripping off his street clothes, hanging them up carefully. He gave Ray Negron a large roll of bills to secrete in a floor locker, which closed with a key, and then, turning and twisting that magnificent body of his, he put on a jockstrap, a pair of shorts, and a torn undershirt. He walked into the trainer's room.

He hopped onto a long table. Trainer Gene Monahan came over, put his fingers into a jar of Vaseline, and began rubbing and soothing Reggie's heavy legs. He first worked on his legs, then pulled and tugged at his arm, loosened his back muscles, twisted and turned at his neck. Reggie fell asleep on the table for fifteen minutes.

Soon he was at his locker again, lifting up a couple of black bats, thirty-five inches long, thirty-five ounces, swinging them lightly, squeezing the handles tightly, meshing mind and matter around the finely cut instruments of his profession. Fran Healy, already dressed in his uniform, walked over.

"This is my gamer, feels gooood," Reggie said, stretching the word out.

He finished dressing, tucking the uniform shirt, with the large "44" on the back and the bold "NY" across the front pinstripes, deep into his pants. He carried a couple of bats out to batting practice. One bat, the gamer, leaned against his locker. "Made in USA 302 Adirondack Pro Ring," it said near the top of the bat, and "Big Stick Reggie Jackson Personalized Model" at the top.

Now he was at work in the batting cage, rattling one after another of coach Yogi Berra's soft serves over the wall in right, deep into right-center on a huge arch, or one time rattling the small protective screen in front of Berra's face.

"Watch that stuff," said utility infielder Fred Stanley. "Yog's face is his fortune."

Jackson simply grinned. Berra's next serve went into the third deck. Carrying his bat, Jackson walked toward the dugout.

Soon the Red Sox were moving slowly out of their dugout onto the field. Slugger Jim Rice sauntered to the batting cage to watch the Yankee hitters. Jackson moved toward him. Reggie asked to examine Rice's bat. The brooding black outfielder handed the bat to Jackson and said, "Don't take any hits out."

"I wish I was strong enough to swing this," said Jackson.

"It's six forty-five," shouted Boston coach Johnny Pesky.

The Yankees began coming off the field, and the Red Sox moved on. In one hour and fifteen minutes they would meet again out there with a little more intensity.

*   *   *

The game began and proceeded to the ninth inning without a score. Ed Figueroa, a Puerto Rican curve-balling right-hander, had been brilliant all night. A burly pitcher named Reggie Cleveland had shut the Yankees out as well. In the bottom of the ninth inning Thurman Munson walked to the plate.

The Red Sox considered Munson the best hitter on the Yankees. He didn't have Jackson's power, but he could hit good pitches. In a tough spot Cleveland had to make perfect pitches on Munson to get him out. He didn't make a perfect pitch. He threw the Yankee catcher a high fastball, and Munson lined it to center field for a single. The winning run was on.

At once a thunderous chant of "Reggie, Reggie, Reggie" filled the cavernous old park. There were 54,365 people in the building, and they all seemed to be calling Jackson's name.

"Can you bunt?" Billy Martin asked Jackson as he stood on the top step of the dugout.

"Yeah, I can bunt. Do you want me to move him?"

"Let's try it on the first one."

Martin, to his credit, never let his personal animosity toward Reggie carry over into a game. While he would get back at Reggie by not permitting him to play in right field, Martin was compelled by Reggie's awesome batting ability to use him in the designated hitter's spot. He might make fun of him to the press, but once the game started, his managerial instincts dictated his moves. Personality had nothing to do with it.

"I'd play Adolf Hitler if I thought he could help me win," Martin once said.

Martin thought a bunt was the play. He ordered Jackson to bunt. The pitch was high and away, and Jackson bunted it foul. Now he looked down at third base coach Dick Howser. Howser rubbed his shirt, rubbed his sleeves, touched his cap, rubbed his hand, and touched his cap again. The bunt was off. Jackson had Billy's permission to swing for the downs. Jackson gripped his bat tightly.

"Please God," he said quietly, "let me hit one. I'll tell everybody you did it."

The next pitch was low for a ball. Jackson moved out of the box, dropped his bat between his legs, adjusted his glasses, stepped back in, and pumped the bat again. "Reggie, Reg-gie, Reg-gie," flashed the scoreboard. The next pitch was inside, Jackson faked a bunt, pulled back, and the count was 2-1. The next pitch was a curve on the inside part of the plate for a 2-2 count. Then a fastball missed for 3-2.

Cleveland studied catcher Carlton Fisk's sign. He looked over at Munson, who had a long lead, thought about throwing over, decided not to break his rhythm, and fired a low outside fastball toward the plate.

"A perfect pitch," Cleveland would say later. "I don't know how he hit it."

Jackson harnessed all the power in his 208-pound body, exploding the head of the bat, the fat part, at the baseball, catching it flush, driving it on a rising line over the fence in right field for a two-run game-winning homer. He stood at the plate for an instant to admire his handiwork, dropped his bat gracefully, bent his head down, and began sauntering around the bases, his arms pumping slowly, his legs hopping in a proper gait, his eyes filling with tears of emotion. The shattering noise rang through the night air. Cleveland seemed transfixed on the mound long after most of his Boston teammates were jogging for the sanctity of their dugout. It would not be their shame. It would only be Cleveland's.

There were some thirty reporters, some radio men with microphones, and the glaring ever-present television camera around Jackson's locker. He was still on the field, standing in front of the dugout, waving to the crowd, soaking up the adulation he desperately needed. He was an opera star, a veritable prima donna, taking his curtain call to 50,000 bravos.

"I was supposed to hit a ground ball on that pitch," he was telling the press now. "When I hit it out, it was like a fairy tale. It was an exciting feeling. You can feel everybody loving you; you can feel your friends feeling it, the people who are pulling for you feeling it. I had the feeling I was sharing it with everybody, my friends, my family, my business associates."

Reporters scribbled as fast as they could. Phrases danced off Jackson's tongue. No player in baseball could so articulate his emotions, was so willing to share his sensitivities, was so anxious to make a speech after a good game as Reggie Jackson. Among his teammates, except for Healy, there was a consensus. They disliked him. They thought he was arrogant, a phony, aloof show business-type, disdainful of them. Among the working sportswriters there was never a consensus. Some thought he was charming, brilliant, and witty. Some thought he was full of hot air. All admired the way he hit a baseball, handled a postgame interview, and used the language. In a business controlled almost exclusively by white men, Jackson's rich, deep voice, his choice of words, his poise and passion as he talked astounded them. Few of the reporters had heard blacks speak that well.

In some six months as a Yankee, Jackson had received more attention than any athlete, save Muhammad Ali, in his time. Ali wasn't around New York and being written about by New York writers every day. Jackson was. His speech that night was over.

"If bullshit was religion," one reporter said, "he'd be the Pope."

"That was the biggest homer of my life," says Jackson now. "It was the most important, the most dramatic, the one that turned the season, earned me respect. I don't know where I'd be today if I had failed that night."

The Yankees had moved into first place on August 23 after a tumultuous summer. They held it shakily through mid-September. They had moved up by as much as four and a half games. The Boston series began with the Yankees one and a half games ahead. Guidry's victory and Jackson's homer enabling Figueroa to win had given the Yankees a three-and-a-half-game lead with seventeen games to go. The Yankees simply do not lose leads in September. They won the American League East race by two and a half games over Boston and Baltimore.

In 1976 the Yankees had won the pennant on Chris Chambliss's dramatic ninth-inning home run in the final game of the American League championship series. Now they were playing Kansas City again. The two fine teams split the first four games. The American League pennant would be settled on Sunday afternoon, October 9, at the Harry S Truman complex in Kansas City.

George Steinbrenner, Yankee president Gabe Paul, and Billy Martin sat in Steinbrenner's suite at the Crown Center Hotel in Kansas City a half hour before the team bus was to leave for Royals Stadium at the complex.

Martin was tight-lipped, his eyes appearing hollow, his skin seemingly pulled tight on his bony body as he addressed his two baseball superiors.

"I'm not starting Reggie," he told them.

"You're the manager," said Steinbrenner.

"I don't think he can hit this guy," Martin said.

"You're the manager," Steinbrenner said.

A left-hander named Paul Splittorff was starting for
Kansas City. He had compiled a 16-6 record and had been
a difficult pitcher for Jackson to hit.

"The records show Reggie doesn't hit him," Martin explained to the press.

Jackson was deeply wounded. "I know what I can do,"
he said. "If he did, we might be a lot better off."

Reporters, tattletales all, raced to Martin's office to relay
Reggie's reaction. They had baited the hook again. Billy,
compulsive always about the last word, naturally snarled
back. "I'm the manager of this club. I make out the lineup
card," he barked. "If he doesn't like it, he can kiss my dago
ass."

Splittorff remembers his elation at finding out Jackson
wouldn't start.

"I had good luck against him, but my God, he was Reggie Jackson. He could hit it out on anybody," Splittorff
says. "I thought that was an edge for me. You know what
else was important? Billy Martin had told the world Reggie Jackson was afraid of me. Can you imagine what that
did for my ego?"

Steinbrenner and Paul sat together before the game in
the stands behind home plate. When a reporter asked
Steinbrenner what he thought of the benching of Jackson,
he said, "Billy's the manager. See me after the game."

The pennant was on the line. The message was clear.
Billy Martin was gambling his Yankee managerial career
on that move by starting Paul Blair in right field.

Splittorff led by a score of 3–1 into the eighth inning.
When he tired, the Royals' best relief pitcher, Doug Bird,
came in with two on and two out. Martin sent Jackson up
as a pinch hitter. He fought off a high fastball and lined
a single to center. The Yankees closed the lead to 3–2.
Three Yankee runs in the ninth inning gave New York a
5–3 win and the American League pennant.

Jackson sat in his locker, alone, away from the tumult of the pennant celebration. Only Fran Healy and a few reporters came by to talk with him. In that noisy room, a wild scene where champagne was bubbling, adult baseball players were acting like high school kids, and blazing television hot lights were matting tousled hair, Reggie Jackson was an outsider. The man was a solitary island.

In the opening game of the World Series against the Los Angeles Dodgers, Paul Blair, in as a defensive replacement for Jackson, singled in the bottom of the twelfth inning to give the Yankees a 4–3 win.

Catfish Hunter, struggling to maintain his brilliant skills as his career was fading, was crushed in the second game. He had not pitched since September 10 because of a sore shoulder. He allowed three Dodger home runs in less than three innings as the Dodgers evened the 1977 Series at one game apiece. Reporters raced to Jackson for an opinion on the pitching of his former Oakland teammate.

"Billy embarrassed him," Jackson said. "The man never should have been in there."

Before Jackson's quotes could reach the papers, the Yankees flew west to Los Angeles. Martin dined at La Scala in Los Angeles with Dodger manager Tommy Lasorda and a well-known popular singer. Somebody asked Martin the next morning who picked up the tab. "When you go out with Frank," he said, "Frank pays."

Before the game Martin was in his office at Dodger Stadium and Jackson was standing on the grass in front of the Yankee dugout. Groups of reporters surrounded each man. Jackson was repeating his criticism of Billy's use of Hunter. Martin was livid in his own defense.

"I'm the manager of this club," Martin was saying, his voice thin and high, the nerves in his neck twitching, his eyes raging with fire. "If he doesn't like it, he knows what he could do." In his usual hair-trigger fashion, Billy was building up to another confrontation with Jackson.

Most of the other Yankee players couldn't have cared less about the latest Jackson-Martin fuss. They had more

important things on their minds. Thurman Munson, the
team captain, spoke for them. "Look at these seats they
gave us," Munson was saying, waving a dozen tickets for
locations in the upper deck at Dodger Stadium for wives,
family, and friends of the Yankees. "If these seats aren't
exchanged for better locations, I'm going home."

Playing baseball seemed incidental to the Yankees.

After Hunter's loss the Yankees won the next two
games. Jackson, who had homered in the fourth game, hit
another home run his last time up in the fifth game. The
Dodgers won, 10–4.

In the sixth game of the 1977 World Series, despite all
the turmoil and anguish, Reggie Jackson hit three consecutive home runs on three pitches. It was the ultimate
vindication of this torturous summer and one of the most
spectacular feats in modern baseball.

Jackson walked the first time up. Then he hit a long
home run off a high fastball by Burt Hooton. As the crowd
howled and cheered his next appearance, he smashed
Elias Sosa's hard, low fastball deep into the right-field
seats. Two swings, two home runs. Then he was at the
plate again, the fourth time in the game, the crowd conscious that this remarkable man, this marvelous home run
hitter, was on the threshold of an incredible feat. Only
Babe Ruth had ever hit three home runs in one Series
game. Ruth had done it twice. "Everybody knew what I
had to do," Jackson says.

Charlie Hough threw a high knuckle ball. The ball
floated toward the plate. Jackson, as disciplined a hitter as
there is in the game, held his bat back for the precious
instant that the soft pitch floated toward his eyes. Then he
unleashed that majestic swing, the ball racing off his bat,
climbing for the deepest portion of the huge ball park,
racing out for the wall in straightaway center field, and
finally crashing into the bleachers high over the 417 mark.
When the ball cleared the wall, Jackson, his bat at his feet
now, his eyes following the entire flight of the ball, bent
down low and went into a slow jog toward first. His body

tilted slightly toward his left as he moved toward second, the crowd noise growing louder as he circled third toward home. He started walking fifteen feet before home, jumped on the plate with both feet, and walked the rest of the way toward the dugout. Then he held up three fingers, caught by the television cameras, to his mother, watching in Baltimore. The noise would not cease for well over a minute. He came out and waved his cap, went back into the dugout, and listened to the surge of sound again. He came out a second time, waved, and finally disappeared into the corner of the Yankee dugout under a massive outpouring of respect, if not affection, for this enormous triumph.

Some three years later the memory remained sweet. Jackson's eyes were alive as he recalled the heady evening of October 18, 1977, at Yankee Stadium.

"I never related to it as three in one game. I related to it as five in one Series," he says now. "Four straight homers, five in a Series. Impossible to repeat."

Elias Sosa pitches for Montreal now, and he has the memory of the Jackson World Series home run embedded deep in his psyche.

"A very strong man," he says. "A great long-ball hitter. I made my best pitch. I cannot be ashamed. This was not lucky. This was Reggie Jackson. He has done this thing to everybody."

The home run off Sosa is the one that Jackson admires most. Hooten hung a high pitch. Hough threw a soft knuckle ball. "Room service," kids Jackson. But Sosa threw a hard fastball, low, at Jackson's knees, on the outside part of the plate, a ground ball pitch for most humans.

"I could see the mustard on it coming to the plate," Jackson says. "It should have been by me, but I did all the mental and mechanical things correctly. I overwhelmed that baseball by the sheer force of my will."

He had held up one finger, then two, and finally three as he came toward the dugout after each home run, greeting his mother on television as his effervescent father sat proudly in the twelfth row of the stadium and smiled.

It had been fifteen years since the New York Yankees had won the World Series. As Steinbrenner and Gabe Paul and New York City Mayor Abraham Beame and singer Robert Merrill and Steinbrenner's pal Cary Grant were pulled into the raucous clubhouse celebration, Jackson let his guard down. Some players came over to him now, and some reporters, who had thought his act was more talk than show, listened patiently for his winning speech.

"After everything we have gone through here . . ."

His voice trailed off. He carried an opened bottle of champagne into the manager's office. In front of a dozen reporters Billy Martin stood up to greet him. He leaned over to shake Jackson's hand, and soon the two men were bear-hugging. "You did a hell of a job, big guy," Martin said.

They slugged from the same bottle of champagne. They posed for pictures. They patted each other on the back. All the anger, the animosity, the pain, the jealousy seemed to run out of both their bodies.

On the streets of New York, car horns were being honked loudly, kids were dancing, water bags were being flung from second-story fire escapes, and old women leaned on the edges of their windowsills to share in the joy. Nowhere in the city was there more noise and joy and music than on the corner of 125th Street and Seventh Avenue, the main intersection of the city's black ghetto in Harlem. Small children held up baseball cards and newspaper photos and glossy pictures of Reggie Jackson.

"Why not?" asks black Harlem Congressman Charles Rangel. "Who else do these kids have for heroes, Sammy Davis, Jr.? Of course they love Reggie. He's the black Babe Ruth."

Father and Son

MARTINEZ JACKSON, SON OF A WHITE SPANISH mother and a black American father, a Merchantville, New Jersey, policeman, whose roots were in slave beginnings in Virginia, was born June 6, 1910, at the Merchantville General Hospital.

"I remember walking the beat with my father," says Reggie Jackson's father, Martínez, a husky, light-skinned, and mustachioed self-employed businessman in Center City, Philadelphia. There is a small sign above his store at 1623 Ramstead Street reading "Jack the Tailor," and underneath that line is another, "Reggie Jackson's Daddy."

The author visited the elder Mr. Jackson on a summer afternoon in 1980. Resurreción Jackson, Martínez's second wife, was busy at a small table sewing clothes. The pile of dirty clothes awaiting the afternoon pickup was on the floor. Martínez Jackson, Jr., the five-year-old son of Martínez and Resurreción ("We call her Cion," says Mr. Jackson), holds a Little League bat in his hand and waves it at a visitor. "I'm a baseball player," says the youngster.

Cion Jackson was born in the Philippines, taught school, came to the United States some twenty years ago, and married Reggie Jackson's father seven years ago. He taught her the tailoring trade, and today she is an industrious woman in her late forties. Reggie's half brother is their only child.

"We'd have more," says Mr. Jackson, "but who would make them for me?"

He laughed heartily at his small joke about his advancing years and turned to a pile of scrapbooks he keeps on his large desk against the back wall of the store. He showed pictures of Reggie as a youngster and asked Junior to pose. "This boy is much bigger than Reggie at the same age," he says. "He'll be a good player."

Martínez Jackson as a boy spoke his mother's Spanish and his father's English at home. He was a strong, witty youngster, never really bothered by his race, passing for white if it mattered, sliding easily between the two cultures he inherited.

He attended Bordentown Manual Training and Industrial School in Bordentown, New Jersey, learned the tailoring trade there, went on to all-black Hampton Institute in Virginia for two years, and came back to New Jersey in 1930.

He held assorted jobs in Merchantville, working as a grocery deliveryman, a shoeshine boy, and an apprentice to a tailor. There were other things he liked more. He was a dashingly handsome fellow, not unlike his son, and was a dead ringer for black singer Cab Calloway. He had a glib manner and could bed down almost any young lady he set his mind on. He was a constant gambler and lived by his wits. As the Depression deepened and Franklin D. Roosevelt was elected President of the United States in 1932, he turned to bootlegging and gambling as a full-time vocation. Every once in a while the police would crack down, and he would wind up in prison for short stays. But he would soon be freed by black lawyers who worked the jails as both legal representatives of the minority class and bail bondsmen.

Martínez Jackson began to see that there was no future for him in gambling, bootlegging, or philandering. He had been a good baseball player in school and soon heard that the Newark Eagles, the highly respected Negro league baseball team, were looking for recruits to fill out barnstorming squads made up of their stars.

In 1933 Martínez Jackson, a quick, lithe, tough second baseman, joined the Eagles. He played professional baseball for five years.

"Seven dollars a game," he says. "That's what I got. When Reggie signed for three million dollars, I had to remind him of that, seven dollars a game."

He played with and against all the great stars of the Negro leagues—Josh Gibson, Cool Papa Bell, Satchel Paige, Judy Johnson, all of them—and he held his own.

"I was young," he says. "I didn't mind the life."

He was the team driver, as the youngest man always was, and he drove with six or seven of his teammates through the South, watching out always for rednecks with shotguns, who used the black players as target practice for sport. The players ate cold sandwiches pushed out the back windows of diners, slept in black flophouses, where whores offered bed and board in exchange for anticipated gate receipts from the games. Moving on and playing another game made up the pattern. He played in thirty or more states, in Cuba, in Venezuela, in the Dominican Republic, and in Mexico, earning little money, having much fun, reading every day of the doings in the faraway romantic big leagues.

Judy Johnson, a Hall of Famer from that era, remembers Jackson well.

"Sure he was a good player, or else he wouldn't have been on those teams. You don't think we took guys with us just to fix the cars, did ya? Now what are you gonna pay for this interview? You guys were the same then, and you guys are the same now. You want things, but you ain't willing to pay good money for it," Johnson says.

The Negro leagues peaked in the 1920s and early 1930s. But they soon began losing out because of lack of facilities, the move toward integration of the big leagues, the coming of the Second World War, and the chance to make more money in other businesses. With the signing of Jackie Robinson by the Brooklyn Dodgers in 1945, the death knell for Negro league baseball had sounded.

Martínez Jackson had left baseball years before and had moved back to the Philadelphia area shortly before World War II. He lived in Germantown, bought a small tailor shop, married Reggie's mother, Clara, a light-skinned black woman, and began rearing a family. Six successful children rose from the marriage. Reggie's oldest brother, Joseph, is a career Air Force officer. His next oldest, James, is a graduate of Harvard Law School and practices law in California. There is an older sister, Dolores, a housewife in Baltimore, and two younger sisters, Martina, an airline stewardess, and Beverly, who works in her husband's furniture store in Baltimore. Reggie's five brothers and sisters have produced twelve grandchildren for Martínez Jackson.

Magazine covers of Reggie's baseball feats and James's law school awards and citations receive equal prominence in Martínez Jackson's tailor shop.

In 1940, with three kids, a small house in Wyncote, and growing responsibilities, as well as increased harassment from the law brought on by gambling charges, Martínez Jackson joined the Army Air Corps. He was thirty years old. He figured he could make more money in the Air Corps than in the tailor shop.

"I entered the service as a private, and I came out as a lieutenant," he says proudly. "I flew P-51s with the Ninety-ninth Bomber Squadron and participated in the invasion of North Africa."

After being injured during a mission over North Africa, he returned home to his wife and children. He bought a two-story wooden house at 149 Greenwood Avenue in

Wyncote for $9,000, moved his family there, and soon opened a tailor and clothes cleaning shop in the attic of the old building.

Shortly after the war, on May 18, 1946, a fourth child, a son, was delivered to Clara Jackson at Abington Memorial Hospital. The doctor's name was Reginald Peterson.

"My wife decided she liked the name, so we named the baby Reginald after the doctor and Martínez after my mother," Mr. Jackson said.

The world of 1946 into which Reggie was born was troubled. The exhilaration of the war's end had begun to wear off, and the United States faced the sobering task of restoring political order and economic stability to a destroyed world. On the home front President Harry Truman was pitted against a staunchly conservative Congress and was forced to confront an economy which showed signs of staggering inflation. Life was never easy at the Jackson house, where Martínez and Clara struggled to feed four young children and stall off the numerous bill collectors.

Reginald Martínez Jackson weighed eight pounds nine ounces at birth, was slightly darker-skinned than either of his parents, had large, deep-set brown eyes, large hands, and a cherubic, round face.

"He wasn't a real big boy as a child," says Mr. Jackson. "But he liked to play ball early. I remember that. I taught him how to be a presser in the shop when he was a little kid, but he wasn't there often. He was out playing ball, running to this game or that."

Despite a bad war injury, the elder Jackson was still capable of playing ball. He and young Reggie would go out on Sundays and throw a baseball around in the woods and clearings near the home.

"We all called him Skipper, you know, from being the skipper on a plane in the war," says Donald Feinstein, owner of a grocery near the Jackson home in Wyncote. "We'd see them together with a ball and glove, Skipper and son, always together."

All was not, however, content within the family. Martínez Jackson still liked to gamble, still liked to stay out
late, still liked to drink and chase women as his family
grew. One day Clara Jackson had had enough. She moved
out with three of the small children, leaving Reggie and
his two older brothers with Skipper. They were divorced
a couple of years later, and Mrs. Jackson resettled in Baltimore.

"My father never talked about her, and I never saw her
as a small kid," says Reggie. "That hurt me a great deal.
It took a long time before I understood the whole scene.
I was a grown man before I forgot it. Now she lives in
Baltimore, we see each other every time I'm there, and
we get along fine."

Rearing three sons with him and paying support for his
wife and three more children, Martínez Jackson hustled
a buck wherever he could. He delivered dry cleaning. He
did sewing in the attic of the house. He laundered shirts.
He hustled, hustled, hustled to keep his family together.

"I practically raised myself from the time I was seven
or eight," says Reggie. "I never ate breakfast. There
wasn't anything to eat. I took some leftovers for lunch. I
played ball after school. Then, when my dad got home
eight, nine, ten o'clock at night, we all cooked and
cleaned up together."

The deep wounds from this life without a mother contributed to some of Reggie's early anger as a youngster.
With his father also gone most of the time, he was mature
beyond his years, self-reliant, extremely proud and independent. The separation—which Reggie considered a
personal desertion—made him suspicious of women,
sometimes fearful, always alert for another wounding
blow.

Wyncote, which dates back to 1682, is a small subdivi-
sion of Cheltenham Township outside Philadelphia. It was
a fashionable rural area of Philadelphia through the late
1880s. One of its more distinguished citizens at that time
was Cyrus H. K. Curtis, founder of the Curtis publishing

empire. Young Alexander Graham Bell, the Scots-born inventor, attempted to get Philadelphia bankers interested in his newfangled telephone in 1875, but even though they thought it might be an interesting scientific phenomenon, a history of the area reports, the bankers decided Bell's invention was "of no practical or commercial value." Bell, disappointed but not discouraged, moved to Boston, where more visionary men backed his invention.

Made up mostly of members of the Episcopal Church, the Presbyterian Church, and some Quakers, Wyncote's religious community began changing shortly before the First World War. German Jewish families began moving in. Soon there was in the town a synagogue, a Jewish social community, and an active summer community of Philadelphia Jewish industrialists. By World War II the village became more than fifty percent Jewish, and it is now nearly sixty percent Jewish, one of the more predominantly Jewish suburbs around Philadelphia.

"Most of the kids I grew up with were white and Jewish," says Jackson. "That was my background. Those were the kids I knew."

"He's got a Jewish *kup,*" says Mr. Jackson, using the Yiddish word for good sense.

Both on and off the field, Jackson has been an aggressive businessman and hard bargainer. Many of his commercial endorsements have been made with Jewish businessmen. He is comfortable around Jewish businessmen, well liked by them, often throwing around Yiddish phrases he heard as a kid in Wyncote.

Reginald Martínez Jackson entered the Wyncote Elementary School in 1952. The assistant principal then— later the principal and now retired—was a woman named Mary Ellen Rockefeller, a tenth-generation American Rockefeller and a relative several times removed of the John D. Rockefeller oil, banking, and political family.

"I remember Reggie from Wyncote Elementary," recalls Mrs. Rockefeller. "He was one of those youngsters

with a lot of ability. He used it only when he wanted to.
He had to have the urge. He had a nice, sweet personality.
You have to remember he didn't have a lot of motivation
at home. His father was in jail when he was in my school.
That affected him some. Sometimes I felt Reggie was like
a caged animal. He was a tiger who wanted to get out. I
also remember he was very verbal at the time for a youngster of his age."

Mrs. Rockefeller has kept in touch with her then-fledg-
ling academic star. She was a surprise guest on the *Mike
Douglas Show* when Jackson was on as a guest, and she
has visited and talked with him at the stadium a couple of
times since he became a Yankee.

"He was a very good athlete. That's the memory that
has stayed with me all through the years. The best in
school. One time the boys were playing with a round ball
in the school grounds. One of the boys kicked it up a tree.
The teacher came over and asked if there was any way to
get the ball down. It was too high for a ladder. I asked the
youngsters if they had any ideas. 'Sure,' one boy said, 'get
Reggie here. He'll get it down.' I summoned Reggie out
of class. He came over, took a look, got another ball the
same size, threw it up once at the ball in the tree, and
knocked it down. All the children applauded him and
went, 'Wooo, Reggie, wooo.' I think he liked that attention."

When he was fourteen, Reggie entered Thomas Williams Junior High School in Wyncote. There his athletic
ability began showing itself.

"We had competitive teams at the school and played
other schools," says Robert Trimble, who taught physical
education there and later taught and coached at Cheltenham Township High.

"Reggie was a great natural athlete. He was good at
every game he tried," says Trimble.

His grades at Thomas Williams were average, but he
was a noted athlete and a noted talker. He was the kind
of kid who was immediately singled out of a crowd.

"You couldn't help noticing him," says Trimble. "A good athlete, a good talker, a pretty good student. I coached the teams there, and I had a little bit of trouble disciplining him. He always liked to have his say. He wouldn't take things as they were given. He questioned everything. He had an opinion. One thing about Reggie, if he had something to say, he said it. What was on his lung was on his tongue."

Reggie's peers had similar impressions of the high school star. A classmate of Reggie's at Thomas Williams, George Beck, who works for U-Haul in Philadelphia, began running with Reggie and a couple of other kids during his junior high years.

"Reggie was cocky, like his father," says Beck. "He didn't take any guff from anybody. He knew he was good, and he knew even in junior high he was an exceptional athlete."

Like most of Jackson's school friends, George Beck is white and thought nothing of bringing this black young man home to his house in the early 1960s.

"We were on the football team together. Reggie was a back, and I was a guard. I guess the only time we ever talked about race was when he said Willie Mays was his favorite player. Then I sort of realized he liked him because he was a black hero. Mine was always some white player from the Phillies."

Beck and Jackson delivered papers together throughout Wyncote, but it wasn't a very successful enterprise. "We would get all these papers piled up on the corner all set to go. Then somebody would pull out a ball, and we'd start having a catch. Then a bunch of other kids would come over, and all of a sudden we'd have a game going," says Beck. "Those papers never would get delivered, and those people who wanted them would holler to the company."

Beck, another friend, Irving Stevens, and Reggie would hang out after school at the Jack Frost ice cream stand in Edgehill or down by Kenyon's diner, eyeing the girls, talking sports, dreaming about their futures. It was a fairly typical teenage world, not unlike that of *American Graffiti, Bye Bye Birdie,* and Elvis Presley movies.

"Reggie always knew he'd be an athlete. The rest of us never had any idea. Reggie knew, he just knew," says Beck. "I admired him for that."

Beck says Jackson never was embarrassed about being black in a white society. He had white pals, dated white Jewish girls (to the consternation of some of their parents), and was an important man about town.

"Skip always had money. He gave Reggie dough. One year Reggie drove to high school in a 1955 Chevy. Skip had bought him a car. I think he was the first kid in our gang to have a car."

Beck, Stevens, and Jackson soon began breaking down that car and rebuilding it.

"Reggie made that thing into a hot rod. It could fly, I mean, really fly," Beck says. "And Reggie could take the whole thing apart and put it together blindfolded."

Jackson's love of cars has never faded. At last count he had four cars in New York, another two in California, and a half dozen antiques he drives for fun, and he is the owner of two car dealerships in Arizona and California.

"I love cars," says Reggie. "I love the sound of them, the speed of them, and the beauty of them. Fine cars, fine wine, and fine women."

Beck, Stevens, and Jackson continued as classmates at Cheltenham High and remained in touch through the years. Reggie, however, considers only his business associates and baseball mates true friends.

"Reggie's a pretty busy fellow these days, but we still get together once in a while when he comes into town. I'm not surprised by anything he's done. He could always make it in anything he tried. As an athlete he's the best. As a friend he's very loyal," says Beck. "I'll tell you, he hasn't changed much through the years. If you are his pal, he'll give you the shirt off his back. But if you cross him, watch out. He knows how to be mean if he has to."

Cheltenham Township High School, a sprawling, attractive suburban school serving several Philadelphia bedroom communities, including Wyncote and Glenside, was built in 1959. There are some 1,750 students at the school. Reggie Jackson entered the school in 1960.

"It's an upper-middle-class school," says Joseph Guarneri, the acting principal, who was the assistant principal when Jackson was there. "Most of our students were children of professional people. Our minority enrollment is small, maybe five percent."

Under the influence of strong athletic coaches—Robert Trimble, football coach John Kracsun, basketball coach Ed Delator, football assistant and baseball coach Chuck Mehelich—Jackson received and willingly accepted discipline. With his father working hard to keep the family together, Jackson turned more and more to his coaches for inspirational male role models.

"He had a pleasant personality, but when he was riled up," says Guarneri, "he could shoot from the hip."

When a classmate mistakenly stole his lunch one day, Jackson leaned the frightened boy up against the blackboard and threatened to smash his face.

"Man, don't do that. Why do you want to do that?" the boy said.

"Because I'm crazy," Jackson told the boy. It was Reggie's way of creating fear, the intimidation factor, a psychological war he has fought and won many times in his professional career. This time it resulted in a three-day suspension.

"They were really easy on me in school because they wanted me for the sports teams, and I was good at sports," Reggie says.

Cheltenham Township High—like most high schools in America—would hardly admit to a double standard. But athletes are the chosen people. They receive and expect privileges. They become important personalities in school. They are undoubtedly spoiled. They are heroes to their classmates. They win attention, prizes, and girls. A varsity letter is still more significant to adolescent success than the grade of A on any exam. Jackson excelled in baseball, basketball, football, and track.

"We knew he had the potential to be a successful professional athlete," says Robert Trimble. "All he had to do was keep his head together."

"When I had him in freshman football," says Ed Delator, "he was accident-prone. He didn't care if there was a wall in front of him, he just kept going."

Jackson was a star running back on Cheltenham's football team in his junior year of 1963. The team was preparing for its big game against Abington Township High on the Saturday before Thanksgiving. On Friday afternoon the news spread through the halls of the school that President John F. Kennedy had been assassinated in Dallas.

"Of course, everyone remembers that day vividly," says Guarneri. "I remember the game the following Thursday on Thanksgiving for another reason. We had moved the Saturday game to Thanksgiving, and early in the game Reggie was severely injured. He twisted his leg and had to be carried off the field. We rushed him to Abington Hospital. I tried to reach his father on the phone to get him to the hospital. I couldn't reach him. I had to sign the papers allowing the doctors to perform the necessary work on Reggie. He was very brave. He just looked up at me and asked, 'Will I be able to play again?' I assured him he would."

"Football was very important to me," says Reggie. "It was a way out, a way to an education, an opening to better things."

He was more of a football player than a baseball player in high school. He was a high scoring guard on the basketball team, an important track man, but football was his favorite sport. He enjoyed the physical contact of the game.

"He was as tough a kid, as determined a kid as I ever saw," says Ed Delator. "He wanted to get better. We had a baseball game against Abington coming up. We finished practice, and Reggie stayed to take extra batting practice. I threw some to him and then he asked one of his teammates, a left-hander named Gene Waldman, to throw to him. He wanted more work against tight left-handed pitching."

It was nearing seven o'clock and the sun was setting behind the school buildings as Jackson swung against Waldman's pitches.

"Throw it high and inside, real tight, move me back," Jackson said to Waldman.

The left-hander kicked and threw a high, tight fastball that flew toward Jackson's head. Reggie lost sight of the baseball, hardly moved away, and the ball crashed into the lower part of his face.

"I ran up to him at the plate. Blood was rushing from his mouth. His eyes were aglaze," says Delator. "I picked him up and carried him to my car. We rushed him down to Abington Hospital. He had a severely broken jaw. They wired him up and said he probably couldn't play the rest of the season. He missed three practice days and one game before he pulled the wire out of his mouth. He wanted to play so badly."

When he was a junior, college recruiters began appearing. The University of Alabama and the University of Georgia made inquiries, each willing to integrate its football team for this flashy Philadelphia suburban product. In his senior year, as his baseball skills improved, professional baseball scouts began showing up. A constant visitor in the spring of 1964 was Hans Lobert, a veteran scout for the San Francisco Giants.

"A lot of us thought Reggie would sign with the Giants. He liked Willie Mays, and when Lobert came around, we all thought that was the team Reggie would go with," says Trimble.

Jackson was interested in a college education. He didn't feel he was ready to play professional baseball. He was a much better football player than a baseball player. Professional football was his goal, and he needed a good college program that would help him toward that end.

His football coach, John Kracsun, had been friendly in western Pennsylvania with another local coach named Frank Kush. One day he put a call into Kush, who was now the head football coach in a growing program at Arizona State University at Tempe.

"Frank, I think I got a kid you might be interested in," Kracsun said.

"I'll be in the East next week on a scouting trip. What's his name?"

"Jackson," said Kracsun. "Reggie Jackson. I gotta tell you a couple of things about him first. He is a hell of a football player, but he also likes baseball."

"I think we can work something out on that with our baseball coach, Bobby Winkles," said Kush.

"One other thing. He's a black kid."

"Can he play?"

"He can play."

"We won't have any trouble with that," Kush said.

If a black kid could play, most coaches in the middle 1960s were able to overcome whatever prejudice they or their institutions may have had. Blacks could be recruited. A white southern basketball coach, reflecting on the prejudices of an earlier period, was once asked how many blacks played on his team. "Two at home, three on the road," he said, "and five if we are behind."

Talent was the equalizer. Frank Kush offered Reggie Jackson a full football scholarship within NCAA rules and the promise of a chance to play baseball if he kept his grades up. Jackson signed a letter of intent at Arizona State.

On June 20, 1964, Reginald Martínez Jackson was graduated from Cheltenham Township High School, a young man clearly knowing the direction his life was taking. In the 1964 Cheltenham High School yearbook, *The Panther*, next to a smiling picture of Jackson, it was written, "Football Holden Award winner and co-captain, future All

America, basketball and baseball star, hopes for professional sports career. Hobby, cars." And underneath his
biography, in large letters, was written Reggie Jackson's
motto: "SOVEREIGN INDEPENDENCE."

3

Big Man on Campus

ARIZONA STATE UNIVERSITY HAS BEEN KNOWN FOR years as a top baseball school. Its honor roll includes Rick Monday, Sal Bando, Duffy Dyer, Lenny Randle, Craig Swan, Alan Bannister, Ken Landreaux, Gary Gentry, Bob Horner, Floyd Bannister, and Reginald Martínez Jackson. These young men stepped off the campus of Arizona State into almost instant major-league stardom.

In the fall of 1964 Reggie Jackson, wooed and won by Frank Kush, went to Arizona State. He wanted to be a professional football player. Arizona State could help you do that, too.

Frank Kush is in private business in Tempe now, a manufacturer's representative, after his twenty-two-year coaching career at ASU ended in 1979 under a cloud. He was accused of striking punter Kevin Rutledge after he had shanked a kick and of covering up the incident.

"Reggie was one of the toughest athletes physically and

mentally I ever had," Kush says. "He was very strong, very durable, a leader in every way. He could have played tight end on any professional team. We used him as a defensive back. That's where we needed him most. He was our regular strong safety in his sophomore season."

Jackson had clearly expressed to Kush his desire to play baseball as well as football at ASU. After his freshman football season was finished, Kush talked to Bobby Winkles. Winkles said he would look at the youngster from Cheltenham.

Winkles, who now coaches for the Chicago White Sox, started at Arizona State in 1959. "Reggie got permission in 1965 to skip spring football from coach Kush and work out with the freshman baseball team," he says. "He was very aggressive as a baseball player, very strong, a fine young man."

Winkles's posted rules included: "WE DON'T ARGUE WITH UMPIRES, WE RUN EVERY BALL OUT UNTIL THEY PUT US OUT, WE RUN ON AND OFF THE FIELD."

"We also made sure all our young men spoke the English language properly to the coaches and their school instructors. Our players said, 'Yes, sir,' and 'No, sir,' and they attended all their classes. Reggie once missed an ROTC class when he said he was ill. I told him if he was too ill for ROTC, he was too ill for baseball practice," says Winkles.

Winkles and Jackson stayed close through the years, a warm, dignified, scholarly baseball man and a dedicated, intelligent, driven baseball player.

"Reggie was always mature beyond his years. I remember when I was fired as the California manager. The first call I got was from Reggie. He reminded me that life had peaks and valleys. This was one of the valleys. 'Go home,' he said, 'and stay with your family. They still love you.' Imagine a kid counseling me like that."

Jackson's varsity football career at ASU began in the fall of 1965. Winkles's baseball team had won the championship, and interest in the school was high. Early in fall practice Kush switched Jackson to the starting cornerback position, a spot for hitters.

"I liked football, I liked contact," says Reggie, "but I realized when I was switched football wasn't for me. I wanted the offense, the glamour position. I was a glamour guy. I didn't want defense."

By the spring of 1966 Jackson had become more serious about baseball. He began practicing harder and longer. He began catching the eyes of scouts who crowded the front-row seats of ASU's Packard Stadium.

"Rick Monday had set all the home run and strikeout records here in 1965," says Dick "Moon" Mullins, the sports information director. "Reggie broke them all in 1966."

More than his huge home runs, his dramatic strikeouts, his ferocious swing, and his wonderful running speed, Reggie's personality and character were most remembered by his ASU teammates and friends.

"I go back to 1965 with Reggie," says Rick Monday, now a Dodger outfielder, "but I guess I don't go far enough back to remember when he was shy."

Monday, the first player ever drafted in baseball's free agent draft in 1965, initially spotted Jackson on the football field at ASU after a baseball practice.

"We used to work out in the fall and then go over and watch football practice," says Monday. "We wanted to see Curly Culp knock somebody down. This big kid comes to me and says, 'Hi, I'm Reggie Jackson. You'll be hearing a lot about me.' "

Monday was the starting center fielder with the A's when Jackson joined the club. "I was in center, Joe Rudi was in left, and Reggie was in right. I used to wave him in and out and remind him not to let balls go over his head. A month later he was waving at me not to let balls go over my head. Reggie never lacked confidence," says Monday.

Monday said that Jackson always handled pressure well. That was what he most admired about him.

"Pressure is the test of a human being," says Monday. "When the houselights go on, Reggie is at his best."

Some fifteen years after he first met Reggie Jackson on the football field at Arizona State University, Monday was asked if he liked Reggie. He paused for several seconds. Then he spoke very slowly.

"Reggie Jackson is at least three different people," says Monday. "One of them I have always liked and admired and respected very much. The other two I can't stand. The trouble with being with Reggie is you never know which one of him you get."

* * *

Arizona State University lost Sal Bando and Rick Monday off their team in the 1966 season. No fewer than seven regulars on the 1966 squad, including Jackson and Duffy Dyer, signed pro contracts. The best pitcher was Gary Gentry, later to sign with the New York Mets and star in the 1969 Mets world championship season.

"What helped Reggie a lot," says Gentry, now in the real estate business in Tempe, "is having Winkles as a coach. I remember Reggie standing up taking bows at the basketball games and being noticed all around campus. There had been a couple of black players before Reggie, but he was the first one to be noticed. All that changed on the field. Only Winkles was noticed. He was gung ho teaching kids, and he did it his way, no nonsense. Nobody was independent; everybody was on time for practice, Reggie Jackson, Gary Gentry, or Babe Ruth, always on time."

Gentry says that Jackson was raw as a player at ASU, unschooled, strong but undisciplined as a hitter.

"I had played baseball every day of my life. Reggie was basically a football player when he came there. The first time I faced him as a freshman he was no hitter. I threw nothing but sliders at him and struck him out three times."

And now?

"Now," says Gentry, "I would throw everything in the dirt."

More and more, scouts began watching Jackson crash those long home runs, raw as he was, through the spring of 1966. The New York Mets had the first draft pick and sent scout Nelson Burbrink to watch him. The Kansas City A's had the second pick, and owner Charles O. Finley was a constant visitor. The draft was scheduled for June 12, 1966.

In New York's Plaza Hotel, the city's most elegant home away from home for the wealthy and the famous, the second baseball free agent draft was being held in 1966. Bob Scheffing, director of player development, Joe Mc-Donald, administrative assistant, and Harold Weissman, publicity director of the team, represented New York. The Mets had the nation's first pick. Charles O. Finley, owner of the Kansas City A's, represented his club.

McDonald walked to the microphone and said, "The New York Mets draft negotiating rights to catcher Steve Chilcott."

A huge smile came to Finley's face. He quickly walked to the microphone and said, "I take Reggie Jackson."

Finley got the man he wanted, the big slugger from Arizona State. The Mets were happy with Chilcott. Who knew what Reggie Jackson would become?

"We wanted a catcher," says McDonald. "Casey Stengel had scouted Chilcott in high school. He said he was the best young catcher he had seen in years. We needed a catcher."

At the 1969 All-Star Game, after he had become a star, Jackson said, "Scouts told me the Mets didn't draft me because they heard I had a white girlfriend. I believe that."

There may be some truth to support Jackson's bitterness. The Mets have never had an admirable record regarding blacks. They have no blacks in significant front-office posts. They have never had a black manager or a black coach. They have usually had less than the unwritten quota of blacks on the team, hardly ever more than four or five in any of their first fifteen years.

"There was absolutely nothing to Jackson's charge," says McDonald. "We simply drafted the first player we thought could help us."

The Mets chose an eighteen-year-old high school catcher, while the A's, picking second, grabbed a twenty-year-old college sophomore who was setting home run records at ASU. Racism or a simple mistake in judgment? Chilcott came up with a sore shoulder and never played in the big leagues.

"We expected Chilcott to be our regular catcher for ten or fifteen years," says McDonald. "Remember we had some good young pitchers [Tom Seaver, Jerry Koosman, Nolan Ryan] coming along. We thought a catcher would be most important for us. As soon as we got one, Jerry Grote, we started winning."

Fifteen years later it would be nearly impossible to evaluate honestly the motivation of the Mets in their selection of Chilcott over Jackson. Certain facts are irrefutable.

Racism is built into the fabric of baseball.

There are no black owners of baseball teams; no black general managers; one black manager, Seattle's new man, Maury Wills; no blacks, except for the occasional showpiece ex-player (Hank Aaron, the vice-president at Atlanta with somewhat nominal duties is the best example), in positions of executive authority.

"Off the field, " says Bobby Bonds, a friend of Jackson's from his Giant training days at Phoenix while Reggie was in school and working out at nearby Tempe, "nothing has changed since Jackie's days."

Jackie Robinson came to the Dodgers as the first black player in 1947. It took Frank Robinson, no relation, twenty-eight additional years to come to the Cleveland Indians as the first black manager in 1975. He lasted two and a half years. Larry Doby served as the Chicago White Sox manager for less than half a year. Wills took over at Seattle on August 5, 1980. In the National League, where

Jackie Robinson started and where blacks have dominated play for more than two decades, there has never been a black manager.

"There will only be more black managers," says Jackson, "when there are black owners."

Baseball owners are, for the most part, wealthy white industrialists over the age of fifty who have made fortunes in outside business and buy ball clubs for fun and ego. Men such as Gussie Busch, the beer baron in St. Louis, George Steinbrenner, the shipping magnate in New York with the Yankees, Nelson Doubleday, the publishing giant who owns the majority share of the New York Mets, and William Wrigley, son of the founder of the Wrigley gum fortune, are typical. They are middle-aged men who generally relate to blacks as they did during an era in their youth. Most can deal with blacks as ballplayers because they are, after all, only ballplayers who are owned by the owners themselves. Yet when Curt Flood fought baseball's free agent system and declared himself "a ninety-thousand-dollar-a-year slave," he found himself being scoffed at.

It would be impossible for such men to conceive of the indignities—despite huge salaries—they have heaped on black players by ignoring them for front-office jobs after retirement, by demeaning them in private conversations with their associates, by ridiculing many of them with the tired clichés of shiftlessness, laziness, stupidity.

"The media are white; the fans are mostly white," says Bonds. "They see black players the same way. When Pete Rose leaves Cincinnati to become a four-million-dollar free agent and slides on his face for Philadelphia when the play is at another base, he is described as colorful. When Reggie leaves his club and signs with the Yankees for three million and watches a home run at home plate, he is called a hot dog. That's racism; that's clear evidence of two standards, two sets of rules, two separate and unequal ways of judging men."

This antagonism, felt by most black players but articulated by few for fear of reprisals in subtle ways, still exists a quarter of a century after Jackie Robinson's arrival in Brooklyn.

"I remember when I was a small kid," says a black Mets scout named Ed Charles, who starred on their 1969 team and was released in 1970 without a spring training chance to make the club again, "and Jackie came through my hometown of Daytona Beach, Florida. The Dodgers played an exhibition, and all of us came out to see him, little kids, old folks, blind people being led to the park by a friend's hand, and old people being wheeled up the ramps. When the game was over, a bunch of kids followed Jackie down the street and walked with him to the railroad station. Then he got on that train, and we ran down the tracks after it, and when it was gone, we put our head on the tracks to listen to the fading sounds of that train, to hold a piece of Jackie with us as long as we could." Most white baseball team owners could hardly begin to understand this emotion.

It was Robinson, ailing with diabetes and going blind, a frail shell of his once-athletic build, standing on the field at the World Series game in Cincinnati in 1972, about two weeks before his death, who said, "I will not be happy until I see a black face on the field managing a big-league club." There was embarrassed silence from the crowd and stillness from the gathered baseball executives, who had expected to honor Jackie for stealing bases, not for abusing them on their racial standards.

Thirty-four years after Jackie first played for the Dodgers, few teams have more than a handful of black players. Even the game's great stars worry about their future when they can't hit the ball any longer.

"We've talked about my postplaying future," says Willie Stargell, the marvelous Pirate slugger, a bright, articulate, and thoughtful man. "I have an understanding I can stay here the rest of my life. Doing what? I don't know. That hasn't been spelled out."

Nobody has promised Stargell he will manage the Pirates or be groomed as the general manager or be asked to organize a group of wealthy men to buy the Pirates from the Galbreath family.

It is certainly true that not all white stars will wind up with jobs. Babe Ruth died a bitter man because baseball refused to give him a manager's or general manager's job after he could no longer hit home runs. But Stan Musial became an instant vice-president of the Cardinals, Ted Williams managed the Washington Senators, and Willie Mays was kicked out of baseball when he took a job with the operators of a gambling resort in Atlantic City. Mays had been an occasional batting coach for the Mets.

The racism of the 1980s is not quite of the same vitriolic tone as that of the 1940s. Manager Ben Chapman of the Phillies called Jackie a "nigger" so often it became tiresome. He threw a black cat on the field near him and described it as a relative. The St. Louis Cardinals organized a boycott against Robinson which was quickly squashed by Commissioner Ford Frick. One of the leaders was Enos "Country" Slaughter, then a fiery racist from Foxboro, North Carolina, who paid for his action, it is widely believed by sportswriters, by being denied a place in Baseball's Hall of Fame by sportswriters who remembered.

Still, in 1981, observers in big-league clubhouses can hear white players describing opposing black players to teammates in a derogatory fashion. Black players on most teams still sit together in small groups apart from their white teammates. White players rarely go to dinner with black teammates, spend much off-the-field time with them, or double-date.

"How can you double-date with them?" asks one white player. "They are always looking for a good-looking blonde to screw, and so are we."

So it was in 1966 that consciously or subconsciously the New York Mets chose the handsome white eighteen-year-old catcher Steve Chilcott, a pro baseball nobody as it turned out, over Reggie Jackson, bright, black, and opinionated, a certain Hall of Famer.

* * *

Shortly after he had been selected as the second draft choice in the country but before he had signed anything, Reggie Jackson was sitting in room 311 of Sahuaro Hall on the campus of Arizona State University.

A soft-spoken, well-dressed blond young man knocked on Jackson's dormitory door.

"I'm Gary Walker," he told Jackson. "I'd like to talk to you about insurance."

"Not interested," said Jackson. "I'm too busy."

"This won't take long. It will change your life," Walker said.

There was something in his manner, his quiet aggressiveness, his determination that caught Jackson's fancy. He told the insurance salesman to sit down.

"I came for five minutes, and I stayed an hour and a half," says Walker. "When I walked out of that room, I knew I would be a friend of Reggie Jackson's for the rest of our lives."

"He is my best friend," Jackson says of Walker. "He is there when I need him."

Walker, typical of most of Jackson's friends, is a deeply sensitive man. He is intelligent, low-key, unpretentious, easy to be around. His gentle demeanor seems to mesh well with Jackson's flamboyance. People like Walker, Fran Healy of the Yankees, teammates Brian Doyle and Tommy John, and many other business associates bring out the gentle, introspective side of this complex man. On the baseball field Jackson is all flash and fire. Off the field he is often soft and soothing and is most comfortable in his associations with men and women of a similar nature.

All his women friends seem to be of a generally sedate nature, content to wait for his game-high enthusiasms to change into postgame calm. He usually shuns actresses,

models, show business types. "I hate actresses," he says
bluntly. "They bore me."

Walker had graduated from Arizona State University.
He had gone into the insurance business in Tempe. He
had done well, if unspectacularly, and sensed that selling
life insurance policies would not be his life. He had followed Jackson's career in the local papers and read of the
draft selections. He knew a college kid needed help in
many areas in dealing with the powerful baseball industrialists.

"We sat and talked that day of life and love, of philosophy and psychology, of all of the aspects of human behav-
ior," says Walker. "I could immediately see Reggie's cha-
risma, dynamics, his incredible mind. It was a beautiful
experience."

There was something that kept coming through from
Reggie to Walker, some sense of himself, some significant
thread that colored all his conversation.

"Reggie had a sense of destiny," says Walker. "Even
then, even as a college kid, he saw something special in
his future; he knew the directions his life would turn."

Walker convinced Reggie he could handle a policy for
$1.5 million as soon as he signed with the A's. He also
convinced him their lives would be interwoven from that
day on. Today they are partners in United Development,
a land investment company in Tempe worth maybe $20
million with some sixty employes in the busy selling season.

"We deal in raw land," says Walker. "Reggie has a desk
here in the off-season and goes out with buyers. We get
the raw land and sell it to developers for residential, commercial, and industrial properties."

Jackson spends less time in Tempe than he did in the
early years of his career. His outside business interests—
commercials, television appearances, film schedules—
keep him moving from late October until late February.

"He comes out here to breathe. We talk religion and
history and philosophy," Walker says. "Sometimes, when

he is down, we just get in a car and drive up to a stream, go out for a walk, stop in a roadside cabin for a cup of coffee. We enjoy talking business. Reggie must transcend the image of an athlete."

Walker has been consulted on every business move Jackson has made, sat in on the negotiations with owners when Jackson was shopping for a club after free agency, advised him on where to put his money, soothed his battered soul during the interminable Billy Martin-George Steinbrenner battles, and cheered his triumphs. It has been a deep, serious, lasting friendship between two very dedicated, motivated, intelligent men, one white and one black. Jackson's name has helped the land business prosper. The relationship has also given Gary a status in the community he could not have otherwise gained. These two men like and respect each other and enjoy each other's company. "My family always thinks Gary is ripping me off because he is white," says Reggie. "Some things are hard to explain."

How deep is the relationship, how meaningful, how lasting?

"I have one son," says Walker. "He is two years old. His name is Reggie Jackson Walker."

The time had come for Jackson, the college sophomore who saw himself as a person with a chosen destiny, to make his decision. Jackson entertained thoughts of finishing school and waiting until his senior year to accept a professional contract. Reggie hardly understood the powers of a man named Charles O. Finley.

"We're a lot alike," says Jackson of his first boss. "We are both good businessmen."

Tough, abrasive, and independent, Finley fought with his players over salary and conditions, with league officials over changes he demanded, with the press, the public, and his Oakland Coliseum landlords. The A's dominated baseball in the early 1970s, winning three straight World Series championships in three years, the only team outside the 1936–1939 Yankees and the 1949–1953 Yankees to set that record. Finley's contributions were enormous: night World Series games; night All-Star games; colored uniforms; mustaches (the A's started wearing mustaches and beards for a Finley promotion); the designated hitter. He also embittered many of his own players, all of whom waited for a chance to break away.

On a contract technicality, in an instance when Finley forgot to make an insurance payment owed him, Catfish Hunter was declared a free agent. The Yankees signed him for $3,750,000 over five years. During the next season, with free agency for all veteran players finally a reality, Finley began losing players in trades, releases, and the reentry draft. The A's finished last in the American League West in 1979. Finley attempted to move the club to Denver. When that deal fell through because the Oakland Coliseum Commission would not allow the A's out of their lease, Finley retrenched and started again.

He hired bombastic Billy Martin as his manager, and the A's were building again toward another championship. Finley was to sell his club in 1980, but his impact on baseball would linger for years.

This was the dynamic figure who entered Reggie Jackson's life in June 1966.

"He chased me; he romanced me; he finally wore me down," Jackson says.

Finley flew Reggie and his father to his La Porte, Indiana, farm. He put on a magnificent show, spreading steaks on a long barbecue table, bringing corn from his own fields, serving Reggie and Mr. Jackson while wearing an apron. And he talked at all times about the A's, about the future of his team, and about how rich and famous he would make Reggie Jackson.

"I wondered," says Jackson, "if he would ever get around to talking money."

Finley started his bargaining at $50,000. Jackson started at $100,000, the figure he knew Finley had paid for Rick Monday.

"Let's not argue," Finley said. "I'll give you eighty-five

thousand dollars, and you'll be with the A's next year."

For ten seasons, through much success and much hell, Reggie Jackson and Charles O. Finley shared joys and triumphs. They battled publicly and privately, grew exceedingly close and then extremely far apart. The constant was Finley's begrudging admiration for Jackson's talent, temperament, and intelligence.

Jackson respected Finley's business acumen, admired his innovative methods, and appreciated his boss's good life-style.

"He was a man with a tremendous sense of humor," says Jackson, "but he was also a man who forced me always to be on guard."

The relationship would end with Jackson's being summarily dismissed in Oakland, sent to Baltimore because he refused to sign a new contract, dispatched with hardly a note of thanks.

"Charlie Finley brought us all together," says Sal Bando, the captain of those marvelous A's in the early 1970s, "and Charlie Finley broke us all apart. He's the Humpty-Dumpty of baseball."

Reggie Jackson met with two of Finley's assistants, Hank Peters and Ed Lopat, the former Yankee pitcher. He was brought to Kansas City to sign his contract formally.

"You're going to be a great one kid," Lopat said. "Don't let us down, and don't let yourself down."

"Tell Charlie not to worry," Jackson said. "He hasn't made a mistake. Reggie Jackson will make him proud."

In private Jackson, a bright, articulate, glib college kid, was brimming with confidence. In public it was a little different.

"I remember the signing press conference at the old ball park in Kansas City," says *Kansas City Star* sports editor Joe McGuff. "It wasn't as much a fuss as the one for Rick Monday. Monday had been the first in the nation, first ever. When Reggie got to be big, I kept thinking back to that day. He seemed so wary of all us, his first exposure

to the big-league press. He was quiet really, a little shy.
But he seemed to stare down at everybody before answer-
ing anything. You could see the wheels in his head turning. Wary. That's the only word I can use to describe it."

After the signing in Kansas City, Jackson was supposed
to fly to Spokane, Washington, and drive on to Lewiston,
Idaho. His professional baseball career would begin in
Lewiston with Finley's Lewiston A's. He had to make one
stop before he entered pro ball. He went back to Tempe
to see a woman.

Her name was Juanita Campos. She would soon be Jennie Jackson.

The One and Only
Mrs. Reggie Jackson

I T IS AS IF ONE COULD LOOK UP ON THE SHARP, STARK red-tinted rock above Highway 60 east of Phoenix and see the Indians in full battle dress perched on the cliffs. The sun is high in the early morning of a late summer day in 1980, the temperature climbing to 108, and the road is empty except for an occasional small truck passing in the opposite direction toward Arizona's largest city. There are huge puffs of white clouds in the sky above, figures and shapes clearly seen in one man's eye, a map of the United States here, a familiar face there, patterns emerging from the distant skies.

The road winds and twists, climbing upward to five thousand feet above sea level, as the highway stretches some ninety miles from Phoenix to a small copper-mining town called Miami.

Across the highway, past the copper mines, opposite the hills white with copper waste, lies a small blue stucco home protected by a small metal fence. Juanita Campos, once Mrs. Reggie Jackson, is home on vacation from her teaching job in Japan, a gracious woman who is not used to giving interviews.

"Why would you want to talk to me?" she asked when we first talked by telephone. "It's been so long ago. I don't know anything about Reggie's life now."

* * *

Juanita Campos, who has called herself Jennie since her high school years at Miami High, is darkly attractive. Her hair is worn in tight curls; her eyes are a rich brown; her nose is small and slightly upturned. As we talk, she is without shoes and wears no makeup. Her voice is warm, with a slight Spanish lilt from her Mexican-American background, when she introduces her mother, Jovita, a registered nurse and a slightly older, heavier version of the dark-haired beauty who is her daughter. "And this is Natsuki," she says of the Japanese child who giggles at the introduction to the stranger. Natsuki Ito is ten, her father is a wealthy cement jobber in Nagoya, and Jennie is warmed by her cheery presence. Jennie, her mother, and Natsuki have come to Arizona only a few days earlier after a demanding vacation trip through the Far East. Jennie has traveled alone through Japan, Vietnam, Cambodia, Thailand, and Nepal on other journeys in her pursuit of information as she concentrates on Asian studies. She is on leave from the University of Honolulu, where she is at work on her master's degree, while teaching in the international school in Nagoya. She has no children of her own but has always felt comfortable around them.

"My degree," she says, "will be involved with the study of Asian children, children as failures, children who are not bright, do not do well in school, are not beautiful, are not select. I want to understand them, to help them, to improve them."

Juanita Campos was born in Miami on April 30, 1946. Both her parents were born in Arizona, her father, José, a husky, handsome man of Mexican heritage, and her mother, Jovita, a pretty woman also of Mexican parents. Both families arrived in Arizona from Guadalajara shortly after Arizona was admitted to the Union in 1912. Mrs. Campos's mother, who is ninety-five years old and remembers the Indians roaming free through the nearby reservations, lives alone next door in a neat stucco home.

"She understands a few words of English," says Mrs. Campos. "She liked Reggie a lot. He spoke Spanish. She didn't know from baseball; he was just a nice boy who spoke Spanish."

José Campos worked in the copper mines. He had only a grade-school education, but he was sharp and worked hard. Still, he couldn't become a foreman, advance in his job, allow his abilities to take him higher on the economic scale. He was a Mexican. "The Anglos ran things," says Mrs. Campos.

One of the ways they ran things was by keeping Mexicans out of important jobs. They were discriminated against in jobs, in housing, in social arrangements. "There were separate drinking fountains in town, separate bathrooms, segregated seating in the movies," says Jennie Campos. "I have always been influenced by my Mexican culture. I have always felt this pull inside me. I have also felt the discrimination."

In 1940 José Campos left the copper mines and joined the Army Air Corps. He returned from the service in 1945, married Jovita, his hometown sweeheart, and they soon settled down with their only child, Juanita. In 1947, feeling restless on the job, unable to advance, angered at the conditions in the mine, José spoke to his local priest.

"Father, will I ever have a future here?"

"That is only for God to say," the priest said.

"I feel I may have a better future in the service," he said.

"That might be the correct decision," he said.

José Campos joined the Air Force, served at nearby Williams Air Force Base for two years, and then was shipped to Japan in 1949. Jovita and Juanita, a cherubic three-year-old, soon followed. They lived a comfortable military life, José becoming an accomplished bombardier on B-29s, Jovita and Juanita enjoying the companionship of other Air Force families.

On June 25, 1950, North Korean troops poured across the thirty-eighth parallel. President Harry S Truman ordered American troops into combat under UN auspices. On June 27, 1950, American bombers from Japan took off for the first foray against enemy installations north of the parallel. The antiaircraft fire was heavy with many planes going down. José Campos was killed when his B-29 exploded and crashed into the rugged mountains of North Korea, not unlike the jagged hills near his home in Miami, Arizona. He was first reported missing in action. It was three months before Jovita Campos was notified that her husband was dead. She soon flew home with her four-year-old daughter.

Like Reggie Jackson, Jennie grew up without one parent. "I remember when I first started school," says Jennie, "and the teacher would begin asking the children to tell something about ourselves. My palms would break into a sweat, and my body would shake. All the other children would tell what their fathers did for a living, mostly worked in the mines, and that their mothers stayed home and cooked. Then I would be called on, and I never knew what to say, and I would blurt out, 'My father is dead,' and sit down."

Jovita Campos was receiving a government pension. It was not enough, so she studied nursing. Jennie was sent to a Catholic boarding school in Phoenix for two years while her mother completed her schooling.

"I think that bred selfishness on my part," she says. "I was so alone. I had to learn how to watch out for myself."

Her high school years, back in Miami, where her mother worked as a nurse and she spent much time talking Spanish with her grandmother (she talked English with her mother), were happy times. She had developed into a dark-eyed beauty, and the boys were after her. She always had a steady boyfriend, usually the season's sports hero, though her own sports interest was limited to swimming and pompom cheerleading. She read extensively, dreamed of becoming a teacher in some faraway exotic land, and soon matriculated at Arizona State University in Tempe, about seventy miles from home. She was smart enough to receive a scholarship but didn't. "Only the Anglos received scholarships," she says matter-of-factly.

Jennie Campos was eighteen years old when she entered Arizona State. She was keenly intelligent and attractive.

"I was walking across campus one afternoon on my way home from class. This big black man was walking toward me. He had this intense stare. He scared me to death. His eyes seemed to be riveted on me. We got close together, and he didn't say anything. He just sort of nodded at me, unsmiling, those eyes beating down on me. It was weird. The next day I saw him again, and this time we stopped to talk. He asked me to meet him in the school cafeteria. I was intrigued by him. We met, and I soon found out he was this football hero. We talked a little. He was very nice, very sure of himself, aggressive without being annoying. I think we had our first real date in the spring at a dormitory dance," Jennie says.

Reggie Jackson, deserted by his mother, and Jennie Campos, who had lost her father, were soon a recognized campus item.

"He talked often of his mother," she says. "He couldn't seem to understand what happened to him. He said he remembered when she was leaving his father. She lined the children up to say good-bye and was going to pick out two or three of them, and then she didn't pick Reggie and he stayed with his father. He felt that deeply, sort of being unpicked, unchosen, unloved, as she left with his sisters and a brother."

Jennie had dated many high school boys, but Reggie was the first man in her life who was strong, tender, and protective of her. Reggie, in turn, was still trying to come to terms with his mother, trying to understand the causes of his abandonment. He needed to relate to women easily, openly, fully.

In the tradition of a college romance, Reggie and Jennie were soon linked, eating lunch together, attending movies, going to school dances, sipping coffee on their class breaks, drinking beer at the Sun Devil Lounge. They shared their hopes and dreams and fell in love, paying no mind to their racial differences.

"I knew he was black," Jennie says. "I just didn't make a point of it. Nobody did. He was Reggie Jackson, campus athletic hero, and I was his girl. That was all there was to it."

Jennie Campos is sitting curled up on the sofa of her mother's living room, her eyes deeply intense, as Reggie's often are, the years slipping by easily as she attempts to re-create her emotions of a long-lost love.

"I would have been content to have been just his wife," Jennie says. "I didn't need anything else then. Those were the values I had. Those were the things I lived by. I never dreamed there was any more for a woman than to live and love a good man, to cook and sew, to have babies, to do the things our culture has taught us to do. That would certainly have been enough for me."

Jennie Campos is thirty-four now, a woman of a new generation, a strong, intelligent, opinionated, self-confident young woman whose values are no longer those of an ASU freshman. "Now," she says, "that kind of relationship would not be enough. My interest level is high; my energy level is high. There is a man in my life. His name is Paige, and he lives in California. He is a master electrician, a yachtsman, a sailor. He wants me to give up my teaching and sail around the world with him. That's a bone of serious contention now. I can't do that. I simply can't. I want to work with the children. Besides, I hate sailing."

No such conflicts of the 1980s entered into the relationship with Reggie Jackson. There were other conflicts though. Jennie and Reggie were on divergent courses, but they could not see it then. "It is not enough to love each other," journalist Walter Lippmann once wrote, "two people must also love sharing what they do." Even in their college days, once the facades of athletic hero and campus beauty were torn away, the conflicts were clear. "I wanted to see westerns, and Jennie liked foreign films," Reggie once said. "She read serious books; I read the sports pages."

The major conflict, however, though it was not apparent to them, was race.

"I knew he was black," Jennie says. "I just never considered it important. I just considered Reggie, the man, not the black man, not the ballplayer, just the person I loved and admired."

Though it was not a problem for Jennie or Reggie, the racial question was very much a problem for the athletic department of ASU. It frowned upon the relationship. Things were turbulent enough in 1965 and 1966, what with the country's agitation over civil rights. Having a talented black jock on campus was enough of an issue. A white girlfriend only compounded the situation.

"An uncle of mine, Fernando Guerrero, a successful businessman, is a strong supporter of the athletic program at ASU, a contributor, a man who has some say on the athletic council. One of the assistant football coaches, I don't know who, came to him one day and asked him to intercede with us. 'It won't be good for Reggie's career or for the school.' He told us what was said. He did not push it. Reggie and I talked about it. Reggie said, 'People really care about this?' He couldn't believe it; he couldn't believe anybody could get worked up over who he was dating. Then we just started talking about something else."

Marriage is a difficult human relationship. Good ones demand time and attention to detail, understanding, compassion, selflessness. Communication is vital. Interracial ones demand even more of these values and skills in the America of the twentieth century. Reggie and Jennie did not deal with the problem. They avoided it. They were in love, and that, they thought, was enough.

"We never really cared about it; we ignored it," says Jennie. "I don't think it ever came up in our relationship except for one time. Reggie was playing in Birmingham. Joe Rudi was on the team there. Sharon and Joe invited us over for a barbecue in their apartment when I was visiting Reggie. We had a wonderful evening, lots of laughs. Then we left, and the landlord was in front of the apartment. 'I don't want no niggers in here anymore.' What could anybody say? This was Birmingham in 1967."

Reggie left Arizona State to play professional baseball in 1966. Jennie continued her studies. There were long-distance phone calls and passionate letters and surprise visits. "Marriage wasn't really discussed in any formal way," says Jennie, "it was simply just understood to follow. This was the way things were done in a college relationship."

Her visit to Birmingham, the season Reggie was playing there prior to being brought up to Kansas City, seemed to bring their relationship to the marriage stage.

"I saw the way baseball players lived. It was a comfortable life. I enjoyed it. I would have been very happy doing that for years. Marriage to Reggie just seemed natural after that. Athletes should have wives. That just seemed to be the way it was," she says.

Reggie was brought up to the A's at the end of the 1967 season in Kansas City and played his rookie year in the major leagues with them in Oakland in 1968. The All-Star Game was scheduled for July 9, 1968, at Houston. There was a three-day break for the players not on the All-Star teams. Reggie and Jennie scheduled their marriage for July 8, 1968, in the hometown of the bride, Miami, at Our Lady of Blessed Sacrament Catholic Church. The bride was gorgeous in her long, flowing white gown.

"It was a traditional wedding," says Jennie. "We had all our relatives from around here, many friends, about two hundred people in all. Reggie's daddy was there, and his best man was Gene Foster, a football player from ASU. Three other ushers were also football players at ASU, friends of Reggie's—Ben Hawkins, John Pitts, and Ron Pritchard. At the reception later we sang and danced. Everybody wanted me to get up after a toast. I was too nervous for that. Reggie got up, turned to his friends, and said, 'Thanks for coming to *my* wedding.' The priest leaned over to my mother, shook his head, and said, 'I'm afraid these young people will have trouble.' Then Reggie finished talking and asked all his friends to autograph a plate so he could keep it as a memento of *his* wedding."

Mrs. Campos still had her doubts about the marriage. She knew the racial problems would only aggravate the situation and was cool toward Reggie. That all changed.

"He's welcome in this house anytime," she says. "He still calls me occasionally, on my birthday or something, and says, 'Is Jennie married?' When I tell him she isn't, he always seems relieved. He was always just a nice young man with us, no star, nobody to fuss over. He would come in, go in the bedroom, and take a nap in Grandma's room while we made dinner. It didn't work out, so it didn't work out. It was nobody's fault. He always played with the kids around the house when he came here. He always seemed most comfortable with young kids and old women."

After the wedding Jennie and Reggie returned to Oakland for a series against the Indians. They moved into Reggie's apartment in the Lake Merritt district of Oakland. Jennie went to the game every night. By day they shopped together, bought furniture, hung up drapes, cooked, cleaned, made love, and enjoyed the early days of their marriage with deep affection for each other. Jackson was having a very successful rookie season.

"We were in love. That seemed all that mattered," she says. "The star thing, the superstar thing, that seemed so foreign to me. I would wait for him in the ramps under the stands, and the kids who had seen us together would ask for my autograph. I never could understand why. I couldn't see this need for touching somebody who had touched a star. But I did it without a fuss. I enjoyed the life. The games were fun. We would have dinner in the apartment alone together or with Sandy and Sal Bando, Joe and Sharon, all of us young, starting out, excited about our new lives. There was no thought about myself as a person. I was Reggie's wife. That was enough. Truly, enough."

Jennie Jackson was twenty-two years old, a bride, in love with this home run hero. She was content to be with him when the team was at home, happy enough to be alone when the team was on the road, waiting for a phone call or a letter from him, going to a movie with Sharon or Sandy, watching television, shopping for new clothes, living a life on the fringes of this image. She wanted Reggie. She didn't particularly want what went with him. It started with the required socializing with the other wives. She was forced to attend parties and showers and social activities with the wives of other players. Jennie Jackson of Miami, Arizona, didn't feel quite comfortable with these heavily made-up, strong-willed, pushy, opinionated veteran baseball wives.

"These parties were dreadful things," she once told writer Herb Michaelson. "There were a lot of petty jealousies to cope with. A lot of silent dislike was going on, a lot of backstabbing. If this husband had a higher batting average than that husband, well, if your husband the pitcher was appearing in more games than my husband the pitcher, well. The wives never wanted to go to these affairs, but everybody went."

And they competed with newer clothes, better cars, brighter dresses, smarter kids. The war was always on. Casey Stengel once said, "I lost more clubs over the wives than over the players." Stengel's team always had a ticket rule: No more than two seats together for players' wives. "Keep them apart," Stengel once said, "and keep the club."

Jennie Jackson hated playing the role of wife of player.

She didn't want to dress the way the others did, sit the way they did, talk the way they did, think the way they did. She wouldn't compete. She saw herself still as Jennie Campos of Miami, Arizona, and she knew who she was, what her values were, what really mattered in her own life. The only thing that mattered to her in Oakland was Reggie.

"Things started getting away from us in 1969, the home run year," Jennie says. "I hated it."

Jackson was making a run at the home run record of Babe Ruth and Roger Maris, and the pressures were incredible. The sportswriters fussed over him. The fans called his name from the stands. The owner, Charlie Finley, gave endless interviews praising Reggie, hoping millions of fans would come out and see the kid from Arizona hit home runs. Jennie was pushed further and further into the background. She was a piece of property in this great stage play about baseball being played out in the Oakland Coliseum and every other American League baseball park. She had too much sense of her own self, sense in her own worth, pride in her own person to accept this fringe role. Some wives are naturally gifted for this act. "I don't care what he does," a famous baseball wife once told this reporter, "as long as I get a new fur coat." Jennie Jackson didn't want a new fur coat. She wanted her man.

"He didn't have time for me. He didn't have time for anything outside hitting the ball. I tried to participate in his life. I knew that was what he wanted. I imagined how he wanted me to act, so I did it. If he had a bad day, I would tell him he was standing too far to the left or too far to the right or he was standing up too high. I didn't quite know what I was saying, but I wanted to try."

Reggie Jackson hit forty-seven home runs in 1969, but almost ended the season on the threshold of a nervous breakdown. He bitterly contested his contract over that winter and started off miserably in 1970.

"He blamed it on me," Jennie says. "He said I was bothering him; I was after him to do things; I wanted things from him. All I wanted from him was his love."

Baseball players, by the nature of this short, lucrative, childish profession, are selfish human beings. They have been heroes since childhood. They know little failure. There was much failure for Reggie in 1970. He couldn't cope. The baseball problems were too much. His marriage was only a hindrance to his professional advancement.

"Some couples deal with it in baseball," Jennie reflects. "How do they do it?"

Whatever the formula, Jennie and Reggie Jackson no longer had it. Love was no longer enough. In fact, it was no longer there.

"It began," Jennie says, "with the letters from other women, the phone calls, the notes dropped to him at the ball park, put in the car, stuffed in his hand as he walked out the gate. I confronted him with it immediately. He said, 'It's none of your business.' I wasn't raised that way. I wanted him to stop, just promise he'd stop. He wouldn't."

Infidelity is as common in baseball as a curve ball. It's just the way things are. Some players flaunt it; some don't. Most participate. Most wives know, but most of them ignore it. Some are destroyed by it.

"I knew wives of players who would say, 'Oh, that's just what goes on with them on the road, doesn't mean a thing,' and live with it. I couldn't. I wouldn't."

After confronting Reggie with the evidence of his philandering, Jennie Jackson waited for a response. There was none. Reggie Jackson, a man who never seemed at a loss for the proper words, was. In this one aspect of his life, terribly saddened because he did care for Jennie, Jackson was speechless.

"He would sulk and grow silent. He would sit around for a while listening to music or staring at the walls," Jennie says, "and then he would get up and suddenly leave. He wouldn't return, and I would go out after him. I would find him leaning against the wall of the local

Laundromat, watching the clothes wash and spin and dry."

There would be natural separations—a road trip, spring training, winter ball—and Jennie would hope for a change.

"I kept having this same terrible feeling all the time, this horrible guilt, that I was damaging his career. I was hurting him, and I didn't want to do that," she says.

The marriage was in a shambles almost from the middle of 1969. They tried for another three years. In 1972 Jennie and Reggie Jackson were legally separated. In February 1973 the papers were final, and they were divorced. Reggie Jackson gave Jennie a cash settlement of $75,000. There were no further payments or alimony.

"It had gone back and forth for several months before the final decree. I was suffering from anxieties. I wasn't sure I was doing the right thing, for Reggie, for myself, for the marriage. But I had to end it. I couldn't live in this state of limbo."

Jennie was at home in February 1973, the night before the final papers were signed. Reggie phoned. "Are you sure you want to go through this?"

Jennie Jackson moved from the Tempe campus, where she had received her degree in education, to a bilingual preschool teaching job in Fountain Valley, California. Reggie knew where she was after the divorce, called fairly regularly, invited her out for dinner, asked her to come to games, sent her birthday cards, pursued her with devotion.

"I had to stop it," she says. "I had to get on with my life. There was just no sense in that any longer. I asked him to stop calling, stop writing me. He finally did. I think it is about four years since I have talked to him."

It was the second loss in his life of a woman he loved. His mother and now his wife had left him. As women came and went in his life, there was no serious, lasting relationship with anyone.

"There are a dozen women I could marry," he said in

1980, "but I'm not interested. I'm still young. I don't want to give up my freedom. I'm regimented all year as a ball-player, told when to get up, told when to go to sleep, told when to eat. I want to be able to sleep as late as I want in the off-season, drink a beer for breakfast if I want to, not rush home to anyone. I'll think about it after I'm out of the game."

Resuming her maiden name, Jennie Campos is not the same lady who was once married to a baseball player. Her horizons have expanded. Her experiences are varied. Her attitudes have changed. She is stretching out for her own self, always within reach, helping others, working with children, seeing a full, meaningful life ahead of her.

"Two years ago I went to Honolulu when I became interested in Asian studies. I decided that was the best place to explore it. I would be involved with the Asian culture. I would see the people, feel the differences, understand the motivations. I wanted to work with those children," she says.

Jennie Campos changed and matured and grew. She sensed her own worth now. She was no longer an append-age to a man, a baseball player, a public hero. "Playing second fiddle to a man, a hero, yes, it has its pains," she says, "haunting me always." She moved away from that restricted formality, those preordained rules, those conformable acts that she knew intuitively were destroying her sense of self. As the wife of Reggie Jackson she seemed to have limited functions. As a teacher, a student, a compassionate American dealing with young Asians she could have a bearing on others' lives, and they, in turn, would have a significant bearing on hers.

Reggie and Jennie Jackson were not unusual. Only his later fame and fortune made them unique. They were young, decent, intelligent people who might have survived the early strain had each been willing to sacrifice more of himself or herself for the other. Jennie tried, but Reggie could not even try. His drive for baseball excellence, his passion for success, his intensity of play pre-

vented that. "I once asked him long after we had separated what he wanted out of life," says Jennie. "He said
he wanted to be the best, just the best. I asked him why,
and he seemed puzzled as if the reasons behind being the
best had never dawned on him."

Both Reggie and Jennie have changed through the
years, each reaching a greater peace apart than they ever
knew together. Jennie has a softness, an ease, a spiritual
understanding of her own worth. She is a proud woman
now. Reggie has eased through the fires that surrounded
him, secure in his worth, content, confident, mature, passionate, better able to deal with human beings. He has a
special woman friend in California and some less special
women friends in New York, all intelligent, poised, beautiful. He may even someday make a permanent commit-
ment to one, but that seems unlikely as long as he plays.

What hasn't changed is his role on the American scene
as a hero, his ability to deal with the concept of elevating
a sports figure above the crowd for the simple act of hitting a baseball hard and often.

"There is so much to say and so much screwed up in our
values about hero worship," says Jennie. "I never knew
how to deal with that. But to whom can we say it, what
really should be said about heroes and would it do any
good? I remember one time in 1969 Reggie and I were
driving home from a game with Joe Rudi in the front seat.
Joe DiMaggio was coaching the A's. This great American
hero, and he asked for a lift to his hotel. He came along
with us and sat in the back seat. Joe and Reggie and I
talked about some little thing or other, and Joe DiMaggio
sat in the back and stared out the window. I wanted to say
something to him, to make him comfortable, to welcome
him. I just didn't know what to say. I didn't want to say
something about baseball and sound stupid. I did not
know anything else he might be interested in. He was just
a hero, a great American hero. I sat there and thought I
was a girl from the small copper-mining town of Miami,
Arizona, and Joe DiMaggio was sitting in the back seat,

and I didn't know what to say to him." It is an emotion Reggie Jackson could well understand as his own fame grew. So many people yearn to be physically close to him, and when they make it, however accidentally, they are at a loss for meaningful human contact.

As Reggie has become a legendary superstar in New York, Jennie has fashioned out a career of her own. She will spend two years in Japan and then expects to finish her work at the University of Honolulu and does not know what the future holds. She has worked with the refugee children in Cambodia, will return there on her next long holiday, wants to help these Asian children as best she can. She feels no great pull to return to the United States.

"I've become suspicious of commercialism, and I've grown to doubt the integrity of the American public. I wonder often if we care at all, if we do have principles, standards, or some model to emulate besides ourselves. Shamefully I've grown ashamed of my own country. One of the reasons I returned on this summer vacation here to Arizona was to immerse myself again in its culture, to reappreciate that which I am," Jennie says.

And Reggie Jackson has become the epitome of this crass commercialism Jennie abhors. His face is on ads for Murjani jeans, for Panasonic radio and television, for Getty oil. His instant identification factor also serves much good as he represents several charities, notably the Lou Gehrig disease foundation, the New York City Public School Athletic League program, and many other groups that beg for his endorsement.

There is time now for a long ride from Miami into the rising cliffs toward the Fort Apache Indian Reservation and past the historical markers into the lands of the Indians. Jennie has been here many times, but she is seeing it again as the sun begins to set. The canyon is exciting, and a visitor must shoot some pictures and gasp at the miracles of nature unfolded before him. "It's so beautiful," she explains, "just so beautiful." And one is impressed with the intensity of her emotions as she views this natural beauty. There is no escaping the thought that in the total dedication to hitting and running and catching a baseball these scenes were somehow missed. The day was not long enough for Jennie and Reggie to pause to watch the orange sun slowly sneak behind the canyon.

"I was in Nepal once looking at the mountain ranges, and I walked back to my hotel all filled with the beauty of these natural wonders. I sat down in the lobby for a moment in this faraway land, and I picked up a magazine. It was an old *Time* magazine. It had a picture of Reggie on the cover. I was really shocked seeing the picture on that magazine in Nepal. Am I ever going to get away from that man?"

"Charlie's New Prospect"

IN JUNE 1966 THE KANSAS CITY A'S COMMITTED $85,000 to a husky youngster from Arizona State University who had played fewer than 100 organized baseball games. It was the large bonus money that guaranteed Jackson every conceivable chance.

"Money," said playboy ballplayer Bo Belinsky, "that's the difference between being a prospect and being a suspect. A bonus guy is a prospect, and the trainers rub his arms with secret salve from India. A suspect—a guy like me—got his arm rubbed with Three-in-One oil."

* * *

Less than one hundred miles from Spokane, Washington, across the interstate bridge into Idaho, at the confluence of the Clearwater and Snake rivers, lies the little town of Lewiston. It was a winter camping point during the expedition of Lewis and Clark. Now the town is dominated by the huge lumber mills of the Potlatch Corporation rising high above the hills.

"There's a long tradition of baseball out here," says Bob Barrows, a sportswriter for the *Lewiston Tribune*. "There was a minor-league team called the Lewis-Clark Broncs— a lot of things around here are named after Lewis and Clark—in the old Class A Northwest League. We don't have a lot of people, maybe twenty-five, twenty-six thousand all around here, but most of them are ball fans."

Just down at the end of Main Street, in full view of the interstate bridge, there is a fine, small baseball field called Bengal Field.

"It was the site of the 1973 American Legion World Series," says Barrows. "That was a big time. We were all proud of that."

For several years the Kansas City A's sent their best young prospects to Lewiston to begin their careers playing at Bengal Field.

Early in the evening of June 25, 1966, the owner of a local clothing store, a man named Jack Lee, waited impatiently at the Spokane Airport. Charlie Finley had called Lee personally.

"I got this boy, real good prospect, I want you to take personal charge of him, Jack, see that nobody fools with his style. A real good kid. We just signed him," Finley said.

"What's the boy's name?" asked Lee.

"Jackson, the kid I just signed out of Arizona State, Reggie Jackson," Finley said.

"Oh, yeah," said Lee. "We read the papers, Charlie. A real big one. We'll watch him for you."

The flight from Phoenix was landing now, and Jack Lee moved toward the gate. He watched the people get off the plane. Near the end of the line, wearing a sports jacket, no tie, and dark trousers and carrying a suit bag, was the kid from Arizona, Reggie Jackson.

"Over here, son," said Lee. "I'm Jack Lee."

"Reggie Jackson, sir, pleased to meet you. Thanks for coming out."

Now retired from the clothing business and watching Reggie on television as much as he can, Lee recalls that day vividly.

"He was a real gentleman, a real soft-spoken young man," says Lee. "We had Rick Monday, the other big bonus kid the year before. He was also a pretty quiet youngster. I guess they get up there, they hit a few home runs, and they start talking a little more."

Lee drove Jackson into Lewiston. They talked some about the town, about the weather, and about the nearest movie. Mostly Reggie peered out of the window, staring at the vastness of the great Northwest, alone with his thoughts, on the threshold of the greatest adventure of his life.

Lee took Jackson downtown to the Lewis-Clark Hotel. He introduced him to the desk clerk as "one of Charlie's new prospects" and told him he could walk over to the office at the ball park in the morning to arrange for his pay, his mail, and his tickets. Each player received two tickets for every game.

"We're a quiet town, a successful community," Lee says. "We have no celebrity here. Everybody just does what they do, you understand. I sold clothes and helped run that ball club for Charlie. Reggie Jackson just swung that bat."

Reggie Jackson would have a stay in Lewiston of less than a month before moving to a higher classification. He was there long enough to make a solid impression.

"Nobody ever had any trouble with him," Lee says. "While he was there, he was at home in that town. He had his dinners at Bojack's restaurant, same as everybody else, had the same kind of room in the hotel as the other players, drew about the same money, about seven hundred dollars a month while he was there. He went to the movie we had in town a few times, and I brought him out to my club to play golf. If you're asking if he had any trouble because he was black, I'm telling you he didn't. We are a bush-league town, no fancy field here, but we treated all those kids real well."

Lee said in the dozen games Jackson played in Lewiston, there was hardly a single one in which there was not a Kansas City scout sitting in the stands watching him.

"That was something I'll never forget," says Lee. "Those scouts would come early and watch him in batting practice and sit around the whole game. They were like a bunch of mother hens watching over their chickens."

Jackson played twelve games at Lewiston before moving on. He had 14 hits, 3 doubles and 2 triples, batted .292, struck out 10 times, stole a base, and hit 2 homers. One was memorable.

"You didn't have to be a genius to see that Reggie Jackson was something special. It's not a very big park, but Reggie hit one ball that cleared everything and rolled way down the street beyond. They were talking about that one in Bojack's for quite a few days. Yes, sir, that young man could poleax a baseball, make no mistake about that."

Seven years later Jackson returned to Lewiston for a banquet in his honor after winning the 1973 Most Valuable Player Award.

"He was a little richer, dressed a little better, but we didn't treat him no different. He wasn't a big star to us. He was just a nice kid who could hit a baseball a mile. I guess he still can," Lee says.

On the inside entrance at Bengal Field in Lewiston, Idaho, there are a couple of dozen pictures of baseball players who once played there. The locals call it their Rogues Gallery. Higher and larger than the other framed photographs is a picture of Reggie Jackson in the uniform of the Oakland A's.

* * *

Back in the middle 1960s in Kansas City, Charlie Finley was having his troubles. He ached to leave the town for richer surroundings. He was berated constantly in the press. He antagonized the local fans. By the summer of 1966 it was clear he was determined to move his franchise west to Oakland. Proud of their baseball tradition, local Kansas City boosters reminded Finley of his contractual obligations at Municipal Stadium.

"The team was going poorly," says the *Kansas City Star*'s Joe McGuff, "and the players were being ignored. All anybody wrote about was the fight between Finley and the politicians."

Senator Stuart Symington of Missouri was brought into the battle. He vowed Kansas City would remain in the American League. "This matter will be brought to the attention of the United States Senate," Symington promised.

While he maneuvered for his move west, Finley also was developing his new team. Under the direction of the boss, reputable baseball men such as Hank Peters and Eddie Lopat were discovering talented youngsters and signing them for the A's. The Philadelphia franchise had moved to Kansas City in 1954. Finley had purchased the club in 1960. By 1966 he realized he wouldn't make a large profit there and was determined to start fresh in the west. He wanted to begin in California with a contending club, hoping to steal the spotlight away from the San Francisco Giants, despite the presence of Willie Mays, Willie McCovey, Juan Marichal, and Orlando Cepeda.

In 1962 he signed a Cuban by the name of Bert Campaneris. Two years later he signed a kid pitcher out of Hertford, North Carolina, by the name of Jim Hunter, who had just shot off one of his toes in a hunting accident. "What do your friends call you?" Finley asked.

"Jimmy," said the youngster.

"What do you like to do for a hobby?"

"Hunt and fish, mostly catfish around here," he said.

"Catfish. That's your name, Catfish Hunter."

Early in 1965 he signed Gene Tenace, Joe Rudi, and Rollie Fingers as free agents. With the first baseball free agent draft in 1965 he selected and signed Rick Monday and Sal Bando. Then in 1966 he signed Reggie Jackson. A year later he drafted a high school left-handed throwing quarterback and pitcher named Vida Blue. These players signed as youngsters by Finley became the backbone of the dominating Oakland teams of the early 1970s.

After less than a month at Lewiston, Idaho, Reggie Jackson was called in his room at the Lewis-Clark Hotel by Jack Lee early one morning and told, "Pack your bags, Reggie. You're going to Modesto."

Jackson arrived at Modesto, California, about eighty miles east of San Francisco, on a late July evening. He was proud that he had proved capable of advancing closer to the big leagues in so short a time.

"Modesto would be a good test for any young hitter," says Fred Schwartz of the Modesto *Bee.* "The dimensions of the park are quite fair, very similar to a lot of big-league parks."

The Modesto Reds played their games at Del Webb Field. Webb, an Arizona real estate magnate, had been a longtime owner, with Dan Topping, of the New York Yankees. The club had been sold to the Columbia Broadcasting System, and Webb had confined his interest to his real estate and land dealings. He always maintained a strong association with baseball. Local businessmen approached Webb for a low-interest loan to help finance a field. He contributed some money, he lent out some more at low interest, and in return the new home of the Reds was named Del Webb Field.

"The foul lines are relatively short," says Schwartz. "Only about three hundred ten feet but the power alleys to right-center and left-center run about three hundred fifty feet."

Under Finley's rapid development program most of his young prospects would make a stop in Modesto. The best pitcher on the team, when Jackson arrived in July 1966, was a tall, thin, sandy-haired, smooth-skinned right-hander by the name of Rollie Fingers.

"I remember the first time I saw Reggie at Modesto,"

says Fingers, now the relief ace of the San Diego Padres and a man as famous for his flowing handlebar mustache as for his nasty sinker. "He was so incredibly strong. That's what you had to notice about him. He had muscles on muscles, and for a kid he really had a decent idea at the plate. He struck out too much, but if you are going to get the long ball, you have to strike out trying for it. Reggie never stopped trying for it."

At Cheltenham High, Jackson had been an exceptional athlete—a football hero, a track star, a no-hit pitcher in baseball, a .550 batter in his senior year. He had repeated that cycle of success at Arizona State. It was a little different in professional ball.

"We are all selfish about our own careers down there," Fingers says. "We want to win, sure, but we are more concerned with making an impression, moving up, getting the chance. Reggie didn't just want to hit a lot of home runs; he wanted to hit home runs the organization would recognize. I guess that hasn't changed. Now he wants to hit home runs the world will recognize."

Playing every day, riding buses from town to town, eating in grubby diners, sleeping in small, sometimes ugly, dirty hotels, playing under poor lights and before angry local crowds—these are the difficult adjustments each young player must make.

"Reggie was cocky then, the same as now. He knew he was damn good. He had that incredible power, and he could run and throw like hell. What he didn't have was a tough skin. He didn't like to be kidded much. So naturally everybody kidded him when he didn't execute a play just right," Fingers says.

Fingers remembers a tough game he was pitching into the bottom of the ninth. The score was tied 1–1. Modesto loaded the bases. Jackson was up.

"Even then he loved that challenge, loved that attention, lived for the chance to win the game as the big hero," says Fingers. "The pitch came in, and he was jammed. But he is so damn strong that he was able to fight off the ball and hit a blooper to left field for the gamer."

Jackson ran to first as the winning run ran home for a 2–1 Modesto win. Then Reggie turned back to the Modesto bench, all smiles, waiting for the hero's greeting. All he got was derision.

"You really hit the shit out of that, big fellow," Fingers said.

Jackson's jaw slackened. His eyes turned down. His face grew taut. He angrily grabbed his glove and headed for the locker room.

"He was really hurt," says Fingers. "You could see that. He wanted a hero's welcome. Instead, he got a needle. That was something he had to learn to deal with as much as he had to learn to deal with the good fastball or the hard slider. He had to learn to live and laugh as a professional."

In a few weeks, as he began hitting home runs and driving in runs and winning games for the Modesto Reds, Reggie's confidence grew.

"You could see he was someone special," says Schwartz. "We had a lot of the college boys in Modesto, a lot of All-Americas, and not many of them panned out. Kids would come into town with big reputations for hitting .500 in some cow college somewhere or for being a phenom in some small high school. Then they would see some tough professional pitching, and in a few months they would be shipped down."

The screening process was at work. Fingers and Jackson had it. They would advance; they would move up; they would survive the test and travails. They would ultimately prosper and develop into marvelous players, help anchor the great Oakland teams, star in the World Series, play out their options, and become wealthy free agents. Others would return home in a year or two, back to the farms, back to the insurance offices, back to the steel mills and grocery stores. They had not survived. The memories would always linger, and when Fingers or Jackson would show up on a television screen in some big game in New York or Oakland or San Diego, some insurance salesman, grown fat and lethargic, would quietly mutter, "That could have been me." They could never admit they lacked the talent. It was easier to say, "If I had only gotten the same chance Reggie got."

At Modesto now, deep in Stanislaus County, in one of California's lushest areas of farmland, the Modesto baseball team, now officially called the Modesto A's, still develops young players for the Oakland organization.

"There was a lot of hoopla when Reggie came here," says Schwartz. "He was a big bonus kid with a lot of attention. He was a very tough hitter, had that same aggressive swing, never got cheated at the plate. And he was always exciting on the field, always exciting."

It is about fifteen years since Jackson played at Modesto. Was it obvious then he was headed for stardom?

"I guess I have to admit I was surprised he became as good a player as he did," Schwartz says. "I think he really talked himself into being a star and talked everybody else into recognizing it."

In 56 games Jackson batted .299, the closest he has ever come to finishing a season at .300 before 1980. He hit 6 doubles, had 60 RBIs, and hit 21 home runs. He also struck out 71 times.

"When I left there," says Reggie, "I was ready for bigger and better things."

He soon returned to the campus at Arizona State, where he settled into a town house in Tempe, attended classes on a part-time basis at the university, and drank some beer in his off hours downtown at the Sun Devil Lounge. He played basketball with Lenny Randle and Jim Palmer and Bobby Bonds in early February and reported to the A's training camp in Bradenton, Florida, on March 1, 1967.

Most ballplayers adore spring training. Veterans can work a couple of hours a day in the warm, friendly sun after a winter in the cold, and kids can get a chance to live for a few weeks with big-leaguers, draw the same meal money, stay in the same luxury, vacation hotels. Fringe players do not fear spring training until three or four weeks have passed and rosters start being cut down.

For a youngster like Reggie Jackson in the spring of 1967, the adventure was thrilling.

"We were all kids, excited about our opportunities, confident about our abilities," says Rollie Fingers. "On that A's club everybody got attention. We were all young, good players. Reggie was no different from the rest of us. That's why Reggie never had the trouble in Oakland he had later in New York. With the Yankees he was a stranger, an outcast, an outsider. With the A's we were all guys who grew up together, separate but equal, you could say."

In some few weeks, after getting a chance to play in half a dozen spring games in which he hit one home run, Jackson was moved to the minor-league camp down the road at Bradenton. It would be the last spring training he would experience with a minor-league club. He had been assigned on option to the A's Triple A farm club in Birmingham, Alabama.

* * *

The fires were still burning across the South in 1967. Martin Luther King's bus boycott, the catalyzing event of the post World War II civil rights movement, had begun in 1955 in Birmingham. Then in 1963 a bomb had killed four little girls inside a Birmingham church. Emotions were still at a fever pitch. The memory of Bull Connor siccing his dogs on blacks in church meetings remained vivid. Black neighborhoods were considered occupied enemy territory by white residents. Fear was the most recognizable emotion—fear by the whites of the blacks, fear by the blacks of the whites, fear by law enforcement officers of demonstrators, fear by the demonstrators of law enforcement officers fighting to hold on desperately to a hundred-year tradition of legal bigotry. The dream that Martin Luther King had of a free, equal, open society, built on law and love, was far from realization.

On April 12, 1967, the Birmingham A's baseball team

arrived in town from spring training. Three black players were separated from the group, given cab fare, and told to report to the Gaston Motel in Birmingham's black ghetto. The rest of the team boarded a bus and was taken to a Holiday Inn in the downtown section of Birmingham. The black players rode silently to their ghetto hotel. Separate but not equal.

"I remember when I first joined the Yankees in 1955," said the late Elston Howard, the first black player on the team, "and we were in spring training staying at a black hotel called Sir John on a trip to Miami. We were playing the Dodgers, and the black players on both clubs were there—me and Roy Campanella and Don Newcombe and Jackie. 'Are you guys here, too?' I asked Jackie. 'Not for long,' Jackie said."

Through the efforts of Jackie Robinson and later Bill White of the Cardinals and George Crowe of the Cincinnati Reds, spring training hotels were forced to accept an entire team or none of them, black and white. Southern hotels were actually integrated earlier than northern hotels in major-league cities.

"I remember staying with the Yankees in Kansas City and being sent to a black hotel the first trip in. I didn't complain. I just accepted it," said Howard. "Then Casey Stengel asked the traveling secretary, Bill McCorry, 'Is he on this team or not?' The next trip into town Casey said, 'Go up and get your key.' My key was there like everybody else's. I got it, locked myself in my room, and called my great white father, Phil Rizzuto, to come up and eat with me because I was scared."

There was nobody to push the Holiday Inn to integrate for the Birmingham baseball team. Jackson rode silently with his fellow black players to the Gaston Hotel. He wasn't there to make a fuss. He was there to impress on the field, win a job, escape the minor leagues.

"My idea," says Jackson, "was to show the people I could play as well as anybody."

Later, in Oakland and in New York, Jackson would contribute his money, time, and fame to the cause, appearing at banquets, lending his name to the movement, working for the betterment of his people, speaking out on the game's double standards, adding his powerful voice to the cause.

"When I came up to the big leagues," says baseball's first black manager, Frank Robinson, "bigotry was overt. They called you names. They did ugly things. You stayed together for defense. Now it's different. Prejudice is still there, the double standard, the difficulties blacks have in getting baseball jobs. They swept it all under the rug. Pick up the rug. You'll still see it."

In the spring of 1967 Reggie Jackson saw first hand what he had only heard and read about. As a boy in a predominantly Jewish community he had experienced little prejudice. At Arizona State he had been too big a hero for anybody to make a fuss. At Lewiston and Modesto there had not been enough blacks in either town for any problems. Birmingham was different. Birmingham was black, black enough for the whites to be frightened, aroused, and, in some cases, vicious.

"Black players realized where they were," says Wayne Martin of the Birmingham *News.* "A lot of those kids were afraid to go in the street. They would get a cab to the park, a cab back to the hotel, and eat in their rooms. It was not an easy life."

Birmingham had a long baseball tradition. Casey Stengel had left Birmingham in 1912 on a slow-moving train to New York to report to the Brooklyn Dodgers. Jimmy Piersall had starred for the team before joining the Boston Red Sox. Walt Dropo had played for the team and hit a light tower 470 feet from home plate with one of his huge drives. Gus Triandos had once hit the round Hanna Paint neon sign, broken the green lights, and won $1,000 from the company for bringing it so much attention.

Black baseball had as much tradition. The Birmingham Black Barons were one of the finest teams in the old Negro leagues for more than two decades. A short, stocky man named Willie Howard Mays played on the Barons in the late 1930s and 1940s and was joined after World War II by his amazingly agile fifteen-year-old son, Willie Howard Mays, Jr.

"I remember the first time I ever came up to New York," Mays once said. "It was with the Barons. I was sixteen, and my father was still playing. We were on this bus, and we broke down in the Holland Tunnel. I was the youngest guy on the team. The other players chased me out of the bus to push while they sat back there and drank beer. But I had the best laugh. The bus caught fire, and you should have seen those other guys falling out of that bus."

There was only one major baseball field in Birmingham, Rickwood Field, originally built in 1910, refurbished several times since, and appearing similar to Detroit's Tiger Stadium. There was one deck covering the right-field stands.

"That's where the blacks had to sit," says Wayne Martin. "They had their own section and their own heroes. Later on Charlie Finley bought some old seats from Yankee Stadium and put them in here. They still had the New York emblem on them. I think after the park was integrated, everybody thought the blacks would come pouring through the gates. It didn't work that way. Not any more of them came after the park was integrated than had come before. There were all the baseball fans in the town there were going to be, black or white. Nobody was about to get rich because the black folks could sit anywhere they wanted."

Each afternoon a cab would leave from the Gaston Motel in the old west end of town, and Reggie Jackson would travel to the ball park. He would return the same way after the game. But in between he would be a member of the Birmingham A's, a marvelous player, an exciting personality, a man who was beginning to feel his destiny was within reach.

Trying to make the ball club, Jackson kept his racial

attitudes to himself. Years later he expressed resentment of that experience, anger at the living quarters, concern that baseball officials didn't force integrated housing. He later discussed the impact of Martin Luther King on his life and the lives of all blacks and once said, "I may be invited to lunch at the White House with President Ford or President Carter, but Martin Luther King was my President."

"You could see his confidence growing," says Rollie Fingers. "He was gaining it on the field, and he was gaining it off the field. When he hit a blooper to win a game now, he could go back to the bench, smiling. 'I hit the shit out of that, didn't I?' With that body, with that power, with his ability to express himself, Reggie was headed for something big."

In 114 games for the Birmingham A's and 413 at bats, Jackson led the league in runs scored with 84 and triples with 17. He had 26 doubles and 17 homers, struck out 87 times, and stole 17 bases. He had 58 RBIs and 121 hits. His average was .293.

"We have this strange habit of painting a huge X on the seat in the stands where a big home run is hit," says Wayne Martin. "There are about a dozen of them, the one Dropo hit and Triandos and Piersall and one Dave Duncan hit a little later. The highest, biggest, largest X is for the one Reggie hit, up on the light tower, way up on top, where no one had ever hit one before. We had the damnedest time getting a painter to go up there and put it up there. It's a long time since Reggie hit it up there, but when someone reads about him hitting a big one in the big leagues, they just point out to that light tower."

There would be another distinction for Jackson from his season in the Southern League. When the year was over, the sportswriters held a secret mail ballot to elect the Southern League Player of the Year. The voters included two sportswriters from each of the eight teams in the league.

Sixteen white sportswriters from eight league cities

unanimously elected the black star from Birmingham, Reggie Jackson, as the league's Player of the Year.

"I think," says Jackson, "if I went there to prove a point, I proved it."

In Kansas City Charlie Finley, making plans for his move to Oakland, summoned farm boss Eddie Lopat to his office. It was late in August.

"I want you to go down to Birmingham and take another look at Jackson. I'm thinking of bringing him up," Finley said.

"Charlie, you want to save some money?"

"Sure. What do you mean?"

"You don't have to bother sending me to Birmingham. I saw the kid in July. He's eating up the league. He's ready."

Finley picked up the phone and dialed the offices of the Birmingham A's. "I want Jackson here on the first available plane," Finley said.

In Birmingham Jackson rested on his bed in his room at the Gaston Motel. The phone rang. Manager Gus Niarhos was on the line.

"They want you in Kansas City, Reggie," Niarhos said.

"When?"

"You're on the four o'clock plane. Good luck, kid."

Fourteen months after he had signed with the A's, less than three years out of Cheltenham High School, and after 182 professional baseball games, Reggie Jackson was on his way to the major leagues.

"The feeling was overwhelming," says Reggie. "I wasn't sure I was ready. Then I thought a little more about it. The A's thought I was ready, Charlie thought I was ready, or they would not have brought me up. I could hit. I could always hit."

Jackson reported to the A's in Kansas City and was completely ignored by the fans, the press, and his teammates.

"Too much was going on in town to make a fuss over a kid joining the club late in the year," says Joe McGuff, the

Kansas City Star sports editor. "We were a terrible club. The manager, Alvin Dark, had just been fired. We were finishing last, and Charlie was moving. If a kid was joining us, he wouldn't be noticed."

It was the last time Reggie Jackson would be in any big-league clubhouse without being noticed.

"About the only thing we were worried about was getting another club if we lost the A's to California," McGuff says. "Symington had promised us he would bring pressure through the Senate. We had heard things like that before."

Soon Finley was burning his Kansas City lease on the field, engaging in confrontation journalism with local sportswriters, attacking local politicians, bragging about the fortunes he would make in Oakland.

"There's no there there," Gertrude Stein once wrote derisively about Oakland, the unspectacular neighbor city of San Francisco.

There didn't have to be any there there. Reggie Jackson would be there for eight years. That would be spectacular enough, even for Gertrude Stein.

"Home Run Hitters Drive Cadillacs"

IN THE FALL OF 1967 REGGIE JACKSON RETURNED TO the campus of Arizona State University. He attended classes full time, with a major in biology. He had promised his mother and his father he would finish school and gain his degree.

The mornings were pleasant. He walked to class in the crisp fall air from his new apartment, met Jennie for coffee between classes, studied hard to stay up with his classmates, rushed over at noon for a couple of hours of accelerated baseball training.

"He was a shoemaker in the outfield," says Eddie Lopat, who was Charlie Finley's general manager that year. "This was a kid who was a football player in high school. When he played baseball, he usually pitched, so he hadn't put in much time as a fielder. We had to teach him everything: how to hold his glove; how to catch a fly ball in the sun; how to pick up a line drive off the bat. I'll say this. The kid worked like hell."

"I was determined to improve my fielding," says Jackson. "I wanted to be the best. It wasn't enough to be adequate. The best, man, that's what I had to be. In everything. I didn't want anybody getting on me about my fielding. I was going to be a complete player, a great hitter, a great fielder, a great runner, a great thrower, the best, man, the best, like Willie Mays."

Eddie Lopat scouts for Montreal now. He sees young baseball players almost every day of his professional life. He never saw a better young baseball player than Reggie Jackson.

"He took a few swings, and you fell in love with him," says Lopat. "Only a handful of them, one or two every five years, can swing the bat like Reggie. And that speed, wow, he could run to first in three-point-five; he was the fastest big fellow I ever saw. And that arm, he could fire that thing."

Lopat sat in the stands before a game at Yankee Stadium and he thought back to the fine-looking young athlete he had first seen at Arizona State fifteen years earlier.

"He was such a wonderful young kid, that's what I really liked about him. A gentleman. Soft-spoken, pleasant, very bright, very professional. Then Charlie started to mess with him, push him, fight with him," Lopat says. "It completely changed his personality. Reggie had to get hard, get defensive. All that bragging bullshit, I think it all started because of Finley. I think Reggie has become a great player, the best in the game when the chips are on the table. As a kid he was really likable, really soft and sweet. Now he has that hard shell, that arrogance, that heavy-handed way of doing things. Charlie did that to him. Charlie changed him. Sad. That's why when they moved the franchise to Oakland, I quit the A's. I told Charlie I didn't want to go to California. Hell, it wasn't that. I just didn't want to work for Charlie Finley anymore. The man could just take the heart out of you."

In his quiet moments that winter at Arizona State, Reggie would think back to only one event in the final days

of the 1967 season, the time as a major leaguer and the late
days of the season and the struggle to impress.

"You go through a month, month and a half of that
adjustment early in your career," Jackson says, "and there
is only one memory, just one, that first tater you hit. That's
what I remember about 1967. Reggie Jackson hit a tater.
There would be four hundred, five hundred, who knows
how many to follow, but without that first one, you can't
get that second one. That's what has to be Reggie Jackson's memory of the 1967 season."

It was September 15, 1967, in a meaningless game between the fifth-place California Angels and the tenth-
place Kansas City A's. A handsome left-handed pitcher by
the name of James Brian Weaver, who was to last a little
more than a season in the major leagues with a lifetime
3-1 record, was pitching in relief for California at Anaheim
Stadium. He threw a fastball at the outside part of the
plate.

"Low and away," remembers Jackson, who can visual-
ize with clarity each of his 410 home runs. "It was a good
pitch. I hit it good. Never in doubt. It rose high and far and
sailed into the seats, four hundred, four-twenty, a real
good one. I watched it go, and then I started moving
around those bases. I knew I'd get a hell of a lot more of
them, but I wanted to savor this one."

On February 28, 1968, Reggie Jackson was driven to the
Phoenix Airport by Jennie Campos, kissed warmly at the
gate, wished well, and sent on his way to his first full
spring training as a big-league player. The A's were now
an Oakland franchise, but they would train for the last
time in Bradenton, Florida, before leasing new quarters
in Mesa for the next season.

*   *   *

The Boston Red Sox had won the 1967 pennant, one of the
most thrilling pennant victories in baseball history, on the
final day of the season with a win over the Minnesota
Twins. The New York Yankees, after finishing tenth and

last in 1966, had climbed to ninth. Carl Yastrzemski had won the batting title and the RBI title and had tied for the home run crown in leading the Red Sox in 1967. He had been denied a unanimous selection as the American League MVP by a strange vote cast by a Minnesota sportswriter for Twins utility player Cesar Tovar. The Cardinals had beaten the Red Sox in a stirring World Series.

As a result, little attention was paid to the struggling Oakland Athletics when they gathered for spring training. On their 1968 roster, most of them for the first time, were some young players who would later gain much recognition. They included a relief pitcher named Rollie Fingers, a right-handed starter named Jim Hunter (it would be awhile before Finley's new nickname of Catfish would be recognized), John "Blue Moon" Odom, Dave Duncan, Sal Bando, Bert Campaneris, Dick Green, Rick Monday, Joe Rudi, Chuck Dobson, and Reginald Martínez Jackson.

The manager of this young tenth-place team was a man named Robert Daniel Kennedy.

Bob Kennedy was forty-seven years old that spring, a man who had broken in as a professional baseball player before his seventeenth birthday at Vicksburg, Mississippi.

"I thought Reggie was going to be a hell of a player, a real superstar," Kennedy says. "I think he has been something less than that. I think all the fussing has taken something from his game. He always had that great power, but he struck out too damn much. We tried to work on him, get him to cut down on that swing a little, be a little more selective at the plate. He was interested in hitting home runs. That was the way he saw the game. It was frustrating. I wanted him to be a complete player. He'd go out and take batting practice and hit a dozen home runs. Then he would be slow getting out to the outfield, busy talking to a writer in the clubhouse or shooting the breeze with another player at the cage."

Bob Kennedy has always been one of the nicest, brightest, most accessible executives in baseball. He has had a successful career since his Oakland days, and as executive veep of the Cubs he has little contact with Jackson.

"Reggie makes a lot of money, but he should have been twice the player he became," says Kennedy. "He had the best potential of any player I ever saw. He should have been a brilliant fielder with that speed and arm. He should have hit three hundred, and forty homers a season, for ten years. Reggie never realized his full potential because he couldn't take suggestions. Hitting home runs came easy to him. He was always home run crazy. There's more to the game than that. He resented any suggestions about learning fundamentals. You know why Reggie excels in October and doesn't do it all season, why he doesn't hit three-twenty or three-thirty? He doesn't have the constant challenge. I think someone has to say to him, 'Reggie, you never hit three hundred and you never will. You just can't.' Then he would be motivated. Then he would hit three hundred."

It is a criticism voiced often about Reggie, but Jackson bristles when it is suggested he has not fulfilled the potential imagined for him in 1966 and 1967 and 1968. When he finally hit three hundred in 1980, he minimized the accomplishment, saying, "A lot of guys hit three-thirty and three-forty. George Brett hit three-ninety."

"I've worked damn hard for everything I've made in this game," Reggie says. "Nothing came easy, nothing. When I can't do it anymore, when I can't hit home runs and I can't put people in those seats, they'll get rid of me like a sack of flour. I've worked as hard as anybody who ever played this game. That's why I'm still here at thirty-five. That's why I'll still be here at forty. I'll be another Pete Rose. I'll prove to them age doesn't mean a damn thing. What counts is how good you are, how you deliver the goods, not how many birthdays you have."

* * *

The young man who reported to the A's training camp at Bradenton, Florida, that spring of 1968 was as finely devel-

oped an athlete as ever played the game. He was a shade
over six feet tall and weighed 203 pounds. His muscular
development was incredible; his biceps measured seventeen inches, his waist thirty-two inches. His shoulders,
chest, and upper body were thick and smoothly tapered. His thighs and calves were extremely muscular.
His body, which gave the appearance of a classic build,
had one obvious deficiency: His legs couldn't carry his
torso without pain.

"There were days when I simply could barely walk to
the plate," Jackson says. "My legs were giving me trouble
all the time."

The trainer of the Oakland A's, then as now, was a man
named Joe Romo. He was born in New Jersey and served
as a trainer at many schools, including Columbia University and Lafayette College, before he moved west to work
at the University of San Francisco. He worried about Reggie Jackson's legs for years.

"See, there's only one way to build up your legs," Romo
says, "run on them. Get them used to the pounding they
have to take on those concrete diamonds. In the summer-
time those fields are harder than the playgrounds in New
York. They don't get stronger sitting on the training table.
You have to pound them until they ache. Reggie wasn't
willing to do that. Not a lot of them are. You look at the
records: Reggie breaks down every year, misses ten,
fifteen games. Always with the legs. He always found
some excuse not to run."

Few baseball players run enough. Even the smaller
players, the base stealers, the guys who make their living
with their legs, refuse to run enough. It is too hard, too
much like work, too painful, too difficult. Baseball players,
like most athletes and most people, enjoy doing what they
do well. Reggie Jackson enjoyed hitting the baseball out
of the park. That is what he did best. That is what he
practiced the most. That is where his attention, motivation, and interest always lay.

Jackson's eyes light up when he talks of hitting. He is on

a high, the emotion pouring from him, the attention riveted, the satisfaction complete, the rewards in love and affection immeasurable.

"Home run hitters drive Cadillacs," home run champion Ralph Kiner once said. "Singles hitters drive Fords."

"Hitting that baseball is emotional to me," says Reggie. "It is fulfilling, satisfying, deeply moving. I feel the power in my hands and arms and neck and thighs when I go to the plate. When I hit the ball good, really good, I can feel my spine tingling and my nerve endings jiggling and all my senses participating. It is an unexplainable joy."

That is why Jackson relates so well to the other home run hitters in the league, to Jim Rice and Gorman Thomas and former Red Sox first baseman George Scott and John Mayberry of the Blue Jays.

"Every time we play the Yankees," Mayberry says, "Reggie comes to me and jives me about how many I got. If I'm a couple behind him, he says, 'You'll never catch me, Big John,' and I laugh at him and say I'll catch him that day, but I know I won't. When Reggie starts hitting those taters, he might hit ten, fifteen of them in a couple of weeks. It's no accident the man has four hundred home runs."

It was with George Scott, the golden-toothed ex-Boomer of the Boston Red Sox, a good pal of Reggie's, that home runs were discussed as an art form.

"It was right in my kitchen," Scott would say.

"Did you cook it?" Reggie would ask.

"Smoked it, Buck, really smoked it."

Jackson's face would break into a smile. He would soon be touching Scott's bat and rubbing the handle and inspecting the grains of finely crafted wood.

"Me," he would say, "I gotta go hunt for them. Nobody throws Reggie one in his kitchen."

Home run hitters are very similar to astronauts, men who understand only each other, described by Tom Wolfe as having "the right stuff." They too know when they have the "right stuff" and they understand only each other.

They have their private codes, their private language, their private joys. The crash of the baseball into the seats or over a wall beyond or into a parking lot reveals an act of such depth that singles hitters can merely stop and stare at the performance.

With his violent swing, his tapered, enormous body, his exceptional strength, and his motivation to be an eye-catching home run hitter as well as an important personality, a leader of the A's, Jackson began to swing for the fences.

"We wanted to help him by getting him to hit some balls to left field," says Kennedy. "He was not interested in that. It went right in one ear and out the other."

"Taters," says Jackson, in the baseball jargon for home runs brought into the game by blacks who called home runs long potatoes, "that's where the money is."

Every strong hitter from Babe Ruth to Reggie Jackson has known that if average is to be sacrificed for "taters," so be it. In the summer of 1961, as Roger Maris was driving on Babe Ruth's record of sixty homers in one season, a reporter from *Time* magazine, knowing nothing about the game (often a prerequisite for *Time* reporters for sports coverage), asked him, "Would you rather hit three hundred or sixty home runs?"

When the laughter had died down from the gathered press, listening to the question, Roger simply said, "How many guys have hit sixty homers and how many guys have hit three hundred?" In an attempt to stimulate Maris into controversial conversation (Maris was careful all that summer to avoid offending the muse of the Babe; nonetheless, he still received much crank mail threatening his life if he "dared" pass the immortal Babe) the same *Time* man in typical fashion asked Maris, "You play around on the road?"

"I'm a married man with five children," said Maris, holding his temper.

"I'm married," said the *Time* man, "and I play around on the road."

It is only home run heroes who are attacked by the press, challenged in their private moments, fawned over and fussed over in their daily pursuits.

In the summer of 1968 Jackson became a home run hero.

"He ached to be a leader on that team," says Catfish Hunter, who retired after the 1979 season. "Really there was no one else. The rest of us were young. We were trying to win jobs in the big leagues. Not Reggie. He knew he was hitting those home runs, and he had his job. We let him be the leader, let him deal with the press. We didn't take anything he said seriously. All we were interested in was how he played. And he sure could hit the shit out of the ball."

Charlie Finley, convinced now he had a hot one on his hands with Jackson, spent a great deal of time on the phone with him from his Chicago insurance office.

"Charlie has this problem with the time difference," says Reggie. "I'd be asleep on the road someplace and the phone would ring, and Charlie would go on and on about the game or some home run I hit."

The more home runs he hit, the more Charlie called him. Soon Finley was making pronouncements about him to the press. He called Ron Bergman of the Oakland *Tribune* at regular intervals to ask that he write about Reggie. He was not only Reggie's boss but Reggie's public relations man as well. He knew stories by Bergman, the most influential writer around the team, would help sell tickets.

"I didn't mind Charlie calling me," says Bergman. "It was always a story."

But Finley knew instinctively how to use the press. He also used his players to help him use the press. He gave out his private phone number in Chicago to one or two players (Blue Moon Odom and Bert Campaneris) and had them relay to him conversations they had heard between Jackson and reporters or the manager and reporters or any gossip in the clubhouse. There is not a team in baseball without a Deep Throat. On most clubs he is an innocuous player or a long-serving coach.

Finley and Jackson were alike in one instance. After each big Jackson home run or after each private interview Finley granted to the press, both would sidle up to the nearest newsman and ask, "What did he say about me?"

Since the reporters feed on gossip, controversy, and intrigue, they were quick to report conversations to both sides.

By the middle of the 1968 season Jackson became a media darling. He would never stop being a favorite of the press. He was bright; he was incredibly interesting and articulate; he could describe the most mundane things in the most unusual ways.

"It was as if all the power of the earth and the sky and the sands and the waters," he said once of a home run, "were in these hands."

It would be more likely that a reporter would then write a story about him with such a colorful quote than he would about a player who summarily remarks about a home run, "I hit the shit out of it."

Even Reggie's strikeout descriptions had flair. "You could hear the trains whistle," he once said after a big strikeout. "Hurricanes ain't nothing but soft winds when Reggie starts missin' when he goes for the downs," he said.

Players who can describe routine events in unique ways become personalities, media favorites, more heroic figures than their performances might indicate. A journeyman player for the New York Mets, who had one moment of on-field glory when he made a miraculous World Series catch for the champion Mets in 1969, Ron Swoboda, had many moments off the field. His best use of the language came about one day when the Mets split a doubleheader and Swoboda struck out five times. "It's a good thing we won one or I'd be eating my heart out," he said. "As it is, I'm only eating out my right ventricle."

Late in the 1968 season Reggie told Bergman something

of even more importance than how he could hit home runs off good pitching.

"I'll be rooming with Dobson from now on," he said casually.

Chuck Dobson was a twenty-four-year-old right-handed pitcher from Kansas City. He had attended Kansas University and had been signed by the A's in 1965. By 1968 he was one of the better starting pitchers on the team and had finished 10-10 in 1967. He was witty, bright, well spoken, and white. That was the news.

Twenty years after Jackie Robinson's start in baseball, few black players ever socialized with white players off the field, and very few ever roomed with them. There was a more significant reason even than color difference, racial prejudices, and tradition: sex.

"The road will make a bum out of the best of them," a baseball philosopher-journalist named Harold Rosenthal once said. Like traveling salesmen, baseball players have much time to fill on the road. Some read. Some visit museums. Some go to movies. A great many of them drink. Almost all of them chase or are chased by women, Baseball Annies. Those are the young women (some not so young) who throw themselves willingly at baseball players in exchange for any sign of recognition—a free ticket, an autographed ball, a personal letter.

When Reggie Jackson announced he would room with Chuck Dobson, tremors could be felt throughout the game. It was one thing to put your arm around a black player publicly, as Pee Wee Reese had done dramatically to show that the Dodger captain from Louisville accepted Jackie Robinson; it was yet another thing to room together. Now white women would be in a room with a black player. Now black women might be in a room with a white player.

"A lot of people made a fuss over it except me and Dobber," says Jackson. "We just got along well, so we roomed together. We were young players trying to make a living."

The game survived.

A few days later Jackson hit another home run, and the attention of the press was turned away from the social delicateness of integrating a hotel room.

Interest was increasing in the A's. Reggie was hitting home runs. He was also striking out at a record pace, just missing Dave Nicholson's 175 mark set in 1963. Reggie was to end the 1968 season with 171 strikeouts.

"Every strikeout angered me," says Reggie. "It was a wasted time at bat. It was a loss. I didn't do anything to help my team or myself."

The strikeouts were a show all by themselves. The bat would whirl around, and the ball would crash into the catcher's glove. The umpire would boom, "Strike three, yer out," and Jackson would heave the bat toward the dugout. It would force a batboy to jump or a teammate to scowl. Reggie would march to the dugout in anger, knock over the batting helmets, empty out the bat rack, kick a water cooler, or heave a glove.

"Intense," says Sal Bando, a longtime friend and third baseman of the A's. "I guess that was the word. Reggie simply didn't know how to deal with failure or frustration. He hadn't seen much of it."

The other players on the A's knew enough to stand clear of Jackson when he went into one of his tears, giving him extra room in the dugout and allowing him extra space in the clubhouse. Bando was very important to him.

"Sal was so mature, so in control, so reliable a friend," says Jackson.

Salvatore Leonard Bando of Cleveland, Ohio, was the captain of the winning Oakland A's teams. He met Reggie first at Arizona State, signed in 1965, came to Kansas City in 1966, anchored the championship Oakland teams, played out his option in 1976, and signed with Milwaukee in 1977. Someday he will be one of the most successful managers in the game.

"Reggie is one of those very exceptional human beings," says Bando. "He needs understanding and affection. He has to be listened to when things go badly for him. He has such a drive for success, such intensity, such emotion. At the same time he is one of the kindest, most understanding, most emotional people I have ever met in my life."

Soon Bando, Jackson, and outfielder Joe Rudi had become extremely close. They would be the pillars on which the great Oakland teams would be built.

"I expect Reggie and I will be close all our lives," says Bando.

Are there any problems over race?

"I judge a man by his actions," says Bando, "and Reggie does also."

The 1968 season, with Detroit winning the pennant, was drawing to a close. Jackson had played in 154 of Oakland's 162 games. He had batted only .250, but he had hit 29 home runs, more than half of them titanic blasts into the farthest points of several stadiums. He had struck out 174 times and led the league with 12 errors, most of them on wild throws. He had scored 82 runs, had 138 hits, and stolen 14 bases, a very high number for a slugger.

"He was such a talented player, so strong, so capable of doing so many wonderful things in this game," says Bob Kennedy. "He could have done more."

He had established himself as the best young home run hitter in the game. He had become a personality with the huge home runs and dramatic strikeouts. Less than two years out of Arizona State University he had shown he could hit big-league pitching.

More important, despite his flaming temper, he had handled himself well with the press, established himself as a leading personality on the team, and won the affection of the Oakland fans and the Oakland owner.

"There's nothing Reggie can't do," Charlie Finley told the press that winter. "This kid is going to be one of the greatest."

Several days before the season ended, Finley called Jackson in his hotel room.

"Son, I want you to play winter ball. I want you to cut down on those strikeouts. We got a program all worked out for you," said Charlie.

"Mr. Finley, I'm tired," Reggie said. "I'm going home to Arizona. Then I'll be spending the winter in school."

"School? I want you in winter ball," said Finley.

"I'll be at school," Jackson said.

Then he hung up the phone. Jackson would do what he wanted in the winter, as he always had, in his own way. He knew how to get ready for the next season. He didn't need Charlie to tell him.

Besides all that, he didn't like to be called son.

That Bitchy Lady Named "Ruth Maris"

THE YEAR OF 1969 WAS A MEMORABLE ONE IN THE ebb and flow of recent history. It was the year a failed politician named Richard Nixon was installed as President. The war in Vietnam was twisting itself into the psyche of Americans, who became increasingly angered and frustrated and embarrassed by what they saw on television every night. Lyndon Johnson had been forced out of the White House in January, and Hubert Humphrey had failed to attain the presidency, his legacy of good works forgotten by a public haunted by the impending disaster in Vietnam.

The memories of the assassinations of Martin Luther King and Robert F. Kennedy lingered painfully. The counterculture movement, drawing much support from the children of America's white middle class, was in full bloom in San Francisco's Haight-Ashbury district.

In 1969 man walked on the moon.

The Mets won the pennant and then the World Series.

And Reggie Jackson made a brave chase after a grand old bitch named "Ruth Maris."

* * *

Snow fell heavily on the streets of Chicago in the biting cold days of January 1969. Charlie Finley sat in his Michigan Avenue office. Spring training for the first time for his A's in Mesa, Arizona, was a little more than a month away. Finley, a man of constant motion, incredible energy, and reckless adventure, was hit with an idea. The more he thought about it, the more he loved it. He knew he could pull it off. He phoned the offices of New York Yankee president Michael Burke.

"Mike, this is Charlie, how are you?"

"Fine, Charlie. How you doing?"

"Freezing our asses off here in Chicago."

Burke, a dignified, distinguished former Columbia Broadcasting System executive and OSS hero in World War II, knew Charlie hadn't called to discuss the weather. He waited for the man to make his move.

"I'd like to talk to DiMaggio," Finley said. "Can you put me in contact with him?"

* * *

Joe DiMaggio. The name alone conjures up pictures of grace and style and class. From 1936, as a rookie out of San Francisco, through 1951, with three years out for Army service, DiMaggio had personified excellence. He had been the quiet leader of the Yankees, the successor to Babe Ruth as the most significant player on the most significant team of all. He had crossed that invisible threshold which divides the baseball player from the pop hero, cultural figure, major American star. He had retired from baseball, sore-kneed and sore-legged after the 1951 season. The Yankees had wanted him to continue as a part-time player, but he had too much dignity for that. Once, with the waters of San Francisco Bay lapping at his restaurant at Fisherman's Wharf, brother Tom DiMaggio was asked why Joe hadn't taken the $100,000 from the Yankees for another season. "Don't you know?" he said incredulously. "He wasn't Joe DiMaggio anymore." DiMaggio then drifted into television, found himself quickly unsuited for that, and moved across the country. He became America's perennial guest, available for celebrity golf tournaments and banquets and businessmen's dinners.

His fame had risen, rather than diminished, in retirement. There had been a storybook romance with movie star Marilyn Monroe and a crashing divorce nine months later in 1954.

In the angry, ugly days of 1969, Joe DiMaggio seemed still pure and untarnished, the last American hero.

Charlie Finley called DiMaggio and offered him a job as a special batting coach. The new Oakland manager would be a close friend and former teammate of DiMaggio's, Hank Bauer. It had often been said of Bauer he had a face like a clenched fist. His features were rugged, masculine, tough. He had been a real World War II hero, bouncing around islands named Saipan and Guam and Okinawa and Iwo Jima with the Marines. He had starred as a player for the Yankees from 1948 through 1959 and ended up with Kansas City. He had managed the A's for Finley there, coached at Baltimore, managed the Orioles to their first World Series victory in 1966, and been fired in 1968. He was replaced by a dumpling named Earl Weaver.

"I had always gotten along with Charlie," Bauer was saying early in the summer of 1980. "I thought that would be a good ball club. I was glad to go back. I was glad Charlie had gotten the big guy to help us."

Bauer remembers the end of the 1969 season. Finley used to call him almost every day. Then the calls stopped.

"I knew I was gone. That's one thing that pissed me off about Charlie. He didn't have the guts to tell me I was through," Bauer says.

When asked about young Reggie Jackson, Bauer leaned back in his chair, ran his hands through his old-fashioned crew cut, now thin and white, and spoke softly.

"What a great athlete. He had incredible power, a marvelous arm, could run like hell. I never had any trouble with the kid. He played hard for me. I told him if he played hard, hustled, gave me everything he had, I'd be his best friend. Then he started making big money later on. Changed him a lot, I hear. But in 1969, in the only year I had him, he was one hell of a baseball player."

* * *

In spring training at Mesa, Bauer told Jackson, "Joe will work with you. Listen to him. He's the best."

They sat together often in the clubhouse and leaned on an outfield fence or sipped a few beers together at night. DiMaggio was reluctant to offer advice. Jackson pumped him. DiMaggio became more open, less suspicious.

"He really helped me," says Reggie. "He knew so much about the game."

As the season began and the A's traveled from city to city, DiMaggio gave out interviews to the press. He was often asked about the young slugger, and he would say, "A fine young hitter, great power, he has a chance to be a wonderful player."

Jackson was still uncomfortable with a glove, and DiMaggio, the smoothest fielder of his time, worked often with him on that aspect of his game. Reggie was less interested in that than in hitting the baseball. In the summer of 1969 few second-year players ever hit as well.

"You could see that he was going to have a great year," says Bauer. "He had that enormous power and that grooved swing. He was out there hitting rockets."

Soon he had ten, fifteen, twenty, twenty-five home runs. The numbers began moving across the country, twenty games ahead of Ruth, twenty games ahead of Maris, a home run today, another yesterday, driving, driving, driving on baseball's most honored mark.

Babe Ruth had hit sixty homers in 1927, a mark every schoolboy can recall. Maris had hit fifty-nine homers in

154 games in 1961, ending his chase, his nerves frazzled, his
hair falling out, his eyes burning. In game 159 he had hit
home run number sixty, and in game 163 he had hit home
run number sixty-one off right-hander Tracy Stallard.

"I knew how long it would last," Maris says now, "because I knew how hard it was to get there. A lot of them
get near fifty, and then they fall. Who knows how long it
will last now? Maybe forever."

As the home runs mounted, Jackson moved from being
an Oakland celebrity, a California celebrity, to being a
national celebrity. Pressures mounted. His marriage became shakier. Jennie became an adjunct to the real
woman in his life, that twin devil he named "Ruth Maris."
The more homers he hit, the more famous he became, the
more time off the field was stolen from him. And from
Jennie. His emotions became tied to that simple act of
hitting a baseball. There was no other concern in his life,
not Jennie, not his friends, not his parents back East, not
his teammates or his fans. Hits, home runs, the chase after
"Ruth Maris," that was all that mattered, that consumed
him, that drove him. He was a chosen child of destiny,
reaching out for more home runs, more attention, more
honors. He could articulate these hitting emotions in the
most incredible hyperbole. One day he talked with Herb
Michaelson, a marvelous writer for the Modesto *Bee*.

"I am like a storm when I hit," he told Michaelson.
"First there's sleet. Slow, sharp sleet out of dark skies.
Then comes a mass of clouds and a howling wind. And
thunder. Very noisy, very frightening thunder. The wind
now grows in intensity. Leaves are blowing everywhere
off trees of every description. Limbs and boughs are snap-
ping off and falling. There is a great noise. There is a
heavy, heavy downpour all around. But just you wait.
That's only the way it is now. Only once in a while, like
rain. Someday, though, my hitting will be just like this.
Every day, as sure as that sun is up there, my hitting will
be all there. All around. Everywhere you look."

When Reggie talks like this—and he often does—his

eyes are riveted on the listener; his voice is soothing and modulated; his features are set; his body tightens; his command of a situation, a room, a person is total. He can be spellbinding. He can talk jive with fellow blacks; he can talk loud and brash and full of braggadocio with other players; he can storm through an ugly scene with fans. But when he is emotional, philosophical, deep, choosing his words purely for sound and effect, he can be poetic, plausible, and spiritual.

The home runs transformed Jackson into a national sports figure. He had reached the threshold of his stardom and now knew which direction he was moving toward.

"I joined the club that year," says Gene Tenace, the former Oakland catcher now with the San Diego Padres. "I never saw a hitter with such confidence. He was beginning to realize his role on that team, and everybody else was beginning to realize it, too. We would have a tough game against a tough pitcher, and the guys would be saying, 'I hope I can get a hit today,' and Reggie would say, 'I don't know about you guys, but I'll hit two out today,' and damned if he didn't. Any big hit you needed, any big run you had to drive in, he had to do it. He simply needed motivation. Needle him, kick him, tell him he can't do something, and watch him do it, from driving his car at a hundred miles an hour to hitting a ball five hundred feet."

Tenace says that Jackson probably worried more about what other people thought of him than any player he has ever met.

"It's like being married. Every day isn't perfect. You get on her nerves, and she gets on yours. In baseball you spend six, seven months with the same guys. One bad apple can fuck up an entire team. I don't think Reggie was a bad apple. I think he was a pretty nice guy. He never tried to hurt anybody. He always means well. I remember one time when he was down, not hitting well, depressed, very worried about a slump, and more worried about what the other guys thought. 'Be yourself, Reggie, you'll come out of it. The guys still like you.' He looked at me like a little kid and said, 'You mean it? The guys like me?' Sure, he was insecure, sensitive, easily hurt. This fucking game does that to you. I hit four home runs, as many as Babe Ruth, in the 1972 Series, and I had to fight like a bastard the next spring for my job."

* * *

The All-Star Game is baseball's best summer theater. It began as a newspaper promotion in conjunction with the Chicago World's Fair in 1933. It became a showpiece of the sport. In 1969 it was scheduled for July 22 in Washington's Robert F. Kennedy Stadium, newly named for the martyred brother of the murdered President. Baseball was celebrating its centennial that year. There were several major events in conjunction with the game.

A banquet was held at the Shoreham Hotel. The greatest team of all time was to be named, and the greatest living players, all in attendance, were selected. Babe Ruth was selected as the greatest player, Casey Stengel, doing a small dance as he moved onstage, was selected as the greatest living manager, and Joe DiMaggio was selected as the greatest living player.

All the honorees were invited to a banquet in the Blue Room of the White House. President Richard M. Nixon discussed baseball for thirty minutes with the assembled heroes, moving through an embarrassingly long monologue on how much he had liked the Chicago White Sox as a kid growing up in California. Then all the baseball personalities and news people were paraded through a reception line to have their pictures taken with Nixon.

There was one player in Washington that July day who intrigued the press. Reporters awaited his arrival in the Shoreham Hotel and surrounded him as he walked into the lobby to register. With Willie Mays and Willie McCovey and Johnny Bench and Pete Rose and Hank Aaron and Bob Gibson meandering through the hotel, the press chose to collect around second-year player Reggie

Jackson. They wanted to know how his chase after "Ruth Maris" was going.

"If I stay healthy, I might be able to do it," Jackson said.

More important, the writers wanted to know who in hell this kid was. Oakland's doings were not yet of major national import, but Jackson's homers were filling wire service stories each day. Jackson described his background in Philadelphia, growing up in his father's tailor shop, playing at Cheltenham High, and matriculating at Arizona State. Then came the baseball draft.

"I heard from some baseball scouts that the Mets wouldn't draft me because I had a white girlfriend," he was saying now as reporters moved closer. "That's what I heard. I can't say if it is true or not. But I would have played in New York. My home is Philadelphia. That would have been nice. But if that was true, if that was the reason, I'm glad I'm in Oakland."

The rains came heavily on the night of July 22, 1969. Hundreds of All-Star guests were caught in the downpour under steamy tents across from RFK Stadium. The players sat in their underwear in the clubhouses, autographing baseballs, signing pictures, telling stories, while they awaited word of cancellation of the game.

Reggie Jackson walked up to the locker occupied by Frank Howard, the gigantic slugger of the Washington Senators.

"Let's see that bat," said Jackson.

"Forty ounces, kid. Can you lift it?"

"I don't have to swing a heavy bat like that," said Jackson. "I just swing a quick one."

Howard stared at Jackson as the A's right fielder walked down the line of lockers, talking with his All-Star teammates, examining their bats, moving through the crowd of stars like a casting director through starlets.

"Who is that kid?" Howard asked.

"Jackson, Reggie Jackson of the A's," said Frank Robinson of the Orioles. "Don't mess with him. He's the only one in this room as strong as you."

Jackson, who later hit a memorable All-Star home run, failed to get a base hit in that game in two chances. He started in center field, caught two fly balls, and was replaced by Paul Blair of the Orioles when the game was played the next night before 45,259 people, including the President of the United States.

In San Francisco the story of the game was Willie McCovey's two homers in a 9–3 National League win. In Cincinnati it was Johnny Bench's homer. In Detroit it was catcher Bill Freehan's homer. In Washington it was hometown hero Howard's line drive shot against the left-field seats.

In New York, in the media capital, in the city where the advertising agencies and the networks and the big newspapers and the major magazines make their homes, the story was a young Oakland A's outfielder named Reggie Jackson. Had the Mets passed on him because he now had a white wife? Whether the answer was yes, no, or maybe —and no one would ever really know—that discussion seemed to overwhelm the game.

As it turned out, the Mets didn't need Jackson in 1969. As it also turned out, New York City was still in Reggie Jackson's future. It would be part of his career. But the days of candy bars and New York stardom still were years away.

Jackson had not yet made a dent with his bat on the All-Star Game, but he had come forward as a media personality with the New York press. It had been a successful visit to Washington for him. He came to town as a hot-hitting home run kid. He left town in a splash of prominence, regarded now as a controversial star.

Jackson flew back to Oakland on July 24 with teammates Sal Bando and Blue Moon Odom. He carried a suit bag and an autographed silver tray, a gift from the league for being an All-Star. As the plane climbed smoothly out of Washington's National Airport and moved west toward California, Jackson could now think only of that bitch, that tough old lady he was challenging, that mean task of making the world notice him and his assault on "Ruth Maris."

Babe Ruth had hit fifty-nine homers in 1921. When he hit a home run for number sixty off left-hander Tom Zachary on September 30, 1927, he was only breaking his own home run record. Not much was made of it in the press. He was thirty-two years old, showed no signs of slowing down, and could generally be expected to hit sixty-one, sixty-two, or sixty-three homers in the next season or two.

The record had lasted for thirty-four years when Roger Maris attacked it. Then the baseball world attacked him.

Maris turned twenty-seven years old on September 10, 1961. He was a husky green-eyed Yankee right fielder who had grown up in Fargo, North Dakota. He was a solidly built six-footer, 205 pounds, with thick arms, thick chest, and heavyset legs. He wore his hair in a tight crew cut, spoke in a monotone, and lived quietly with his wife and five children in Kansas City. He had been the American League's Most Valuable Player in 1960. In 1961 he engaged in a titanic home run race with Mickey Mantle, who ended with fifty-four homers when an abscess in his buttocks knocked him out of the lineup and into the hospital.

Commissioner Ford Frick, who had been a ghostwriter for Babe Ruth as a New York journalist, decreed Maris had to break Ruth's mark in his first 154 games for the record to be valid. He said if it went past 154 games, it would be marked in the record books of baseball with an asterisk.

Maris, angered at this insult to his performance, simply said, "A season's a season. I didn't write the schedule."

Two new teams, the Los Angeles Angels and the Minnesota Twins (moved from Washington and replaced by a new Washington franchise), had joined the league that year in an expanded schedule. Maris moved on the Babe's record under enormous pressure from fans, sportswriters, and television. He was demeaned by most of the press. Old-time players protected Ruth's image and denigrated Maris and modern baseball. The entire nation seemed caught up in the controversy. Phony feuds between Maris and Mantle (who shared a New York apartment) were created by the press.

Maris just missed tying the record in Baltimore in game 154 and hit number sixty in game 159 and number sixty-one in game 163 at Yankee Stadium. He received the plaudits of the crowd and the congratulations of Mrs. Babe Ruth. A nineteen-year-old fan named Sal Durante caught the last homer and demanded $5,000 for its return. Maris posed for pictures and told the kid to keep the ball.

In the summer of 1980, a little heavier than he had been, still wearing that crew cut, speaking quietly and selling beer out of a Gainesville, Florida, distributorship, Maris talked of the home run chase. He had earlier enjoyed an animated conversation with Jackson. The subject centered on bat weights and home runs.

"Whether it is Reggie or Dave Kingman or Gorman Thomas or anyone else," Maris was saying, "there is no pressure until forty homers. Then it builds a little at forty-five. After that it becomes tough. Of the last ten home runs I bet not one of them was hit off a strike. The pitchers would rather walk you than answer the questions from reporters. Anybody who does it will have to do it without any help."

As he left Washington on July 24, 1969, Reggie Jackson, twenty-three years old, had thirty-seven home runs. He had played in ninety-two games for the A's. After ninety-two games for the Yankees in 1961, Maris had thirty-six homers. After ninety-two games for the Yankees in 1927, Ruth had thirty homers. Jackson was ahead of Ruth by plenty, ahead of Maris, and driving hard on that most recognizable of all sports records.

"I was too young," Jackson says now. "The pressure was too much. Too many people wanted too much of me. 'Reggie, do this, and Reggie, do that. Reggie, go here, and Reggie, go there.' Now I could deal with it. Now I would know what to do. But twenty-three? Too young for that scene, man, too young."

Jackson hit three more homers in July to end the month with forty homers. He needed only ten in August and ten in September to tie Babe Ruth.

"April is the cruelest month," wrote T. S. Eliot. Nonsense. Any baseball fan knows August is the cruelest month. The heat is blistering. The travel is wearisome. The wear and tear on a player's body are insufferable. The bat grows heavy, and the ball feels like lead to a pitcher.

It was twelve days into August before Jackson could hit a home run in that month, a long smash off left-hander Pete Richert of the Orioles. He got one off Denny McLain, the thirty-one-game Detroit winner of 1968, on August 17, and two in two days off Dave McNally, who was later to gain fame for challenging baseball's reserve clause, and Jim Hardin of Baltimore. He had forty-five homers at the end of August. Ruth had forty-three on August 31, 1927. Maris had fifty-one on August 31, 1961. There was still time if Reggie had a spectacular September.

"He didn't have much left by then," remembers Oakland *Tribune* sportswriter Ron Bergman. "He was washed out. He developed a rash. Everybody knew it was nerves. He seemed more testy. His legs bothered him. There was just no way he could hit fifteen or sixteen homers in September."

He hit two.

The race was over. The hill was insurmountable. That majestic, yet evil bitch "Ruth Maris" had defeated him.

In October it was time to return to Arizona, to escape the daily pressures, to see if he could salvage his crumbling marriage with Jennie, to plunge deeper into business with Gary Walker at the development company, to get away from the hordes of questioning sportswriters who wanted a piece of him almost every waking moment.

In a few weeks, after spending a little time with Sal Bando, after riding into the open lands with Gary Walker, after reading countless stories about his heroic challenge, he began feeling more contented with himself, assured now that he had only begun to make the mark on American life he knew he would someday make.

He had finished the 1969 season with 47 homers, the youngest American Leaguer at twenty-three to achieve that milestone. He had led the league in runs scored with 123. He had knocked in 118 runs and batted .275. He had led the league again in strikeouts with 142, and Harmon Killebrew had passed him in the final days of the season for the home run title with 49.

"You had a wonderful season, son," Charlie Finley told him one day during the winter. "I'll be giving you a nice raise."

"You certainly will, Charlie," Reggie said.

Charles O. Finley didn't particularly like the sound of Reggie's voice. He didn't seem grateful at all at the announcement he was getting a raise.

For the first time in his life Charlie Finley would meet his match, and then some, in the person of a tough, determined, intelligent young Reggie Jackson.

(Left) In his tailor shop in Center City, Philadelphia, Jack the Tailor poses in front of his sign, which reads, "Reggie Jackson's Dad." (*Photo courtesy of Janet Allen*)

(Below) Reggie was a 1966 Arizona State star and soon a big leaguer. His college credentials would later lead to Oakland stardom. (*Photo courtesy of the Arizona State University Sports Information Office*)

Reggie Jackson, OF, 6-0, 197, So., ASU

(Right) Jennie Campos, a different lady today than she was as Mrs. Reggie Jackson. She was vacationing at her Arizona home while school was out in Japan when this picture was taken. (*Photo courtesy of Janet Allen*)

(Below) Jennie (far left) with other American school-teacher friends outside their school in Nagoya, Japan. (*Photo courtesy of Jennie Campos*)

Ex-high-school pitcher Jackson throws batting practice as a young outfielder with the Oakland A's. (*Photo courtesy of the Oakland A's*)

Unleashing that powerful swing, Jackson is shown here slamming a homer for the A's as he matures as a hitter. (*Photo courtesy of the Oakland A's*)

Reggie has extraordinary demands on his time but always finds time for kids. Here he makes a handicapped lad one happy fellow. (*Photo courtesy of the Oakland A's*)

(Above) The historic day, November 29, 1976. Yogi Berra, a smiling Thurman Munson, and Roy White help Reggie get used to Yankee uniform number 44. (*Photo courtesy of Louis Requena*)

(Right) A rare quiet moment for Jackson and Munson, on the field in 1977. Their relationship was always strained if not tumultuous up until Munson's death in 1979. (*Photo courtesy of Louis Requena*)

Reggie's mighty swing has become legendary in New York. Here he unloads a long home run. (*Photo courtesy of Louis Requena*)

(Above) One of Reggie's happiest days after the 1977 World Series triumph and three homers against the Dodgers. Reggie gets some help in drinking his champagne from Cliff Johnson. (*Photo courtesy of the New York Yankees*)

(Left) Reggie draws much of his emotional sustenance from the adoration of his fans. New Yorkers were initially wary of the Oakland slugger, and it took four years for the catcalls to turn to cheers. (*Photo courtesy of Louis Requena*)

(Below) Sluggers often find themselves decked by tough pitchers. No American League hitter goes down as often as Reggie. (*Photo courtesy of Louis Requena*)

ne of the best-liked players among other big-name players, Reggie kids with x-teammate Mike Torrez and Boston slugger Jim Rice before a deadly serious ankee-Red Sox battle. (*Photo courtesy of Louis Requena*)

eggie is often called on to pose for pictures with sponsors and business associ-tes. Here he goes through the ritual without much joy. (*Photo courtesy of Louis equena*)

When the game gets hot, Reggie can let loose all the tensions with a good cu
His strikeouts are as exciting as his homers. (*Photo courtesy of Louis Requen*

(Top, right) That old smoothie Billy Martin gives Reggie some sweet talk, but r
one knows what either man was really thinking about the other. (*Photo courtes*
of Louis Requena)

(Bottom, right) Bob Lemon, the pennant-winning Yankee manager in 1978, l
Reggie play baseball without a fuss. He finished with a flurry as the Yankees wo
the pennant and the Series. (*Photo courtesy of Louis Requena*)

Reggie Jackson, one of the beautiful people, did some disco time at Studio 54. Here he arrives at the disco with model Lisa Ryall (right), who takes a peek and asks Reggie to shut off the photogs. (*Photo courtesy of Associated Press*)

(Top, left) Like the Babe, he promised a dying youngster a homer, and he delivered the next day. A week later the boy was dead of cancer. (*Photo courtesy of Gannett-Westchester/Robert F. Rodriguez*)

(Bottom, left) When the day is done, Reggie goes up to his nineteenth floor apartment on Fifth Avenue, across from The Metropolitan Museum, and gets away from it all with his houseplants. (*Photo courtesy of Janet Allen*)

The kid from Wyncote and Cheltenham High is thirty-four years old, and he cele-
brates with a surprise birthday cake offered by the Yankee staff. (*Photo courtesy
of Louis Requena*)

A Winter in the Sun

O NE OF THE FEW THINGS THAT HAD REMAINED constant for more than 100 years of professional baseball was low salaries. The issue had not been mentioned at the 1969 centennial events of the game in Washington. It was a cloud that hung over baseball as it entered the decade of the 1970s. Salaries were on the move. There was a revolution brewing.

In Oakland, California, Reggie Jackson followed other players' spiraling salaries with keen interest. He had been paid $20,000 for the 1969 season. Now he wanted $60,000, a star's salary. Finley offered $40,000, a young star's salary. Salaries meant more than dollars and cents to players. They were the only true measure of status players had. High averages were fine but meaningless if not accompanied by high numbers on the contract.

The contract battle was difficult. Finley phoned Reggie regularly and sent him letters. He had other club officials call him. Finley leaked stories to the newspapers ridiculing Reggie, suggesting he choked in August and September under the pressures of the home run chase. He pointed out that Reggie was, after all, only twenty-four years old, reminding readers he had paid a lot of money to sign Reggie originally out of Arizona State, and suggesting he was most ungrateful.

There was nothing Jackson—or any of the other players—could actually put his finger on, but the odor of racism lingered in the background of all this. Finley was condescending. Finley was abusive and abrasive in dealing with Jackson. Finley got personal, suggesting that Reggie didn't always run as hard as he could, throw as hard as he could, play as hard as he could. Finley was equally tough in bargaining with white players Sal Bando, Catfish Hunter, Joe Rudi, but there was never quite the same intensity.

"That was the last time I was ever naïve about owner-player relations," says Jackson. "I learned that it was all a business decision. The owner does what he has to do, and the player does what he has to do."

The resentment over the bitter contract hassle remained. Jackson seemed on edge all spring. Writers wanted to talk about any chance for a new challenge on old "Ruth Maris," and Jackson wanted to talk about how Finley had intimidated him. Sportswriters inquired about the chances of the A's, under new manager John McNamara, and Jackson wanted to talk about how much money he would make Charlie pay him next year.

Jackson, thinking only of the soured relationship with Finley, could not concentrate at bat. His swings were listless, his baserunning was odd, and his defense faltered. Finley called him on the phone and berated him. Then Finley called McNamara, a shy and laconic man, and ordered him to bench Jackson and to pinch-hit for him and to embarrass him by using him for defense. McNamara, starting his first full season as a big-league manager, did what Charlie told him. The situation grew more tense each day. McNamara, on orders from Finley, forced Jackson into embarrassing positions. There was even a threat that Finley would send Reggie down to the minors.

It was this situation, this harassment, that hardened Jackson's attitudes about money. Forever. He knew Finley could jerk him around because Jackson still needed the paycheck.

"Money is power," Jackson says now. "When you have it, you are independent. Nobody can force you to do what you don't want to do. People respect you when you have money, real money, big money."

As late as June 11 he was hitting under .200 at .198. There was no climactic home run race in 1970. Jackson had all of 10 home runs through the end of June. He hit only 6 in the next two months. He finished with 23 homers, his lowest big-league total ever. He batted .237, his lowest big-league average ever. He managed 57 runs scored and 66 runs driven in, both again career lows. He struck out 135 times in 149 games. Any way one looks at it, 1970 was a terrible season.

There were moments that year when Jackson actually considered retirement, when he would sit alone in some hotel room or in his Oakland apartment or in a quiet lunchtime café on the road and think about entering the real estate business full time with Gary Walker. The pressures were enormous, and the rewards seemed slight.

A few things still moved him. The fans were booing him in Oakland, but the kids weren't. He had always had a closeness with children, the children of his friends, his nieces and nephews, his teammates' offspring. And he always seemed to get along with old people. Jackson was quiet and gentlemanly with elderly people. He would wink at old women in a hotel lobby and force them to blush. He would stand and talk endlessly with old men, never showing, as most athletes did, obvious signs of boredom. He seemed to find solace in people away from the rigors of his contract, his poor performance, and the pressures on him.

One afternoon during that season, while playing a game

in Washington, he was approached by a young black man named Thad Mumford. Mumford today is a well-known Hollywood television writer, with key credits on *M*A*S*H, The Jeffersons, Maude,* and the enormously successful production of *Roots.*

"I had been a batboy for the Yankees a couple of years earlier," says Mumford. "I had seen Reggie a few times, chatted with him a little, but couldn't really say I knew him. I had an elderly grandfather in Washington by the name of Joseph Jefferson. He was a fantastic baseball fan. He especially liked home run hitters, and he especially liked Reggie. Reggie had hit all those home runs in 1969, and he had turned on a lot of people, especially a lot of old black people."

Black baseball fans for years had argued that Josh Gibson, the bruising black catcher, who was too old to play in the majors when the color line was finally broken by Jackie Robinson, was really better than Babe Ruth. There were legends about the size of some of Gibson's home runs, 450 feet, 500 feet, 550 feet, 600 feet easily. There was talk among old black baseball reporters that Gibson had once actually hit a fair ball out of Yankee Stadium, a feat not ever achieved and documented by a white player before 1947 and not by a white or a black after 1947.

Jackson, with his prodigious wallops, was the closest reminder of Gibson that old blacks like Joseph Jefferson could recall.

"My grandfather was wasting away with cancer," says Mumford. "He was near death when the A's came into Washington one day. I thought if I could get Reggie's autograph, if I could get it on a ball for him, that would make the old man's final days a bit happier."

Mumford stopped Jackson in the Oakland clubhouse after a game. He told him about his grandfather after reminding Reggie he had been a Yankee batboy.

"Where is the old man?" Jackson asked.

"At home. He wants to die at home," Mumford said.

"How far from the ball park?"

"Oh, about half an hour or so," Mumford said.

"Let's go," Reggie said.

"You mean, you'll drive out there?"

"I said let's go."

Mumford quickly walked out of the visiting clubhouse at Robert F. Kennedy Stadium, walked across the parking lot with Jackson, got into his old Chevrolet, and drove off to see his grandfather.

Reggie spent about half an hour out there with the old man, signed the ball, talked to him about some old black players he had seen, promised to try to hit one for him, and was driven back to the Shoreham Hotel, where the A's stayed, by Mumford.

"Thanks, Reggie, that was very kind," Mumford said.

"Glad I could do it," Reggie said.

Mumford let the ballplayer off, turned around toward his own home, and drove off. There were tears in his eyes.

"The old man lived about three more months," he said. "The doctors were amazed. They thought he couldn't last three days. He died quietly one night. That ball was on the nightstand next to his bed. We buried him with the ball in his hand."

* * *

The 1970 season was finally over. Jackson felt relieved of an enormous weight. He had played a little better in the last few weeks. He realized he had let the problems with Finley fester all year. He had fouled up his mechanics. He no longer had that fluid, violent, overwhelming swing. He was defensive at bat and defensive around his team. He had to save his career. At this lowest point of his professional life he would make the decision that would save his career. Reggie Jackson would play winter ball in Santurce, Puerto Rico. His manager would be a man named Frank Robinson. Robinson would turn out to be the most important man in Reggie Jackson's professional baseball life.

Like Jackson, Frank Robinson had been a sensitive, arrogant, and controversial player but a proved star almost from his rookie year. He was born in Beaumont, Texas, in 1935 and grew up in Los Angeles, California. He was signed by the Cincinnati Reds at the age of seventeen and sent to Ogden, Utah. He batted .348 in his first professional season and quickly moved up through the Cincinnati farm system. He came to the Reds in 1956, the last year that Jackie Robinson played in the National League. While Robinson was no relation, he was a close friend and adviser in Frank's earliest days.

Two years later another California outfielder by the name of Vada Pinson joined the Reds. The two have remained close for nearly a quarter of a century.

"What you have to remember about relationships in baseball," Robinson was saying one summer day in 1980, "is that they don't last. Vada and I are close; we talk on the phone; we visit back in California; our families see each other. I played for twenty years. He's the only player I have remained close to."

Robinson led the Reds to a pennant in 1961. He batted .323, hit 37 homers, and knocked in 124 runs. He was named the National League's Most Valuable Player. In 1965, at the age of thirty, he came to Baltimore and had another marvelous season. He batted .316, hit 49 homers, and knocked in 122 runs to win baseball's famed Triple Crown. He was named the league's MVP, the only player ever to win the honor in both leagues. More important, he played hard, tough, aggressive baseball, National League baseball, knocking down shortstops to break up double plays, crashing into walls to catch fly balls, hurling his body every which way. The Orioles won the pennant and defeated the Los Angeles Dodgers in the World Series. Robinson would never again repeat his performance in the 1966 season, but he would remain an important, successful player for another decade.

Robinson was thirty-five years old at the end of the 1970 season. He had always enjoyed the intellectual challenge of the game as well as the physical process. He was a bright, articulate man, a leader on both the Cincinnati and the Baltimore clubs, and was certain he could handle a managerial job. He let it be known that he would entertain a managerial position. The Santurce club outside San Juan contacted him, and he was hired to manage the club in the 1970–1971 season.

Four Americans were allowed on each Puerto Rican team. Late in October, after he had arrived in Santurce and had managed his club for several days, Robinson got a call from Charlie Finley.

"I'd like to send Reggie down to your club. I think you can help. He respects you," said Finley.

"I think he can be a hell of a player. I'd love to have him," Frank said.

"Just one thing," said Finley. "I want him out there playing hard every day. He didn't play hard every day for me at Oakland."

"Everybody," said Frank, "plays hard for me."

*   *   *

Frank Robinson had decided he could make a mark on baseball, establish his credentials, and become the first black to win a big-league managing job as a result of an impressive season with the Santurce club.

"We had a good ball club, and I thought we could win," he says. "I needed a win to get a foothold into managing a big-league club. If they were to break the line, they had to do it with a manager who won."

One of Robinson's best players, one of his most productive and important players toward this end, was Reggie Jackson.

"He came down to help his own career," says Robinson, "but he knew that a good winter season would also help me."

Robinson worked closely with Jackson in the early days of the Puerto Rican season. He gave him extra time for batting practice. He stayed close to him. He watched him hit, run, and field.

"The big break probably came about a month into the season," Robinson says. "I had my wife and kids with me down there for a month. Then they went home to California. I decided to ask Reggie, who was living in a small hotel, to move in with me."

This arrangement would hardly have worked in Oakland or Cincinnati or New York or Cleveland. Managers and players don't live together.

"In Puerto Rico nobody on the team cared. We were just two Americans, and nobody expected I would give him any privileges," Robinson said.

Robinson, thirty-five years old, and Jackson, twenty-four years old, developed an extremely close relationship. Even though Robinson was still playing well and was only eleven years Jackson's senior, he seemed much more mature, experienced, immune to the pressures of the baseball world.

They ate breakfast together, sat around the apartment, walked the streets of Santurce, lunched at sidewalk cafés, drove out to the ball park, spent time together at the batting cage, and sat together most of the game when they weren't on the field. Then they drove back together after the game, had a beer or two, stayed up talking until daylight came.

"I had been through a lot of similar emotions," Robinson says. "I had to convince Reggie the world didn't revolve around him. He was burning so desperately to be the leader on that Oakland team, to be recognized as the head man, to be fussed over by the other players, the press, and the owner."

There was an edge of sadness, confusion, unhappiness in Jackson's voice as he stretched his feet out on a small coffee table in Robinson's Santurce apartment one day and said, "Frank, why won't they accept me?"

"Reggie, there are twenty-five leaders on that Oakland club. Each guy is a leader in his own way. You can't force something like that. You can't force Finley to make you the number one guy just because you hit a lot of home runs."

"If I don't hit a lot of home runs, if I don't drive in the big runs," Reggie said, "we don't win."

"You don't win if twenty-five guys don't do their jobs," Frank said. "One guy doesn't carry a team, not five guys or ten. That's what you have got to accept. Stop putting all that pressure on yourself."

Jackson made it clear to Robinson that he hungered for that leadership role. He was anxious for recognizable stardom, and he was not going to be satisfied until he had that recognition, that appreciation, that love from his teammates.

"What you have to do," said Robinson, "is make them accept you the way you are. Play as hard as you can. Hustle all the time. Never let up. Back off from those public confrontations with the owner. That makes the other players nervous. You haven't been around long enough for that."

Soon Jackson was easing into his role on the Santurce club, hitting home runs, helping Robinson's team win the pennant, gaining the fame and acceptance in Puerto Rico he did not yet have in Oakland, helped no small bit by his Spanish heritage and his ability to converse in Spanish with the local press.

"Reggie's nature is such that he needs attention and affection," Frank Robinson says. "He is a performer, and he enjoys being onstage. In some ways he is always onstage. He likes to do dramatic things on the field, and he likes to say dramatic things off the field. Maybe they call Reggie a hot dog and they don't call Pete Rose a hot dog. Maybe some of it is racial, sure, but a lot of it has to be that Reggie is looking to express his opinion on everything. Rose isn't."

In the ten years since Santurce, Robinson and Jackson have stayed friendly, if not exceptionally close.

"We see each other. We talk. We compare notes. But

we don't go out of the way to socialize with each other," Frank says.

During a summer visit by the Orioles to Yankee Stadium Robinson leaned against the batting cage as Reggie was putting on a batting show for the early fans, a long home run to left field, a couple to left-center, three or four more over the right-field wall in right. He walked out of the cage, all smiles, his Yankee blue warm-up T-shirt soaked with sweat, his neck perspiring, his glasses damp from his own efforts.

"I can't do no better," he said to Robinson.

"Your fans had to love that," said Frank.

"I had to love it," said Jackson.

Then he threw his bat on the ground and walked toward the Yankee dugout. The fans stood and applauded as he ducked his head and walked up the ramp to ready himself for the game.

"Nothing to prove anymore, but he's still a great showman," said Robinson. "Reggie will always be Reggie."

"He Taught Us How to Win"

CHARLES O. FINLEY SPENT TEN YEARS BUILDING HIS baseball team into a contender. By 1971 it was on the threshold of success. Finley ached for a winner. He thought now he had put all the pieces together for a winning team. He had the best young pitcher in the game in Catfish Hunter and the best reliever in Rollie Fingers. He had a fine infield with Sal Bando, Bert Campaneris, and Dick Green as the key players. His outfield was solid with Joe Rudi, Reggie Jackson, and Rick Monday. He had a good catching staff with Gene Tenace and Dave Duncan. Now he felt that all he needed to win was a new manager. Finley always decided all he ever needed to win was a new manager. He had gone through Bob Kennedy, Hank Bauer, and John McNamara in his three successive seasons in Oakland. In 1971 he hired Dick Williams. This time he was right. It would prove to be a marvelous move, putting the right manager in the right place at the right time in Reggie's career.

An intense player, very self-confident, Dick Williams was learning a great deal about the game as he sat on the Dodger bench with those wonderful Dodger teams of the early 1950s. He managed with intensity, struggling over every out and every game, and in 1965 and 1966 he finished third and second in his two minor-league managerial seasons at Toronto.

In 1967 he was hired by the Boston Red Sox to manage a bunch of players long known as country clubbers. The Red Sox had talent but hadn't won since 1946 mostly because of a serious lack of significant discipline. The Red Sox had a good time day and night, home and away, game or no game. That all ended with Williams.

He began by molding Carl Yastrzemski into one of the game's greatest team players. He taught a soft-spoken, gentle, college-educated pitcher named Jim Lonborg how to throw tight at hitters and win. With some talented young kids—Reggie Smith, Mike Andrews, Joe Foy, George Scott—and some still-valuable veterans—Elston Howard, John Wyatt, and Ken Harrelson—Boston won the pennant under Williams on the final day of the season. The Sox lost a tough seven-game World Series to St. Louis. Yastrzemski was the American League MVP, Lonborg was the Cy Young Award winner, and Williams was the Manager of the Year.

Squabbles with some of the players and with the front office, in addition to a disappointing fourth-place finish in 1968 and a third-place finish in 1969, ended the love affair between Williams and the Red Sox. He was fired on September 23, 1969, and moved to Montreal to coach under an ex-Dodger teammate named Gene Mauch.

"This is the man we need to instill pride and discipline in this club," said Finley, who was most responsible for lack of pride and lack of discipline by the way he undermined his players and managers. "I think he will lead us to a pennant."

Finley's all-pervasive attitude had affected every player and each of his managers. Now it was Williams's turn. He was a strong man. Would he be subject to the boss's pressures?

"I'll run the club my own way," Williams announced at his hiring.

"Dick stressed fundamentals in spring training," says Oakland catcher Dave Duncan, now a Cleveland coach. "He made us all managers on the field. Suddenly we saw how things really worked in baseball. It wasn't just hitting, running, and throwing the ball. It was thinking ahead, analyzing the play, anticipating the moves of the other team. He made every player think he was a leader of his own position. He made the players more intense and proud of their performance. He gave us bigger egos. He told us how good we could be. We all knew we contributed, but we were also aware of who contributed the most, who was the one player we couldn't afford to lose, the one player who really was most vital to our success. That was Reggie."

"He was down when I got there," says Williams, "but the man had so much talent it was easy to see how he could carry a club. Having Reggie in an up mood was essential to the success of the Oakland A's. My job was to bring out that talent, remove those doubts, allow Reggie to fulfill his destiny."

When Reggie is asked about Dick Williams, his eyes light up, his pride in those successful Oakland years emerges, and his memories are warm.

"I don't like to go around rating managers," he says. "I can't say this one is better than that one. You learn from all your managers. They all have you at different stages, and you need different things. We had the talent on the Oakland club. We all had our functions on that club, but we would not have won anything without Dick Williams. He taught us how to win. We didn't know how before he came. We were just some guys who could play, but he taught us how to play together."

"Dick had this emotional distaste for losing," says Dave Duncan. "We'd lose a game, and he'd go over certain fundamental things we did wrong. We'd lose two in a row, and you would think we had lost twenty in a row. He would actually get ill, he hated losing so much. He kept stressing pride. 'The Oakland A's don't make mental mistakes,' he would say. Then we'd go over and over the things we had done wrong."

Williams, now a successful manager with Montreal, is a little heavier, with a few more gray hairs in his mustache than he had then. He is still intense and poised as he talks.

"I never had any trouble with Reggie," he says. "He played like hell for me. He was a leader on that ball club. You could count on him. I was proud to have Reggie with that team."

In the early days of the 1971 season Jackson seemed to shake himself free of the trauma of the poor 1970 season. He was growing as a leader, more forceful with the press, more confident with his teammates, more protective of the Oakland pride, more respected by his teammates.

"Some guys didn't like him, sure," says Duncan, "but hell, we all knew he could carry the club for a month by himself. Who the hell else could do that? Mike Epstein thought he could, but that just wasn't so. He came over from Washington, and he thought he would be the big home run guy on the A's, the big hero. There was only one big home run guy, one big hero. That was Reggie. He was born to the job."

In 1968 Finley had signed a left-handed high school quarterback out of Mansfield, Louisiana. He had joined the A's in the last weeks of the 1970 season and pitched a no-hitter in his second big-league start. His name was Vida Rochelle Blue, Jr. Finley once tried to get him to change his name to True Blue. "It will be more colorful, and you'll get famous faster," the owner said.

"I like my name. It was my father's before me," Blue said.

Blue refused to allow his boss to change him in any way until after an incredible 1971 season and a bitter holdout.

They would change Blue's personality, transforming the smiling, gregarious youngster into a suspicious, often bitter young man. That would be Finley's contribution to Blue's baseball lore, more than the failed opportunity for baseball finally to have somebody who was really "True Blue."

Blue lost his 1971 opener and then won ten straight games. The A's were rushing off to their first Western Division title. Reggie Jackson was having a fine comeback season, but most of the attention around the A's in the summer of 1971 focused on Blue. Nationally syndicated columnists pressed close for interviews. *Time* magazine put Blue on a cover. Movie companies made offers to sign the handsome black twenty-one-year-old left-handed pitcher. Denny McLain had won thirty-one games in 1968, the first pitcher to turn that trick since Dizzy Dean won thirty for the 1934 Cardinals, and Blue that summer was being questioned about the recurrence of such a feat.

"That's the one question I won't answer," he told interviewers.

As the All-Star Game in Detroit on July 13, 1971, drew closer, Blue was beginning to feel the pressures of the incredible start. He was 17-3.

"I feel like a prisoner," he told teammate Tommy Davis, the ex-Dodger star now sharing an apartment with him. "I hate it."

As he discussed his plight one day with Davis in their Oakland apartment, the telephone rang. Blue moved toward it.

"Don't answer it," Davis said.

"That wouldn't be nice," Blue said, "and besides, if I don't answer it, how will I ever know who was calling?"

A handsome young man, a bachelor, fond of the ladies, Blue knew that not all the phone calls were from reporters. Some were from women who had considerable skill in obtaining the unlisted phone numbers of Blue and other famous players.

* * *

The All-Star Game had become a favorite of the fans. All the great players of the game would be collected in one place for this showpiece event. The National League, mostly on the strength of its quality black players, had begun to dominate the game. By 1971 the National League had won eight straight All-Star Games. The event was becoming an embarrassment to the American League.

In Detroit the game took on even more interest than usual because it was the first time two black pitchers, Vida Blue for the Americans and Dock Ellis for the Nationals, had ever started against each other. Ellis and Blue were the dominant figures as the game began. Reggie Jackson was the dominant figure as the game ended.

In his only other All-Star Game, Jackson had monopolized the press coverage of the event with the discussion of his nondraft by the Mets in the season he was chasing old "Ruth Maris." In 1971 Blue, 17-3 at the All-Star break, was rocked in the game by home runs hit by Johnny Bench and Hank Aaron. The American League came back with four runs in the third and hung on for a 6–4 win, with Blue receiving credit for the victory. Not many people, however, discussed the performances of Blue, Ellis, Bench, Aaron, or Frank Robinson.

The press was too shocked by the awesome display of Reggie Jackson to think of anything else.

Jackson had hit a home run. Jackson had hit *the* home run. It was the hardest-hit ball of his career. It was the hardest-hit ball anyone, including many of the old-time writers who had observed Babe Ruth, ever remembered seeing. It set off arguments that lasted for days. One thing that is not well documented in baseball, a game of impeccable statistical accuracy, is the distance of massive home runs. Babe Ruth was reported to have hit several homers more than 600 feet away from home. Jimmy Foxx hit one some 590 feet. Mickey Mantle hit a home run 565 feet from home plate by a press agent's measuring stick. Dick

Allen hit a few in Philadelphia that may have traveled 550 feet in the air.

On the evening of July 13, 1971, before more than 500 members of the media and in front of 53,559 paying customers, Reginald Martínez Jackson hit a baseball 590 feet from home plate on a rising arch.

Dock Ellis, a hard-throwing Pirate right-hander with a big fastball and a bigger mouth, was on the mound for the Nationals. Blue had pitched the first three innings and was trailing 3–0. Frank Robinson had homered off Ellis for two runs, and Luis Aparicio was on first with two out. It was Blue's scheduled turn to bat, but manager Earl Weaver looked down the bench and picked Reggie Jackson as a pinch hitter.

Jackson had gotten into the classic on a pass. When Tony Oliva, the great hitting star of the Minnesota Twins, came up with a bad knee, Weaver had selected Jackson as a replacement for the American League team.

"We might need somebody who can jerk one out," Weaver said, "and that kid Jackson is a threat on any pitch."

The crowd cheered Jackson's appearance as he moved from the dugout. He had become a recognized star after his forty-seven-homer season in 1969, and fans knew he was capable of a long shot into the stands. He could entertain, and that was what the All-Star Game was all about.

Jackson made an art of his appearance in a big spot in a big game. He moved slowly to the plate, all eyes in the stands watching him. He spread his legs wide apart, digging the back foot deep into the soft sand of the batter's box. He pumped his bat back and forth, back and forth, stopping for an instant in mid-swing to stretch it out in front of him, pointing directly at the pitcher's head. Now he held the bat high over his ear, his top hand, his left hand, held firmly on the handle, his bottom hand, his right hand, more loosely held so he could whip the bat quickly at the baseball. His knees were slightly bent, and his eyes focused on Ellis's hand, watching for signs of the white baseball as the pitcher twisted and turned toward the plate. The baseball raced to the plate at about 95 miles per hour as Jackson's brain registered the speed, the approximate location, and the absence of a curvature plane in less than one second.

"Hitting is concentration," Jackson says. "Free your mind of everything. Study the flight of the baseball. Do not think of fine summer nights or fine wine or beautiful women. Think of seeing that white baseball, that spinning sphere, those seams turning over and over again as it gets closer to you. See it from the pitcher's hand to the contact of the bat. See it, see it, see it."

Harnessing all the power in his 205-pound twenty-five-year-old body, Jackson exploded in a flash as the ball moved toward the plate, whipping the head of the bat at the baseball, catching it at the exact instant when the thick part of the bat was directly in line with his fully extended arms, driving it on a huge arch toward the green stands behind right-center field. The ball was still rising as Jackson stood at home plate, and the crowd grew silent in its intensity to follow the flight of the baseball. It was climbing over the stands now, up over the roof, and then it crashed with a violent thud into the middle of an electric transformer above the stadium nearly 600 feet from the initial point of impact.

With one swing Jackson had stolen the game away from Blue, from Ellis, from Frank Robinson (even though he was the game's MVP for hitting the two-run homer which started the winning four-run rally), from all the other home run hitters.

The press surrounded Jackson in the American League clubhouse. He stood in his underpants, the rippling muscles on his body soaked with sweat. He spoke with obvious intensity and pride at hitting what many believed was the longest home run ever hit in a big-league game.

"I smoked it, didn't I? I could feel that one from the top of my hat to the tip of my toes," he said. "It was a fastball right down the middle of the plate. That cat wanted to challenge Reggie and see how far he could drive that ball. When I hit that tater, I looked over at him and saw his eyes get as big as grapefruits. He couldn't believe what Reggie had done to the man. Maybe he has learned some respect now. Maybe next time he will know better than to throw a straight fastball to Reggie down the middle of the plate. This game is a show, man, and I wanted to entertain the folks out there who paid good money to see all those great players. They got their money's worth. You don't see none of those folks lining up at the exchange window asking for their money back after that. They paid good money, and I gave them a good show. It will be awhile before anybody kisses that transformer up there again for a while. Will they put my name in white paint up there?"

"No," one reporter said, "they are going to send you the bill for breaking the damn transformer."

Reggie laughed at that and said, "I hope they don't have a power shortage out here because of me."

"Reggie," the reporter said, "one thing they'll never have any place you're around is a power shortage."

* * *

In the second half of the 1971 season the nation's baseball fans continued to focus on Vida Blue. The A's were running away with the Western Division race (they would win 101 games to second-place Kansas City's 85), and the next test would come in October against Baltimore in the American League championship series for the pennant.

Something seemed to go out of Blue's pitching after the All-Star break. It was August before he won his twentieth game of the year, 1–0, over Kansas City, and thirty games seemed by then too remote even to consider seriously anymore. He was burning out in his chase after McLain and Dizzy Dean and old Cy Young, destroyed by the incessant pressure of the press, by the attention of the media in every town, by the constant phone calls and conversations with Finley. It was too much, and Blue, who had started the season as a fresh, enthusiastic new face on the baseball scene, was ending it in a shell, hiding from reporters, reluctant to give anything more of himself to his teammates, disappointed at how sour success seemed to taste.

"Ever since I was a kid," he once said, "I wanted to be a sports star, a football hero, a baseball hero. That's all I wanted; that's all I dreamed of. Then it happened. It wasn't like I expected. They chew you up and spit you out. People use you. Nobody wants you for yourself. They want you for your records, your wins, your numbers. You are nothing but a damn won-lost record, a low ERA, that's all you are."

Stardom—a dream, a fantasy of so many. Then again, a nightmare, bitter, unpleasant, painful. Vida Blue could not carry that heavy burden. It changed him and crushed him. It was a sword that few of them could wear handsomely. He would win twenty-four games, lose only eight, end up with a 1.82 ERA, win the Most Valuable Player Award, win the Cy Young Award, and have his psyche permanently damaged. It hardly seemed worth it.

Another story aptly reflects the phenomenon of winning too much too soon. A mediocre pitcher named Billy Loes had won thirteen, fourteen, and thirteen games for the Brooklyn Dodgers in the early 1950s. He seemed to have more talent than that. One day a reporter asked him, "Why can't you win twenty games?"

"Hell, I can win twenty games," he said. "But if you win twenty games once, they'll want you to do it every year."

Loes articulated what so many felt. The pressures of success were a difficult burden to carry. None of them carried it without anguish, not Babe Ruth or Joe DiMaggio or Ted Williams or Hank Aaron or Willie Mays, not even Reggie Jackson.

Jackson had spent much time with Blue. They had discussed his fame over a beer at night, at the ball park, and on team flights. Jackson had warned Blue of the pressures.

He had seen what it had done to him at age twenty-three as he chased old "Ruth Maris." It had depressed him and debilitated him. It had made him nervous and suspicious. It had caused rashes on his skin, a nervous stomach, and a twitch in his eye.

As the press gathered around Blue game after game, Jackson sat aloof from the scene now, a mature man, intelligent, worldly in the ways of fame, wishing he could help his teammate.

"I know what he is going through. I went through it," he said. "He knows all this attention is unreal. He knows when his success stops, everyone will turn on him."

Baseball fame rarely lasts more than a season or two. There are always new heroes. There are always records to be broken. Soon the pretty women turn to the latest hero; the sycophantic businessmen find another player worthy of a free suit or a white shirt or a free pair of shoes. Soon the covers of magazines are filled with the faces of the next crop of bright young stars.

"I don't know if success is worth it," Jackson said. "I don't know if I want it. I want to win. But I just want to have good years, not great years, and be left to live my life in peace."

* * *

The season was winding down. The A's clinched the division in Chicago, the first triumph for Finley, who they pounded into the clubhouse to celebrate with his players. Champagne bottles were uncorked. Players slugged California bubbly. Some of it was used for hair tonic. Grown men hugged and kissed each other. Reggie Jackson lifted Dick Williams up, after the manager had already dressed in street clothes, and carried him to a cold shower. Jackson then approached Finley, who stared steely-eyed at his right fielder. Jackson thought better of it.

"We had the talent," Jackson was telling a reporter, "but Dick taught us how to win. He showed us what the game was all about. He made us into a team. He made us care more for winning, more for the team than for ourselves. He deserves all the credit."

But Charlie Finley thought he deserved all the credit. He had collected this talented bunch and handed them to Williams. He had scouted Monday and Bando and Jackson at the campus of Arizona State, signed Hunter out of high school, Campaneris out of a tryout camp, Blue out of Louisiana American Legion ball, Dick Green out of sandlot ball around Rapid City, South Dakota.

Finley paraded around the Lord Baltimore Hotel like an overblown peacock, strutting and pronouncing all afternoon, as the nation's baseball press wrote down every word he said publicly. It had finally come together for the insurance magnate from Indiana. Now he was somebody. He no longer was a kook who was simply tolerated by the other owners. No, sir, from now on old Charles O. Finley would be a somebody.

It came down to winning. That's really what it was all about. All of them, all the owners, were in there for one thing: attention. Nobody made much money in baseball, not the kind of money most of them made out of baseball. They enjoyed the attention; they enjoyed the best seats in the best restaurants, the snap-to they got when they picked up phones and announced their names.

"Before I came to New York as the Yankee owner," said George Steinbrenner, "I used to come into town on shipping business. I always wanted to go to a place like '21,' and I never could get in. I bought the Yankees, and we held our announcement press conference there. Suddenly I had a whole room at '21.' That's what it means to own the Yankees."

Now George Steinbrenner and Howard Cosell can often be seen dining together at the best front table at "21." That's what being a baseball owner is all about.

The first game of the 1971 pennant play-offs was scheduled for October 2. A heavy rain postponed the game, and finally, on October 3, 1971, the A's took the field for the first time in postseason play against the Baltimore Orioles. Baltimore was the defending American League champion. Finley, wearing a green suit and waving a gold Oakland pennant, sat in his first-row box seat next to his team's dugout.

For several weeks Blue had been announced as the obvious starting pitcher for the A's.

"He's the key to the series," said Baltimore manager Earl Weaver. "If we beat Blue, we'll beat the A's."

"What made that series tough for us," says Dave Duncan, the graceful catcher on that team, "was that we had cooled down from the pennant race. We had won so easily that we had not really played a competitive game for a month. Dick knew how to get us to win our division, but he didn't know how to keep us hot. We started the play-offs mentally like a team starting spring training. We weren't at our peak."

Since he had become the most dramatic pitching attraction since Sandy Koufax, Blue had pitched in turn all season. He had logged 312 innings in thirty-nine games, an incredible amount of pitching for a twenty-one-year-old rookie. He no longer had the same stuff and stamina in October that he had had in June.

Dave McNally, a crafty left-hander, started for the Orioles in the first game against Blue. The A's jumped ahead, 3–0, but Blue allowed five runs in the sixth inning. Paul Blair, who always responded in big games, bounced a two-run single over third base to lead the Orioles to victory. The score was 5–3 for Baltimore, and Catfish Hunter would be asked to tie it up the next day.

Hunter gave up home runs to Brooks Robinson and two to huge Boog Powell, and the Orioles won, 5–1, for a two-game lead behind veteran left-hander Mike Cuellar.

Now it was back to Oakland. Williams tried to rally the troops, but they were downhearted, faced with the prospect of winning three straight and faced with the hard-throwing right-hander Jim Palmer. Palmer allowed the A's only seven hits, Baltimore batted Diego Segui around, and the Orioles won, 5–3. In the last game of the play-offs, striving desperately to save his team from defeat, Reggie Jackson hit two home runs.

Naturally it was October.

Jackson hit two home runs, a double and a single in twelve at bats for a .333 average, he struck out only once, and he did his best to fight off defeat.

When the last game was over and his teammates walked slowly off the field and up the ramp to the clubhouse, Jackson sat alone in the dugout, his head in his hands. His body was curled up in a fetal position, his eyes were red with tears, and his knees were trembling with emotion. Defeat. He did not know how to deal with it. He had played with such intensity, such emotion, such desire that he was drained as the final score was put on the board. He knew he was the leader of the A's. He felt personally responsible for the defeat.

* * *

The days were quiet in Oakland following the 1971 season. The excitement of the play-offs had ended, and the sports pages were filled with stories about the Oakland Raiders football team. Jackson was winding down after the long season, confident that he was hitting his true stride as a leader of the A's and a main man in the league. He had hit 32 homers with 80 RBIs. His average was .277, and he had led the league for the fourth straight time in strikeouts with 161. No matter. He had come back dramatically from the disaster of 1970 and would never again be embarrassed at a season performance.

Before returning to Arizona after the 1971 play-offs to work with Gary Walker in the land development company, Reggie lounged around his Oakland apartment in a luxury downtown building. He listened to soft soul music on his stereo. Women dropped by, some uninvited, mostly white, some black, and they stayed five minutes or an hour or overnight, depending on how Reggie felt that particular day. His taste ran then, as it still does, to beautiful women, regardless of race, and he still amuses himself by picking them up in department stores, around the ball park, or in restaurants. He often asks autograph hunters for their phone numbers if they are young and pretty. None has refused him.

His apartment was inundated with growing plants, and Reggie attended them with much care, talking carefully to them, warmly and seriously, as he had been instructed to do by the local florists who got him interested.

"I enjoy growing things," he says. "I like to see things being nurtured and matured and changing with the sands of time."

In the early afternoon, after staying out late the night before and sleeping late in the morning, he dressed slowly, picked out a jacket, moved carefully to the apartment garage. He turned the key in his new blue Pontiac Grand Prix, one of four cars he drove and owned, and raced down the street. He turned quickly against the light and roared over to a neighborhood hangout called Lois the Pie Queen. The proprietor, a heavyset black woman, hugged him as he came in and set about cooking up his regular breakfast of pork chops, rice, and scrambled eggs. Years later he cut down on meats and now eats mostly grains, vegetables, and fruits. He says it has made him feel better and stronger.

Kids hang around Jackson everywhere he goes. For no reason at all, he might pull a $20 bill from his pants and hand it to a kid. "Now get on home with that, and tell your mother you earned it being nice to Reggie," he might say. Jackson likes the finer things in life: fancy cars, homes, rugs, paintings, wines, and women. He can also give away money ludicrously, donating to several charities which get him at a giving time, underwriting a school for underprivileged boys in Tempe, Arizona, donating to several charitable organizations in Oakland, paying for a ranch in Tempe for Chicano and Yaqui Indian orphans.

"The thing about money," says Jackson, "is that it can make people happy. It makes me happy. It makes anybody happy that I give it to. If you've got it, spread it around."

The Oakland players used to laugh at him when he pulled a huge pile of bills from his pocket to pay a cab fare, warning him always he would be mugged, especially in New York, Chicago, and Oakland. With the Yankees, the players turned their backs on him when he flashed big bills, snickered, passed sarcastic remarks about his showing off. The first thing he does nowadays when he buys a new $300 cowboy hat for traveling on the road is to stuff the lining of the inside of the hat with $100 bills. "If anybody steals it," he says, "they'll know whose hat it is."

For dinner, he dined in the best restaurants in San Francisco, choosing to skip the one or two Oakland restaurants because he was too well known there.

"It's sometimes funny with Reggie," says Oakland neighbor, close friend, and two-time Cincinnati MVP Joe Morgan. "We would go out together, and more people would fuss over me than him. Maybe that was because he was there all year. I'd take my family out to the Elegant Farmer, because that is a family place, nice but family. With Reggie it's downtown San Francisco, the Blue Fox."

"We got to a lot of basketball games at the Oakland Coliseum together," says Morgan, "and they always asked us to stand up and take a bow. I got the bigger cheers. Reggie got some boos. That always ticked him off and made me laugh."

After dinner at an elegant restaurant Jackson liked to close out those Oakland evenings with some dancing to soul music at one of San Francisco's finer emporiums.

"You'd never find Reggie in anything but the best restaurant in any town, the best nightclub, the best lunch place," says Dave Duncan. "We used to pal around together, Reggie, Joe Rudi, and me, and we could never go any place but the finest restaurant in any town. Reggie was very conscious of his public image, his standing in baseball and with his teammates. It just wouldn't do for Reggie to be seen eating dinner in some ham and eggs place. Reggie was always a gentleman, a stylist, a guy with much class. He knew the public watched him. He wouldn't embarrass himself, and he wouldn't embarrass the Oakland A's."

After a couple of weeks of rest, parties with friends, and visits with some of the business associates he had little time for during the season, Jackson left Oakland. He spent the winter in Tempe, worked with Gary Walker, and watched his assets in real estate grow dramatically. He also played some basketball with old friends at Arizona State, dated a few of the coeds, visited back East a couple of times during the winter, with his father in Wyncote and his mother in Baltimore, spent some time with his brothers and sisters, nieces and nephews, and prepared for spring training.

Everyone knew the A's were the team to beat in 1972. They had improved dramatically with the addition of a fine left-handed pitcher named Ken Holtzman. They were headed for the World Series.

After his marriage breakup, Jackson had undergone some psychiatric therapy. It had helped him mature, appreciate his own worth, and settle down. He had come back strong in 1971, aware that he was on the threshold of some great seasons. Only one thing was missing: a woman to love and love him.

"If I had a wife and family," he mused one day, "I would hit fifty home runs, forty-nine of them for them."

Without the wife, without the family, Jackson became more narcissistic about himself and craved friends. Many of them were inconsequential in his life, there to flatter his image. Others were there for business reasons.

"When you do something in this game," he once said, "you like to have somebody to leave passes for, somebody who cares."

His public life was a smashing success. His private life was still a bit hollow.

"There are times," he once said, "when I'm so damn lonely I feel like crying."

With all that baseball success, all that public acclaim, all that fame and fortune, all the millions of fans, there were times he was so damn vulnerable anyone who cared even a little bit about Reggie Jackson would feel great compassion.

The Mustache Gang

IN MORE THAN 100 YEARS OF PROFESSIONAL BASEBALL fewer than a half dozen teams have become heroically blended into the folk fabric of American life. Winning was not enough. Winning with élan mattered, winning with drama, winning with colorful players under the severe scrutiny of the press. Only a few teams have gained enduring national fame: Connie Mack's Philadelphia A's; John McGraw's New York Giants; the St. Louis Gashouse Gang; the Yankees of Ruth and Gehrig, and later of DiMaggio, and still later of Casey Stengel; the Jackie Robinson Brooklyn Dodgers; the New York Mets.

And the mustachioed, fighting, flamboyant, rousing, raucous Oakland Athletics of Charles O. Finley: Reggie Jackson, Catfish Hunter, and Captain Sal Bando. Only the Yankees of 1949–1953 ever won the World Series five times in a row. Only the Yankees of 1936–1939 ever won it four times in a row. Only the Oakland A's of 1972–1974 ever won it three times in a row.

"We won it three times in a row, and only the Yankees ever did better," said Reggie Jackson as he stood, sweating and champagne-soaked, in the Oakland clubhouse after the 1974 victory over the Dodgers. "I want to win four in a row. I want to win five in a row. I want to win it six times in a row, the only team ever, a new dynasty, the best baseball team in history."

They all were young enough; they were certainly good enough; they were ambitious enough. But their world was changing. A baseball revolution was in full force. Free agency was the keystone of baseball's next half dozen years. Soon Catfish would be gone, and then all the rest, Reggie, Sal, Joe Rudi, Campy, Dick Green, all the rest of those marvelous A's.

"I think back to that team," says relief pitcher Dave Hamilton, the only Oakland player of that time who is still on the team, "and I marvel at how good it was. I didn't have much of a part in it, but I was proud to be connected with it. Reggie was the leader, he was the one we all depended on, but each of us filled our own role perfectly. I wonder if baseball people really remember just how good we were."

* * *

On November 29, 1971, the last link in the chain was forged. Charlie Finley traded his former pet Rick Monday to the Chicago Cubs for a left-hander named Ken Holtzman. Oakland would now have three of the best starters in baseball in Holtzman, Vida Blue, and Catfish Hunter. No team with three starters like them could ever lose more than a few games in a row.

It was Holtzman who best typified the Oakland A's of that year through an incident in the clubhouse. Mike Epstein, known as SuperJew for his faith, his size, and his desire to be important, was struggling at bat. Jackson was trying to help by offering suggestions. Jackson, however, did not have the smoothest manner when he proffered his help. Nor did Epstein have the thickest skin. In a few moments they were knocking each other across the club-house. Holtzman was playing cards. He heard the crash, looked over at his two large teammates rolling around on the floor, and said, "Deal."

In those rousing years of championships and free-for-alls, much like the later Yankee teams of 1977 and 1978, Rollie Fingers fought with Blue Moon Odom, Blue Moon Odom fought with Vida Blue, Dave Duncan fought with Sal Bando, but the best of all, the most significant, and the most dramatic was the battle between Reggie Jackson and Billy North.

North had come to the A's in 1973, a talented, smooth-striding, graceful center fielder who could run like crazy, catch a fly ball, and hit. Jackson soon adopted the hand-some young black as a protégé. He worked with him on the pitchers around the league, guided him through the pitfalls of big-league play, and softened him for the rigors of playing for the rowdy A's.

"Reggie had a paternalistic attitude toward me," says North, who is still a fine player with the San Francisco Giants. "I already had a father."

The two became close friends, but Reggie's pedantic meanderings began to gall North.

"Everything was so intense with Reggie," North says. "It was a love-hate relationship. He was an awesome player, just awesome, a very intelligent man, and he offered some very constructive advice. He was also caught up in his own insecurities, that whole leadership bullshit. Reggie wasn't the leader on that club; Sal Bando was. He was the captain and the most tremendous competitor I have ever seen in the game."

Reflecting on those years with Reggie and the A's, North has generally more positive feelings than negative about Reggie.

"He was basically a very good person, fun to be around. He could play. He could carry the team for weeks. In big games, the real big ones, he was cash, money in the bank. He could do some unbelievable things with that bat. If the

Brooklyn Dodgers were the Boys of Summer, Reggie Jackson was the Boy in October. Nobody could play better in a big October game than Reggie Jackson, nobody."

Jackson, on the other hand, admired North's skills. They actually liked each other, but this did not keep them from fighting.

One afternoon Jackson received a phone call from a white woman. She had been a friend of Billy North. She talked about North, about the way Reggie was bugging him with his unsolicited advice, and asked what was going on between the two of them. Jackson was charming, said some complimentary things about North, and ended the conversation quietly. Later that evening, as he undressed in the Oakland clubhouse and reached for his uniform, North, who had been working out early, came into the clubhouse.

"You're a fucking jerk," North said.

"Hey, what's going on? What's eating you?"

"You are," North said.

A few more hot words were exchanged, and suddenly Reggie, naked, lunged at the fully dressed North. They bounced around on the floor of the clubhouse. Ray Fosse, a newcomer to the Oakland scene, jumped between them. He got a bruised shoulder for his troubles. Sal Bando, the captain, moved in and broke it up.

The version of the argument the white Oakland press heard, now denied by both players, was filled with racial and sexual overtones. Jackson was supposedly bragging to North about taking out a gorgeous white "chick." When North asked Jackson if the woman had a friend for him, Reggie supposedly replied, "Nah, she don't go out with niggers."

Ballplayers do needle each other racially, blacks getting on blacks for their blackness, whites getting on blacks, blacks getting on whites, and whites on whites. Such a dialogue would not be unusual had the tone not been so deadly serious.

"I don't know if that was what was said," said an Oakland newsman who prefers to remain anonymous and out of the racial-sexual fray. "All I know is that is what the other players believed was said."

All sides have mellowed through the years. North is now thirty-two, an aging star with the Giants, playing across the country from Jackson.

"We're still friends," says North. "We only live ten minutes apart on the Coast. We go out to dinner together. We get along fine. Things were said then in the heat of battle. Tension has a way of festering and finally exploding on a hot summer night in a baseball clubhouse."

* * *

Through all this furor the A's were gaining national press attention. They were a talented, exciting bunch of baseball players. Every recognizable authority conceded they were the team to beat in 1972. The boss man, Charles O. Finley, kept the pot boiling with outrageous statements to the press, with constant phone calls to the manager, with advice to the players, with interference in their personal lives. Catfish Hunter once borrowed money from Finley to purchase a farm. Finley harassed him by phone even before he was starting vital games. Jackson and Finley constantly battled over salary. Blue and Finley never could get together emotionally after Blue's brilliant 1971 season. He had held out and threatened to retire to work for a plumbing supply company, which manufactured toilet seats, and Commissioner Bowie Kuhn had to jump into the midst of the negotiations before things were finally settled. After winning the Cy Young and MVP awards in 1971, Blue was 6-10 in 1972, a direct result of poor judgment on Finley's part.

* * *

Yet it was the clever, creative owner who came up with the promotion which separated the A's from all baseball and established them as unique characters. Finley sponsored a mustache day at Oakland. People who grew the best mustaches and beards would win cash prizes. Finley told his players he would pay them each $100 if they grew mustaches and beards. Baseball has always been conscious of its public image. Players could be alcoholics, drug addicts, adulterers, and even occasionally murderers—but they had to remain clean-shaven. Finley changed all that. Almost all the players grew mustaches. Jackson also grew a beard. Rollie Fingers grew the finest handlebar mustache seen on a baseball field since the turn of the century.

Finley expected the players to shave after the promotion. Most did not. Even manager Dick Williams, as conservative as the next baseball man, kept his mustache on. It helped bring him closer to his team.

"The world had changed, and baseball had changed with it," says Williams. "If I could identify with my players with a mustache, why not?"

Soon the sportswriters were calling the A's Charlie Finley's Mustache Gang. Like a band of desperadoes, they were running wild through the West.

Oakland won ninety-three games to finish six games ahead of Chicago in the 1972 division race. Detroit, under fighting, feisty Billy Martin, had finished first in the East. Jackson had another strong year in 1972 with 25 homers, 75 RBIs, and a .265 average. He scored 72 runs and cut his strikeouts to 125.

It was October again, play-off time. The Tigers and A's split the first four games. Detroit went ahead, 1–0, in the fifth and deciding game for the American League pennant. In the second inning with Jackson on third and Sal Bando on first, Williams brazenly signaled for a double steal. Bando broke for second, the throw went through, and Jackson raced for the plate. Burly Bill Freehan, the tough Detroit catcher, blocked the plate as Jackson slid home hard. Jackson's foot touched the plate, he was called safe, and his leg curled up under him in a cloud of dust. Freehan had lodged his spikes into the dirt against the impact. There was a terrific crash. Jackson suffered a torn hamstring muscle. He was carried off the field on a stretcher.

The A's won the game, 2–1, and their first American League pennant. With the final fly ball out to center field, Charles O. Finley stood up and kissed his wife, Shirley, in a deliriously happy moment for him. It would be several more years before bitter divorce proceedings would rock Finley's financial empire.

"That was the unhappiest moment of my life," Jackson says of the injury. "I had worked all those years for a chance at the World Series, and now I couldn't play. I cried all the way back home to the hotel and on the flight to Cincinnati."

Could a man on crutches dominate a World Series? Well, the A's beat the Cincinnati Reds four games to three for their first championship, but Jackson was everywhere. He was given permission by Commissioner Bowie Kuhn to sit on the Oakland bench in crutches and civilian clothes and was regularly interviewed for television. He became close to Pete Rose and Johnny Bench, the two great stars of the Reds, and spent most of his off time with them. Pete's wife, flamboyant and beautiful Karolyn Rose, made a special trip from the losing Cincinnati clubhouse to the winning Oakland clubhouse to kiss Reggie Jackson and congratulate him for his nonpart in the Series. Gene Tenace hit four homers in the Series and received one death threat; he batted .348. Catfish Hunter won two games, Ken Holtzman won one, and Rollie Fingers won one and saved two.

Still, it was Jackson many reporters wrote about; it was Jackson who was seen sitting on the edge of the dugout so many times on television; it was Jackson who spoke for the team in the clubhouse after the last victory, proclaiming the start of a new dynasty.

It was this ability to talk with the press, this desire to be seen, appreciated, and recognized which made so many of his teammates unappreciative of Jackson's great baseball talents. They were simply jealous of the man, jealous of his ability to handle himself in a crowd, jealous of the inordinate degree of fame he received.

By 1973 Jackson had emerged as one of the brightest stars in the game. In a little more than five seasons he had hit 157 home runs, many of them drives of such prodigious impact that they left viewers breathless. The home runs alone, if he were as low-key a personality as, say, Harmon Killebrew, would have been enough to make him a star, even a superstar, in the game. It was more the excitement of what he did, the way he hit home runs, dropped his bat and sauntered around the bases, made a lunging, rolling catch, the way the baseball was thrown, the way it was caught—or missed—the way he ran that separated him from the rest. And the way he talked.

He could draw the press to him. He could interest sportswriters easily. He would say nasty things about Finley or comical things about his teammates. He could express with intense emotions the feelings of being a professional athlete. More and more reporters wrote of him; more and more he became a star.

One day, after hitting a home run to win an Oakland game, he walked around the clubhouse with candy bars. He carried Baby Ruth and O. Henry candy bars, neither of which had anything remotely to do with Babe Ruth or Hank Aaron.

"What kind of candy bar will they name after me?" he asked Sal Bando one day.

"The shithead bar," Bando said.

Soon the A's were engaged in a contest to name the candy bar to be named after Reggie. None of the names selected were anything but obscene.

He would turn on the most, reach for his finest adjectives, his most moving emotions when the A's played the Yankees and the New York press gathered around him. He knew they could spread the word of Jackson farther and faster than anybody. They could make him a superstar regardless of what he did on the field.

"If I played in New York," he would tell them, "they'd name a candy bar after me."

As Finley and Jackson battled over his contract, rumors that Reggie would be traded flew constantly. One place he would never be allowed to go, Finley vowed, was to the hated enemy, the New York Yankees. The Yankees, conservative, successful, and wealthy, had always been a thorn in the hide of the midwestern Finley.

"Maybe," Jackson said one day, "Finley can work something out with the new guy on the Yankees."

The new guy on the Yankees was a Cleveland shipping industrialist named George Steinbrenner.

While Jackson dreamed of being traded to New York and Steinbrenner began the rebuilding of the downtrodden Yankees, Finley worked toward his second championship.

Oakland won easily again in 1973. The A's won ninety-four games and finished six games ahead of the Kansas City Royals. In the spring Jackson, still hampered by his leg, vowed he would have the best year of his career. He was making $75,000 then but wanted $100,000.

"It isn't just the money," Jackson said. "It's the status, the image, the respect of the other players. I want to be the Most Valuable Player. I want players to think of me as they think of Joe DiMaggio, Ted Williams, Willie Mays, and Henry Aaron. The best. I want to be the best."

In 1973 Jackson led the league in home runs for the only time in his career with 32 (he tied for the league lead in 1975 with pal George Scott at 36), led in RBIs with 117 and runs scored with 99. He batted .293 in 151 games. He was unanimously elected the league MVP, just as he had predicted.

After Catfish Hunter shut out the Orioles, 3–0, in the fifth and deciding game of the 1973 play-off, the A's were in the World Series again, this time against the surprising New York Mets.

The Mets had won the World Series in 1969 and slumped badly after that. They were given little chance to win in 1973. In August board chairman M. Donald Grant held a clubhouse meeting. He said the owners had not given up on the team, and they should not give up on themselves. As he walked out of the clubhouse door, relief pitcher Tug McGraw shouted, "You gotta believe." Grant thought he was being made fun of, snorted, and left the room. McGraw continued to walk around the clubhouse, shouting, "You gotta believe."

The Mets believed. In the final week, as things looked darkest, a sportswriter asked manager Yogi Berra, who had succeeded Gil Hodges after Hodges succumbed to a heart attack in 1972, if he thought his club was out of it.

Said manager Berra, "You ain't out of it until you are out of it."

On October 14, 1973, the first game of the World Series, the Mets were pitted against the A's.

Reginald Martínez Jackson was also in the Series for the first time.

"He wanted me there," said Martínez Jackson, Reggie's dad, "so we closed up shop and went out. He sent me a plane ticket, got me a big hotel room, and took good care of me. Sometimes he's got a big head and forgets old Dad, but most of the time he's a good son."

Jackson had wanted a shot at the national attention. He wanted a chance in the World Series. He wanted it especially with the New York Mets as the opposition. Now he would be as big on Times Square as he was on Oakland's Jack London Square.

It was again October, Reggie Jackson's time of the year.

"I don't think there has ever been a player who could do more in a big game than Reggie," says Gene Tenace. "Before that thing started, he said, 'I'll take care of you guys,' and he did."

The Series was one of the most dramatic ever. Oakland won the first game, 2–1, with Ken Holtzman outpitching Jon Matlack. The second game saw Willie Mays, the greatest player of his time, fall down under a fly ball in the sun and then win the game for the Mets with a single in the twelfth inning.

What was more decisive and more representative of the A's was that Mike Andrews, a backup infielder, made two errors on two routine ground balls in the twelfth inning. They led to three New York runs and the victory. Finley went wild. He decided to fire Andrews after the game and had him sign a medical form that he had been injured. Andrews flew to New York for the third game with the team and then was fired and ordered to fly home. Bowie Kuhn stepped into the furor. The Oakland players, led by Sal Bando and Reggie Jackson, arrived at the workout at Shea wearing T-shirts instead of uniform shirts with Andrews's number 17 scribbled in ink. Kuhn soon ordered Andrews reinstated, and he got a standing ovation from fair-minded Shea fans when he pinch-hit in the fourth game.

Meanwhile, Dick Williams, who was under immense pressure from Finley, called his players together for a meeting.

"Whatever happens in this Series," he said, "I'm leaving."

He had taught this team how to win. He was now teaching them how to leave, as they eventually all would, with head held high and pride intact.

The Mets won two of the next three games and returned to Oakland one game ahead. It was a time for October dramatics, willingly supplied by Reggie.

Yogi Berra had a rested pitcher by the name of George Stone ready for the sixth game. He also had Tom Seaver and Jon Matlack. He chose to skip Stone, pitch Seaver in the sixth game, and move Matlack up to the seventh game.

"If you can't win with Seaver and Matlack," Yogi said, "you can't win."

He didn't. Jackson hit two doubles off Seaver, and Oakland won, 3–1, in the sixth game. The seventh game and the Series were a cinch for Oakland. Holtzman doubled in the third off Matlack, Campaneris homered, Rudi singled, and after an out, Reggie Jackson hit the first of his World Series homers, a huge drive over the right-center-field wall.

A small incident, however, in the final days of the 1973 Series had taken attention away from the players. Charlie Finley had always struggled for acclaim. His team had won the World Series twice in a row, but the talk in the press was more about the resignation of Williams than the excellence of the A's. Williams had left the club with an emotional farewell and was being rumored to be the new manager of the Yankees. Their manager, Ralph Houk, had resigned at the end of the 1973 season because he was unable to work for Steinbrenner. Williams was hired by the Yankees. There was one catch. He was still under contract to the A's. Finley asked for compensation in return for the right to sign Williams. The players he wanted from the Yankees were young slugger Otto Velez and young pitcher Scott McGregor. "Never," screamed Yankee president Gabe Paul. "They are our crown jewels." No deal. Williams stayed out of baseball until Finley allowed the California Angels to sign him as their manager in June 1974. As long as the new team was not the Yankees . . .

*   *   *

Finley picked Alvin Dark as his field leader. Dark was grateful for the chance. He had managed for Finley in Kansas City in 1966 and 1967. He was a religious man, a soft-spoken southerner, a marvelous player for the Braves and Giants, a man who was capable of some strange actions. As Giants manager he once threw a stool across a clubhouse and tore off the end of his finger. He (a man who managed Willie Mays) had made some remarks about black and Latin players, suggesting they were not as mentally alert as white players. It cost him the Giants job and a chance at the New York Mets job when sportswriter

Stan Isaacs of Long Island's *Newsday* published the remarks.

"Alvin Dark was very easy to get along with," says Reggie. "At this stage of my career I was just starting to settle
down. I had been a renegade for a while, but now I was
developing a philosophy about life, and Alvin Dark
helped me find some inner peace. I had just started to
become a Christian, and he encouraged me and pushed
me that way."

In some of Reggie's most difficult periods, especially in
the later turmoil with the Yankees, he seemed to turn
more and more toward religion, toward being a Christian,
and toward the Bible. He is not an active churchgoer, but
he does attend baseball chapel services, listens to visiting
Christian speakers in Sunday sessions, reads the Bible, and
encourages teammates along these lines.

The third straight Oakland championship certainly established the team as one of baseball's best ever. The A's
at the end of 1974 had won three World Series in a row,
bested only by the Yankees. They won under two different managers, so it had to be because of the talent of the
players. Jackson had batted .286 in 1974, hit 29 homers,
had 93 RBIs, scored 90 runs, and cut his strikeouts to a
respectable 105. Jackson was distinguishing himself from
the rest of the A's. Even more than the manager, even
more than the owner (and how grating that was to Charlie
O.), even more than the team's success, Jackson was the
dominant personality.

If Bando, Hunter, Rudi, Green, and Fingers all were
excellent players, and they certainly were, Jackson was
that and more. He was a media darling, a personality, a
guy the nonfan, nonsportswriter could appreciate and understand. Jackson had crossed that invisible line from
player to personality. No less a non-sports-oriented jour-
nal than *Time* magazine would affirm that on its cover of
June 3, 1974.

The biggest-selling *Time* cover, in January, was the one
with Judge John Sirica. In February it was the one with

House Speaker Tip O'Neill. In March it was the one with Leon Jaworski. In April it was the cover with Henry Kissinger. In May embattled President Richard Nixon was on the cover with quotes from the Watergate tapes: "I say [expletive removed] don't hold anything back." Nixon's resignation was still more than two months away, the country was immersed in Watergate, and few Americans could think or talk of almost anything else outside their own personal lives. That pattern was broken in the first week of June, when a swinging, dark, slashing figure, Oakland uniform number 9, was on the cover of *Time*. "One-Man Wild Bunch" was the headline on the cover, and below the photo it read "Oakland's Reggie Jackson." In an article entitled "The Muscle and Soul of the A's Dynasty," *Time* wrote, "In the show biz world of sport, Jackson wants the record to show that he is a serious citizen, something more than yesterday's mixed-up kid grown up to be today's hero. Success and psychotherapy have helped give him a strong sense of himself as a person as well as an athlete and celebrity. He means to enjoy all the roles available to him." Two weeks later he would be on the cover of *Time*'s sister publication, *Sports Illustrated*. It was a double play that few athletes had ever experienced. It tended to create more resentment and jealousies on the part of some of the A's players.

Jackson was now making $135,000 a year. He owned an apartment in Oakland and a town house in Tempe. He was worth $20 million in real estate. His clothes closet was filled with enough jackets, shirts, slacks, and shoes to stock a large store. He bedded down almost any beautiful woman he met and desired. His power at the bat was admired and respected by his peers. He was as recognizable a man as any who walked the streets of America.

Still, he fought bitterly with his boss over money. He felt unappreciated in the cold environment of Oakland. He had many lovely women in his life, but he did not have one. He was still trying to sort out in his own mind the reasons for his failed marriage to Jennie. There were moments of fear that it all would crash. He could see the financial structure of baseball changing dramatically. He knew he would never win the status salary—the biggest in the game—from an owner who was jealous of him. He yearned for more recognition. He needed something better than Oakland. He needed Los Angeles or preferably New York. New York was the only city which conjured up images of the Babe, Lou Gehrig, Joe D, Mickey. More and more he thought about New York as his kind of town, the one city with all the media and power.

* * *

The 1974 Series was ending. The A's had whipped the Dodgers easily, four games to one. The most significant play, the one the press wrote about, the one the fans remembered, revolved, of course, around Jackson. Dodger left fielder Bill Buckner had singled in the eighth inning of the final game with Oakland ahead, 3–2, and when the ball got past Billy North in center, Buckner raced past second and tried for third. Jackson, backing North up, grabbed the ball and fired a hard left-handed strike to Dick Green in short right field. The second baseman, without looking, fired a strike to Sal Bando, at third, who tagged Buckner out by several feet. A perfect play, a magnificent example of Oakland defense. "That's why we are the best," Jackson said.

And so they were, with three championships in a row. The best. Then came the first crack and then later a tidal wave. Charles Finley had failed to pay Catfish Hunter $50,000 on an insurance payment due in his contract. Agent Jerry Kapstein told the press at the Series that Hunter would be declared a free agent. He soon was. Every club in baseball bid for the star right-hander. The Yankees won out with a five-year $3,750,000 offer. Scout Clyde Kluttz, who had originally scouted Hunter for the A's, was now working for the Yankees. He convinced Hunter New York would be a good place for him to play. "I've gone hunting a lot of times with Clyde," Hunter explained. "When you walk in the woods alone with a man and you're both carrying guns, you learn to trust him. I trusted Clyde. That's why I chose the Yankees."

Hunter was a marvelous pitcher, but he was a low-key country boy from Hertford, North Carolina. He would help the Yankees win, but he wouldn't become a folk figure. There was only one member of the A's who knew he could do that in the big town.

"If I played in New York," Jackson kept telling anybody who would listen, "they'd name a candy bar after me."

King George to the Rescue

IT HAD TAKEN MORE THAN A DECADE TO BUILD THE Oakland A's and five minutes to bring them down. Catfish Hunter was gone—to the damn Yankees no less —and the other players would soon follow. Charlie Finley had lost Hunter on a technicality, and all the rest of Charlie's Mustache Gang were plotting ways to join Catfish.

In some strange ways the 1975 season may have been the finest season of all for the Oakland A's. They won ninety-eight games. Vida Blue won twenty-two games. Ken Holtzman won eighteen. Rollie Fingers won ten games and saved twenty-four. Sal Bando had 15 homers and 78 RBIs. Joe Rudi had 21 homers and 75 RBIs. Reginald Martínez Jackson tied Boston's George Scott for the league lead in homers with 36 and had 104 RBIs, 5 behind Scott. They did all this with their minds on moving.

The Boston Red Sox won in the East. It was once again October, play-off time, and Mr. October was ready. He batted .417 with five hits in twelve at bats, hit a homer, and knocked in three runs. This time the A's were short of pitching without Hunter and were beaten in the playoff. Boston went to the World Series, and Jackson went home. Boston carried Cincinnati to seven games.

Early in 1976 it was obvious the A's were being torn apart. Most of their players were embroiled in a financial war with Finley. The atmosphere around the team as they gathered in Mesa for spring training in March was unpleasant. Most of the players were surly with the press, each other, and the fans. They had undergone much trauma in arbitration hearings with Finley. Charlie specialized in demeaning each of them as he fought to keep their salaries down. Jackson had won a $165,000-a-year salary in arbitration but felt he was being treated unfairly as salaries were crossing $200,000 for lesser-known players.

Bando, Rudi, Holtzman, Campaneris, Fingers, Tenace, each had refused to sign contracts for 1976. They would be playing out their options. They would be moving into baseball's first free agent pool. Any one of thirteen clubs could pick them out of a shopping basket. The biggest catch of all, of course, would be Reggie Jackson.

The A's were playing an exhibition game in Tucson. Jackson had stayed back in Mesa on the morning of April 2, 1976, to take extra batting practice. The season was only six days away. Jackson wanted his hands strong and ready for the opener. He was called off the field by the clubhouse man. There was a phone call. Charlie Finley was on the phone from Chicago. Reggie expected a new contract offer.

"Reggie, this is Charlie," the breathless owner quickly said. "We've traded you to Baltimore. Good luck."

There were no apologies, no congratulations for a job well done since 1967, no farewell dinners or gold watches. Jackson had earned three World Series rings, the good one from 1972 with the fourteen-karat diamond and the two cheap ones Finley had awarded his club. Reggie also had saved a few baseballs, especially the banged-up one from the 1971 All-Star Game crash against the transformer in Detroit ("Bent," Reggie says). He had some pictures stuffed in a foot locker and a couple of torn shirts he kept in the Oakland apartment for working out in the winter. He was making $165,000 a year in baseball. He also had more than two hundred sports jackets, more than one hundred pairs of shoes, more than a hundred shirts and two hundred ties. He also owned half a dozen cars, had acquired two automobile agencies, and owned a good piece of a $20 million land development company. He had all that. Then he cried.

He cried when he said good-bye to the kids in the clubhouse who shined his baseball shoes and hung up his uniform and put clean socks and underwear in his locker every day. He cried when a fan waved to him as he walked out of the clubhouse with his green Oakland Athletics bag and shouted, "We'll always love you," and he cried when he saw his pal Gary Walker, waiting for him outside the gate.

The bitterness of that moment lingers to this day. "I wanted to be treated like a man," Reggie says. Finley had treated him like chattel, hired property, to be bought and sold at will, no questions asked, no answers given. Almost everybody gets traded in baseball: Babe Ruth, Willie Mays, Hank Aaron, even Christy Mathewson. They all are jolted by the deal, shocked at how easily their lives can be uprooted, angered at the mechanics of a sport that could so callously disrupt a man's life. When free agency came into full force that fall, it would be the players—not the owners—who would be supplying the momentum for a move. It would become the most dramatic change in the game's history.

The team that wanted Reggie Jackson and the man who wanted him most were the Baltimore Orioles and their general manager, Hank Peters.

Hank Peters had been farm director and general manager for Charles O. Finley with the Kansas City A's. He had scouted Reggie Jackson as an Arizona State University freshman and sophomore in 1965 and 1966.

"I always liked Reggie as a player and as a man," Peters says. "I thought he was a dedicated athlete and a fine gentleman. I still do. I regretted that we didn't get him earlier that season. I think we would have won. I was sorry we didn't sign him at the end of the year. We tried awfully hard."

Jackson left Mesa after the deal and went home to Tempe. There he sat and weighed his options. He could quit baseball at twenty-nine and enter the real estate business full time. He could report to the Orioles' camp in Miami, play for the same $165,000 he had coming from his A's contract, and hope for a new and better one. He could sit still, wait for the Orioles to raise their offer, and give himself time to recover from the shock. He took the third option.

"As soon as the deal was made," says Ken Singleton, then starting his second season as the Baltimore right fielder, "they told me I would be the left fielder. As soon as Reggie reported, I knew I had to move to make room for him. I kept waiting."

Jackson stayed in Tempe. The Orioles opened the season without him. Ken Holtzman, who had been traded from Oakland to the Orioles in the same deal, reported and was immediately cut twenty percent of his salary, the maximum allowable by baseball rules for not signing a contract. Jackson asked the Orioles to satisfy him with a huge raise if he reported. They would not consider such an idea, especially for a man who was threatening to quit the game or certainly to play out his option and be with a different club in 1977.

On April 12 Catfish Hunter shut out Ross Grimsley and the Orioles in Baltimore, 3–0. The Yankees moved into first place four days after the season began. They would never be out of first place again. They would win the Eastern Division title by ten and a half games over Baltimore.

"What Reggie did that year was very selfish," says Jim Palmer, the great Baltimore right-hander. "He had been traded to our club and should have reported. He could have fought out his contract battles on the scene the way Holtzman did. We needed him. We had given up a pretty good hitter in Don Baylor and a pretty good pitcher, Mike Torrez, in that deal. He had an obligation to the Orioles to report. It was in his contract that he could be traded. He knew that. We all know that."

While Jackson stayed home in Tempe and the Orioles slipped back in the race, the Yankees were beginning a championship season. Ed Figueroa and Mickey Rivers, obtained in a winter trade for Bobby Bonds, sparked the team. Figueroa developed into the most consistent pitcher on the staff with nineteen wins. Rivers sparked the offense, batted .312, and stole 40 bases. Catfish Hunter won seventeen games, as did Dock Ellis. Chris Chambliss had 96 RBIs, and Graig Nettles hit 32 homers with 93 RBIs. Oscar Gamble hit 17 homers and had 57 RBIs in a platoon role.

The two key men were the catcher and the manager. They would prove inside a year to be significant figures in the life of Reggie Jackson.

The catcher was Thurman Lee Munson, a short-waisted, stocky, unattractive-looking man with a marvelous bat, much style behind the plate, and an abrasive personality. He was filled with insecurities. His teammates called him Squatty Body because of his bulky form, kidded him by calling him Fat Boy to his face, and mailed him newspaper clippings of every fat woman they could find. He batted .302, was probably the finest all-around right-handed hitter in the game, caught 152 games, and won the league's MVP Award.

The Yankees were managed by Billy Martin, ever feisty, nasty, explosive, temperamental, insecure, mercurial, abrasive, pugnacious, and rambunctious. A drinker, a fighter, a lover. All this and, mostly, as several owners found out, a crowd pleaser and a winner.

And then there was George.

George Mitchell Steinbrenner, a Yankee Doodle Dandy, born on the Fourth of July, 1930, is a direct descendant of Great Lakes shipping interests going back to the early 1840s. Young George, determined to make his own way and pursue his own interests, ran track at Williams College, coached high school and college football, joined his father in business in Cleveland in 1960, and restructured the company into the huge American Ship Building Corporation. Always interested in sports, he first owned a basketball team called the Cleveland Pipers, a notable failure, and then, with thirteen partners, purchased the New York Yankees in January 1973. As his Yankee rebuilding program moved forward (the Yankees had deteriorated badly after their last pennant in 1964), Steinbrenner's hold on the club loosened because of a felony conviction. On April 5, 1974, he pleaded innocent to an indictment for illegal corporate contributions to Nixon's reelection campaign. He changed the plea to guilty in August after plea bargaining and escaped with a $15,000 fine. "Will you appeal?" reporters bellowed at his attorney, Edward Bennett Williams, now one of his fellow American League owners in Baltimore.

"Appeal what?" said Williams with a wry smile after he had skillfully helped his client escape jail.

Steinbrenner plunged back into his command of the Yankees with a vengeance on March 1, 1976, after his suspension, imposed by Commissioner Bowie Kuhn, had been lifted. He pushed his manager, and he pushed his players. He was a tyrant around his front-office people, hiring and firing at a moment's notice. He made winning and the pursuit of excellence his only goal. The tension was intensely noticeable when he was in town, and the sighs of relief could be easily heard when he was out of town. But he was charitable. He donated money to many organizations, organized aid for underprivileged kids, helped foster free baseball clinics, bailed his players out of emotional and legal problems, could let his hair down with his staff and his friends.

These personalities—Munson, Martin, Steinbrenner—and the rest of the Yankees would have much to do with Reggie Jackson's future baseball career.

While the Yankees were running away from Baltimore and the fans in Maryland grew angrier at Reggie's absence, Gary Walker continued to advise Jackson to return. He sensed that his value would be increased if he played in 1976, especially under the spotlight of having stayed away for some weeks. Soon the Orioles increased their salary offer to an even $200,000. Jackson agreed without signing (keeping his free agency options open), and Reggie flew to Baltimore on April 30.

"I was glad to see him," says Baltimore manager Earl Weaver. "I thought he could help us win the pennant. I told him to work out by himself. I knew he was a skilled player who knew how to get ready. I was surprised when he came to me a few days later and said he could play."

"You could see he wasn't ready," says Singleton. "But he played. We needed him. Reggie batted third, Lee May batted fourth, and I batted fifth. He seemed to fit in quickly."

Jim Palmer had known Jackson from their days together in Arizona State. He has always been an honest, direct man.

"When Reggie came here, there were no illusions he would stay," Palmer says. "We considered him a superstar, and he didn't do superstar things in the beginning. He simply wasn't ready. All he did was draw a lot of attention to himself. Reggie is Reggie, no matter where he goes. He seemed to feel that there should be a great deal of sympathy for his being traded. He wanted us to concern ourselves with his needs. We all have needs."

Weaver handled Reggie as Dick Williams did, praising him when he did well, correcting him gently when he did poorly. "One time he was on base and ran on his own to second. He got up with a big smile on his face like he had done something wonderful. The next hitter was Lee May. Naturally they walked him. Reggie had taken the bat out of Lee May's hands. I jumped him for that one," Weaver said.

By late June Jackson was in shape. By July he was hitting well, getting eight homers and nineteen RBIs in ten games between July 11 and July 23. He hit home runs in six straight games from July 18 through July 23.

"By next month," he told Weaver, "I'll take over this league."

Soon he was leading the Orioles in a comeback. They were suddenly challenging the Yankees. The Oriole players more and more were impressed by Reggie's awesome offensive power. He grew close to shortstop Mark Belanger and tried to help him at bat. He grew accustomed to Palmer's needles in the clubhouse. He was hit by a pitch by Dock Ellis on July 27, and there was serious concern among all the Orioles. He hit a home run off Terry Forster of the White Sox on August 14 in the first game of a doubleheader; then he hit a grand slam off left-hander Ken Brett in the nightcap. Next time up reliever Clay Carroll knocked him down. Reggie got up quietly but on the next pitch heaved his bat in Carroll's direction, setting off a wild brawl. All his Baltimore teammates were emotionally and physically involved in his fight.

"I think all the credit belongs to Earl," says Singleton. "He kept us all together. He really knew how to handle Reggie."

"It was easy," says Palmer. "He just left him alone. Besides, on this team there was no Thurman Munson."

By late August it was clear Reggie was playing out the year. The Orioles would not catch the Yankees, and Reggie would not stay in Baltimore.

"The last trip into each town was a show business performance," says Singleton. "It was bizarre. All the writers in that town would interview him about moving on, and he would knock down each town. 'Not enough papers here to carry my quotes,' he told the Cleveland writers. 'Too much beer, and I don't drink beer,' he told the Milwaukee writers. He was imposing. Everybody looked at him. He was Muhammad Ali and Joe Namath wrapped up in one. He talked big, but he delivered."

The press had created a terribly negative environment for Jackson in Baltimore. He was booed mercilessly when he first showed up and put on his Oriole uniform. It lessened a little as he started hitting in midseason. It increased almost violently as the year drew to a close and Jackson made it clear he would play elsewhere in 1977. The fans responded by booing him unmercifully and showering him with hot dogs.

"This is a business," he said one day that summer. "I can't worry about the fans. I have to do what I think is right and fair with me. I give them a price. They don't want to meet it, I move."

Rudy May, now a Yankee teammate, joined Reggie with the Orioles on June 15, 1976.

"We grew pretty close. We talked a lot," May says. "I admired Reggie. He did what he thought was right. He made up his own mind. He never said if he would stay or go. All he ever said was that he would see some big bucks before that year was over."

The Oriole schedule ended in early October. Mr. October hit his last homer as an Oriole on October 1 against Boston. Then he had two hits on October 2. He finished the season as he always had, strong. He batted .277 in 134 games. He hit 27 homers and had 91 RBIs. He struck out 108 times and stole 28 bases. He had earned every penny of the $200,000 the Orioles paid him.

Now he was ready to move on. He felt that he had earned his pay and that he owed Baltimore nothing. As the Yankees played Kansas City in the American League play-off, Reggie Jackson worked as a color commentator for the American Broadcasting Company. He was teamed with Howard Cosell. He was the first broadcaster to make Cosell the second banana. Where was Reggie going? That's all anybody wanted to know.

The Yankees won the pennant on Chris Chambliss's dramatic ninth-inning homer over Kansas City in the fifth play-off game. Then they were swept in four straight games by Cincinnati. Johnny Bench batted .533. Thurman Munson batted .435. When asked to compare Munson with his own Bench, Cincinnati manager Sparky Anderson said, "Don't embarrass any other player by comparing him with Bench." It was meant as a supreme compliment for Bench. Munson took it as a horrible insult, displaying a sensitivity Jackson would have to deal with soon.

* * *

On November 4, 1976, baseball's first free agent reentry draft was held in New York's Plaza Hotel. Tables were set up in a huge banquet room with placards marking the names of the teams. There was not much surprise in the room when Gabe Paul, president of the Yankees, said, "New York selects negotiating rights to player Reggie Jackson." Twelve other clubs—Montreal, Los Angeles, Atlanta, San Diego, California, New York Mets, San Francisco, Pittsburgh, Oakland, Philadelphia, Chicago, and Baltimore—all joined the Yankees in securing negotiating rights to Jackson. It would be an intense race.

For three weeks Jackson journeyed across America and into Canada, being romanced by baseball owners, set up in magnificent hotel suites, promised fortunes and even more fame, told by possible new teammates that their town, be it San Diego, Pittsburgh, or San Francisco, would be the perfect place to play. He visited National League ball parks he had never seen. He drank fine wine and was on a first-name basis with baseball owners he had never met. He was front-page news as he came into each town for the purpose of hearing new offers. It was an emotional high for Jackson as the price war escalated, $2 million,

$2.5, $3 million, $3.5, $4 million offered by Montreal, even a little more offered by San Diego.

Jackson came to New York after a Montreal visit, and Steinbrenner picked him up in his chauffeured limousine. They drove into town together to the Plaza Hotel, New York's most elegant and regally traditional resting place for royal personages.

"I didn't talk money," says Steinbrenner. "I talked tradition. I talked the Yankees. I wanted to convince Reggie this was the only place for him to play. I wanted to convince him of the possibilities of business expansion here for him."

Jackson could already see visions of that candy bar named after him.

After lunch at the Plaza, Steinbrenner and Jackson walked outside.

"I want to show you a little of the city," the Yankee owner said.

"I've been here before," Jackson said.

"Not with a chance to be a Yankee," he said.

They walked out the front door of the Plaza. A horse and carriage, one of the symbolic niceties of the Plaza, were parked next to a taxicab.

"Hey, Reggie, hey, Reggie," yelled the carriage driver, "wanna ride?"

Reggie only smiled. They crossed Fifth Avenue, opposite Central Park, and a small black boy, spotting the baseball player, raced after him.

"Sign this, sign this," he yelled, thrusting a scrap of brown paper at the large man.

"See," said Steinbrenner, "everybody knows and loves you already in this town."

Jackson and Steinbrenner talked some more as they walked along Fifth Avenue. Steinbrenner suggested it would be comfortable for Reggie to live in one of those magnificent apartments. He could commute easily to work at Yankee Stadium. He could dine in the finest restaurants in the world. He would be noticed, loved, appreciated. He would help restore the Yankees to their former glory.

The next afternoon, his head filled with New York dreams, Jackson flew on to Chicago. There would be one last day of negotiating. Jackson had told each of the remaining clubs—New York, Montreal, San Diego, and Baltimore—that the auction would close on Thursday at midnight. It happened to be Thanksgiving. Reggie decided he wanted it settled by then.

"After I left him at the Plaza," Steinbrenner says, "I decided Reggie had to sign with us. I knew he would be in Chicago talking with other clubs. I called his agent, Gary Walker, and told him I wanted to see him one more time in Chicago. I wanted to be the first in and the last out."

"He's already got an appointment with another club for breakfast at eight o'clock," Walker said.

"I'll be at the hotel at seven-thirty," Steinbrenner said.

The millionaire owner of the American Ship Building Company, worth about $180 million, of the New York Yankees, worth about $30 million, of horses, hotels, farms, houses, and other property, worth another $40 or $50 million, was in the Hyatt Regency Hotel in Chicago at 7:00 A.M.

"I sat in that lobby Thanksgiving morning, all alone, like some little kid, waiting for my time to call," Steinbrenner says. "I kept thinking how I had promised my kids I would be home for Thanksgiving. This seemed more important."

Steinbrenner got half an hour with Jackson from 7:30 to 8:00 A.M. He repeated his offer of some $3 million with the stress more on New York, the Yankee tradition, and the benefits of Madison Avenue than on dollars.

"By then," says Steinbrenner, "I knew other clubs had offered a million more."

The day dragged on. Representatives of other teams met with Jackson and Walker. Late in the afternoon Steinbrenner went to the coffee shop and had a cup of coffee. It was his only food all day. He was waiting to be paged in the lobby by Walker, so he could be the last out as well as first in. He sat there alone, thumbing through newspapers, talking on the phone back to the Yankee offices in New York, calling his family in Tampa to wish them a happy Thanksgiving, wondering what in hell he was doing in this hotel lobby anyway, realizing he was in the fiercest competition he had ever experienced. That is what kept him there, the competition against the other clubs, the same competition he had always enjoyed as a kid, had thrived on in business, had admired in his better players. He had to come out on top.

"Paging Mr. Steinbrenner, paging Mr. Steinbrenner." He walked to the house phone.

"C'mon up, George," said Jackson, "we're finished."

Steinbrenner walked into Jackson's hotel suite. There was a smile on Reggie's face. He had made his decision.

"You're it, George," Reggie said.

Tears came to Steinbrenner's eyes. He shook hands with the big guy standing in front of him and then impulsively hugged him.

Jackson moved to a small desk. There was a one-page note on hotel stationery. Jackson handed it to Steinbrenner. In longhand he had written out an agreement of acceptance of terms as generally outlined by Steinbrenner. "This will do until the lawyers get to writing it up," Jackson said.

George Steinbrenner has kept that note under glass on a dresser in his Tampa home. Every so often he looks at it, proud of his victory, proud of outhustling every other club that was after Jackson, glad he made that deal.

The four-paragraph note agreeing to terms ended with "We are going on this venture together. I will not let you down." It was signed "Reginald M. Jackson."

* * *

As he leaned back in his thick, deep leather chair, in the shape of a huge fielder's glove, in his Yankee Stadium

office, one day late in the summer of 1980, George Steinbrenner stared at an autographed picture of his friend
Cary Grant. Like his movie pal, he was impeccably
groomed, his hair recently trimmed, his television blue
shirt neatly starched, his trousers carefully pressed, his
leather shoes shining.

"That was one of the hardest days of my life," he says.
"Also one of the most thrilling."

Jackson had homered the night before in another easy
Yankee win.

"It took some time," George was saying now, "but Reggie has finally become the leader of the ball club, as I
always expected. He understands his role now. The magnitude of being a Yankee has superseded the magnitude
of his being Reggie Jackson."

"The Straw That Stirs
the Drink"

THEY LIVE TOGETHER, DRINK TOGETHER, SCREW TO-
gether. They pop pills and down scotch. They fear
death in an airplane crash and the end of their careers with equal intensity. They are thrown together accidentally, redneck farm boys from Alabama, coal miners'
sons from Pennsylvania, husky home run hitters and
skinny utility infielders, hard-throwing left-handers and
junk-balling right-handers, college men and high school
dropouts.

Off the field they share few secrets. Men have played
together for more than a decade without knowing the
names of their teammates' wives or kids. On the road they
might have sex in adjoining hotel beds. At home they may
never visit each other's houses. They walk through those
clubhouse doors in New York or Pittsburgh or Chicago or
Detroit and take on new identities. They seem no longer
to be husbands, fathers, and citizens. They are now .300
hitters, twenty-game winners, relief pitchers, fringe play-

ers, media darlings. They call each other obscene nicknames, talk mostly of sex and money.

At Oakland he was called Buck, a racially motivated nickname given to all black players, or Nine, for his uniform number, or simply Reggie.

In New York, as he joined the Yankees in 1977, it was never Buck or Forty-four for his new uniform number ("I wanted forty-two in honor of Jackie Robinson," says Reggie, "but then I realized there is only one forty-two") or even Reggie. His name seemed to simply become Him. After reading a paper, someone might ask, "Have you seen the latest about him?"

The Yankee players who were joined by Reggie Jackson in the spring of 1977 did nothing to welcome him. They did everything to torture him, led by their manager.

Billy Martin was against the signing of Reggie Jackson. He was concerned Reggie would steal some attention from him. He was concerned he couldn't control him. He was jealous of Reggie's $3 million package, his haughty manner, his boastful drive. He knew Reggie was George's boy. He would get in Billy's way.

"I'll tell you plain out what the whole thing between Billy and Reggie was all about," said Yankee executive Elston Howard, a former player and coach, but never candidate for manager, in an interview shortly before his death.

"Billy was jealous of him, hated the attention Reggie got, couldn't control him. That was part of it. The other part, the big part, was that Reggie's black. Billy hated him for that. I believe Billy is prejudiced against blacks, Jews, American Indians, Spanish, anything, if you don't bow to him. He can get along with blacks if they don't challenge him. But Reggie challenged him in every way. Billy was always hostile to him. Did everything to make him unhappy. Went out of his way to see him fail. I think Billy wanted Reggie to fail more than he wanted the Yankees to win," said Howard.

Elston Howard, fifty-one years old at his death, survived

a serious viral infection around his heart in 1979 and worked in a myriad of insignificant Yankee jobs. He was the longtime Yankee token black for many years because he was never militant. He quietly took what was given him.

"George has been great to me," he said. "He took care of me. He's been a good friend. But I would have liked a managerial offer. I might have turned it down, but I would have liked it."

Now he was finally speaking up, and he saw a clear pattern of racial prejudice in the game. "Frank Robinson, Larry Doby, now Maury Wills, and nobody else," he said. "Billy wasn't unique in the way he dealt with Reggie. A lot of them probably enjoyed it."

When the heat was on Reggie, when the antagonism had grown deep, when the issues had been clearly drawn between Jackson on one side, with some support from Steinbrenner, and Billy Martin, Thurman Munson, and the rest on the other side, Jackson would say, "It makes me cry the way they treat me on this team. The Yankee pinstripes are Ruth and Gehrig and DiMaggio and Mantle. And I'm a nigger to them. I don't know how to be subservient."

"The difference with the Yankees," says Catfish Hunter, an Oakland teammate, "is guys paid attention to what he said. At Oakland nobody listened to him. We just watched him hit. Reggie's really a good guy; down deep he is. I really like him. I always did. He'd give you the shirt off his back. Of course, he'd call a press conference to announce it."

Hunter was one of the Yankee leaders, along with Thurman Munson, Lou Piniella, Graig Nettles, and Sparky Lyle. The others disengaged themselves from the decision making, much too concerned with playing the game.

A baseball team has twenty-five individuals with one collective personality. The manager sets the tone if he is strong. Martin was strong. The players, those accepting the manager's leadership, carry out his edicts and push his policies. It was easy to see Jackson was going one way on the Yankees and the rest of the players, save for Fran Healy, were going another.

"When I was playing for Kansas City and he was with Oakland," Healy says, "I met him outside the players' gate. We talked a long while. I found him very intelligent, very interesting, a unique guy. We became friends, visiting and talking together each time we played. We naturally became friends when he joined the Yankees."

In a crowd of Yankee players, in the clubhouse, on the team bus, in the training room banter, Jackson had to be the first among equals. In a one-on-one situation—and it was several years before any Yankee would allow that to happen with him—Jackson could be low-key, quiet, introspective, even a little humble and insecure.

His signing had been announced at a huge press conference in the Princess Suite of the Americana Hotel. The Yankees had dragged Thurman Munson in from Ohio and Roy White from New Jersey to show solidarity. Reggie had brought along his father, who loved every ounce of attention, his shy mother, his lawyer brother, and several friends, including a blonde girlfriend.

"When I came to that press conference," Reggie says, "we hadn't even put anything on paper. That's how much I trusted George."

* * *

At Fort Lauderdale's Yankee Stadium hordes of press people awaited Reggie's arrival. The grumbling of the other players was noticeable. "You'd think we had just won the fucking World Series or something," said Thurman Munson.

Munson had discovered, after coming to Jackson's January press conference, that Reggie was actually making more money than he was. George had lied to him. It was Steinbrenner's contention that he had not. "I told Thurman he would be the highest-salaried Yankee, and he was," Steinbrenner says. The difference was made up in bonus money. Munson, never choosing the free agent route, had missed out on a $400,000 signing bonus Jackson received.

"You see this," Jackson said as he held court with the press and fondled his black bat. "This is the Dues Collector. This now helps the Yankees intimidate every other team in baseball. That's what I do just by walking into this clubhouse. Nobody will embarrass the Yankees in the World Series as long as I am carrying the Dues Collector."

Soon the Yankees were on the field, going through their exercises, Jackson being watched by his teammates, by the early-arriving fans, by the newspaper, television, and radio representatives. He was clearly being watched, and that was why Reggie Jackson had joined the Yankees in the first place. Among the early-arriving press was a free-lance writer named Robert Ward. He was working on an article about Jackson for *Sport* magazine. It would have much impact on the Yankee season of 1977.

The season started on April 7 at Yankee Stadium before 43,785 fans. Jackson had two singles in four at bats, scored two runs, and was a significant part of Catfish Hunter's opening day 3–0 shutout over the Milwaukee Brewers. Jackson was booed lustily each time he batted, as much for signing a $3 million contract as for not hitting a home run. His first home run came four days later in a losing effort against Kansas City in Royals Stadium. It was hit off Paul Splittorff, a pitcher Jackson would meet later with interesting results.

Munson, still seething over the contract problem, resentful of Jackson's love affair with the press, and uncertain how to deal with it all, whispered sarcastic remarks to his few favorites among the press and made loud remarks to his teammates. Munson, Nettles, Piniella, and Sparky Lyle spent much clubhouse and off-field time discussing Reggie.

Jackson, for his part, did little to win his teammates over. He flashed money on the team bus. He bragged about huge home runs he hit. He flaunted his white

blonde girlfriends at them. No Yankee ever asked him to
dinner save for Healy. He never asked anybody else. He
would eat alone, with Healy, or with one or two sportswriters on the road.

Billy Martin used him as the designated hitter, batted
him fifth, sixth, or seventh, criticized his outfield play
when he played right field, did what he could to pull his
teammates away from him.

Somehow, through it all, the Yankees stayed close or at
the top of their division. Jackson wasn't doing much with
only five homers and a .250 average in mid-May. Then
came a new controversy, the printing of the remark, "the
straw that stirs the drink."

Robert Ward's article was circulated in advance copies
before the June issue came out. The interviews with Jackson, conducted in early March, had almost been forgotten. In fact, Munson and Jackson had even tried to talk
peacefully a few times. Ward's article, entitled "Reggie
Jackson in No-Man's Land," was a bitter pill for a sensitive
Munson to swallow.

"You know," Jackson was quoted as saying, "this team,
it all flows from me. I've got to keep it all going. I'm the
straw that stirs the drink. It all comes back to me. Maybe
I should say me and Munson. But really he doesn't enter
into it. He's being so damned insecure about the whole
thing. I've overheard him talking about me."

Then Jackson said, "Munson's tough, too. He's a winner
but there is just nobody who can do for a club what I can
do. There is nobody who can put meat in the seats [fans
in the stands] the way I can. That's just the way it is.
Munson thinks he can be the straw that stirs the drink, but
he can only stir it bad."

Ward asked Martin if he thought there would be any
leadership problems on the club with Reggie Jackson now
on the team.

"Not a chance," Martin said. "We already have a team
leader. Thurman Munson."

The article was read by every Yankee, even those who

had never read any magazine article that wasn't about themselves. The press fanned the flames. Almost every player was asked his reaction. Each, almost universally, was critical of Reggie. Even Fran Healy found it too difficult to defend. "The straw that stirs the drink" became a catchphrase around the club.

"See, the thing that people forgot," says Fred Stanley, the wonderful utility player on the Yankees, "is that Thurman was the captain. He was Mr. Yankee. He also wanted attention; he wanted it as badly as Reggie wanted it. He just didn't know how to go about it."

Stanley remembers a game early in the season. The Yankees were behind. Thurman Munson hit a homer to win it. The game ended. The press invaded the clubhouse.

"Thurman had this way of walking up and down the clubhouse when he wanted some press attention. If he didn't want it, he could hide. But when he walked, he knew one of those writers would be brave enough to stop him and ask him a question. He was waiting for them. But they never came to him. They all stopped at Reggie's locker, and he discussed the latest rise and fall in the stock market or something, and that just pissed Thurman off real bad."

Stanley is one of the most decent of men. When Jackson finally tried, he won him over.

"I was talking to Piniella or somebody one day about my folks back in Arizona wanting to buy a car. They were quoted a price of eleven thousand dollars, and they were debating getting it. That was steep money. Reggie overheard us. 'You wanna car for your folks?' I told him I did. He said he had a car dealership in Tempe and he could take care of it. He got them the same car for seven thousand dollars. I never forget that favor. He never did either. He made sure eleven guys heard him ask me how my folks were doing with the car he arranged for them. I didn't resent it. That's Reggie. He has to be appreciated."

With Munson, Nettles, and Lyle leading the way, and Martin egging them on, Jackson was almost totally a non-person in the Yankee clubhouse. He may have been the most disliked home run hitter in history.

"Sure, a lot of it was racial," said Elston Howard. "If I was the manager and a guy was black or white or green or blue and could hit thirty homers for me, I'd sure as hell love him to death."

Martin was adamantly sure he could win without Reggie. Gabe Paul, the president, and George Steinbrenner, the owner, were not so sure. As the furor increased, they debated their choices. Steinbrenner vacillated each day. He was almost pushed over the top and into firing Billy after an incident seen by millions on national television on June 18.

The Yankees were in Boston for the emotional Boston-New York series that had been a tradition for more than half a century, ever since the Yankees had acquired Babe Ruth from the Red Sox. The intensity of the Boston fans and the tight confines of Fenway Park increased the drama. The National Broadcasting Company zeroed its cameras in on the game. Suddenly a fly ball hit by Jim Rice was dropping in short right field as Reggie Jackson moved casually for it. Rice was at second base with a double as Boston was coasting to an easy 10–4 win.

Enraged at what he decided was lazy effort, Martin sent Paul Blair to right field and pulled Jackson from the game. The players stared straight ahead on the field as Jackson jogged to the dugout. Now he put down his glasses and moved toward Martin. The cameras followed. Martin screamed, "You show me up, I'll show you up."

Jackson, sweat running down his neck and his eyes glazed with anger, screamed, "What did I do? What did I do?"

Now the large outfielder and the sinewy manager moved toward each other. Elston Howard and Yogi Berra moved between them. Dick Howser, another coach, kept his eyes on the field and his emotions in check.

Pitcher Mike Torrez, who had been taken out of the game, told Jackson in Spanish, "Go inside, cool off, go inside." Torrez, a Mexican American from Kansas City, sensed there would be irrevocable damage done to both men if they engaged in a fight on the bench.

"I think both Billy and Reggie were under enormous tensions at the time," Torrez says. "It was only a matter of time before one or both of them would explode. That was it."

Somebody had to go. These two men could not live together. No other team would take Jackson's $3 million contract. Rumors flew that Billy would be fired by nightfall. George Steinbrenner, who admired Billy's aggressive managing and had no successor immediately available, talked with the player and the manager. The turning point came late in the night when Jackson told Steinbrenner, "I don't want to be the cause of a manager's firing. Don't fire him."

Martin stayed. Jackson stayed. The tensions remained.

* * *

The twenty-three-story white brick building at 985 Fifth Avenue lies across the street from Central Park. Actress Cicely Tyson, wearing a T-shirt, shorts, and sneakers, comes out of the front door, hustles across busy Fifth Avenue, and begins jogging around the reservoir in the park. Writer-producer-director-comedian Mel Brooks and his actress wife, Anne Bancroft, are busy at work on a new script in their fifteenth-floor apartment. The president of a jeans company lives on the twelfth floor. The chairman of the board of an airlines company lives on the eighth floor. There are half a dozen psychiatrists residing in the building. Chauffeured limousines pull up to the circular driveway in front of the building often. Distinguished-looking gentlemen and handsome women, some carrying small dogs, get into waiting cars. Financiers, politicians, and industrialists maintain apartments in the building. Reggie Jackson pays $1,466 a month for a two-bedroom corner apartment on the nineteenth floor of the building.

As Shakespeare would have it, the apartment is furnished "rich, not gaudy." There is a comfortable couch, several tasteful-looking sitting chairs, a small kitchen. There are no signs of baseball in the apartment other than a huge painting of the owner commissioned by his agent, Matt Merola, and a gift presented to him by sports artist LeRoy Neiman. A small patio porch is filled with growing flowers.

One of the residents of the building, Marilyn Barrie, is divorced from George Barrie of the Fabergé fortune. Her son is a writer for Johnny Carson. She is an elegant woman, much younger-looking than her years. She remembers seeing Reggie Jackson often during that stressful period of his life.

"There are two Spanish-speaking doormen, Carlos and Raymón," she says. "I would come down and see him talking to them often in the lobby, just killing time, seemingly with no place to go. Once in a while, at night, he would leave with Raymón, and the gossip would be they went to Studio 54 together. He always seemed like such a poor lost soul to me. The doormen liked him and fussed over him because he was a big tipper. The kids would hang around and ask for his autograph, and sometimes he would give them an autograph, and sometimes he wouldn't. One time a kid asked for his autograph, and he wouldn't sign. He said he was too busy. The kid yelled, 'You're nothing but a bigmouth,' and just ran away. I asked him for an autograph for a nephew once. I wanted it on a ball. He said he didn't have any baseballs, but if I brought him one, he'd sign it. I finally did a year later. He signed, asked who it was for, and wrote a nice note. A very interesting man."

Fran Healy would dine often with Jackson in those depressing summer days of 1977 at Oren & Aretsky's or Jim McMullen's or Rusty Staub's restaurant.

"Most of the time we could eat quietly. Once in a while some jerk would come up and stick a ball-point pen in Reggie's baked potato," Healy says.

*   *   *

By day he would spend time around the apartment, thinking, talking to friends by phone, being consoled by Matt Merola, working on business deals. By night he would be at the ball park, working out early, talking with the press, playing the game, a Yankee, but not very much a part of this famous baseball team. In July, with the tensions still high, Lou Piniella and Thurman Munson met with Steinbrenner in a Milwaukee hotel room. Billy Martin staggered upon the meeting accidentally. He had been drinking heavily. He saw the session as a plot against him, and he threatened to quit. Steinbrenner told him to sleep it off. The meeting had been called by the two players to ease the tension around the team. "Fire Billy or don't," Piniella said. "We can't take this turmoil every day." Steinbrenner agreed he would allow Billy to finish the season. Piniella made one more request, agreed to by Munson. "Let Reggie bat fourth. He thinks it is so damn important to him," Piniella said.

In early August Jackson's name appeared on the lineup card in the fourth spot, the hero spot, for the first time. He said nothing when he saw it. He simply played better than he had ever played as a Yankee. He finished the season with 50 RBIs in the last forty-nine games. He was the leader. He hit the big home run against Reggie Cleveland on September 14. He had received an incredible outpouring of affection from the fans. He loved it.

Reggie Jackson had literally become "the straw that stirs the drink."

He hit two home runs against Detroit on September 17. He had four RBIs against Toronto on September 25. He had four RBIs against Cleveland on September 28. The Yankees, despite the incredible turmoil, despite as bitter a relationship between manager and player as had ever existed in the game, won the division title by two and a half games.

Reggie Jackson had played 146 games. He had batted .286. Only once had he ever batted higher. He had 32 homers and 110 RBIs. He had done it with enormous pressures and expectations.

In the final days of the season, as the pennant was assured and the play-offs against Kansas City still lay ahead, Jackson mused about his future.

"I just might quit," he said. "I can't stand the tension. The only time I'm at peace is when I walk across the white lines. I have money. I have many business deals that will take care of me the rest of my life. I'm not enjoying anything about the game except playing it. I still enjoy that, the competition, the match between Reggie Jackson and the pitcher. The rest of it, the crowds, the fans, the press, the problems, I really don't want that anymore." Then he paused for a moment, seemed deep in thought, and finally said quietly, "Sometimes I just can't understand the magnitude of me."

He had become the most dynamic baseball player of his time. His home runs were thrilling. He could bring a crowd to its feet with a vicious swing. This man who had played golf with President Gerald Ford at the President's request, had caused traffic jams wherever he walked, this man who was wanted by so many civic groups for appearances, who was harassed by so many well-meaning charities, who seemed so visible in his public life, threatened now to withdraw.

It was a passing depression. The excitement of the pennant changed that. The competition of the American League championship series altered all that. The Yankees won again, helped by Jackson's key pinch hit after Martin benched him in the fifth game, and now it was the World Series. It was October. All the attention was on him again.

"You know all this talk about Reggie being a great October hitter, Mr. October," says Mickey Morabito, the former Yankee publicity director who followed Billy Martin to Oakland. "I wonder how many people remember who was the original Mr. October. It was Billy Martin. He had some of the greatest performances in the World Series anybody ever had."

Billy Martin had caught a fly ball off the bat of Jackie Robinson in the seventh inning of the seventh game of the 1952 Series; it had saved the Yankees. He had batted .500 in the 1953 Series and had won the Babe Ruth Award, symbolic of being the outstanding player in that Series. He had batted .320 in 1955 and .296 in the 1956 Series, for a lifetime World Series mark of .333. The Yankees had lost only one pennant between the years of 1950 and 1957. That was 1954, when the White Sox beat the Yankees in the American League race and Billy Martin was in the Army all season.

But nobody, not Billy Martin, not Babe Ruth, not anybody who played in baseball's fall classic, had a series like the one Jackson had in 1977 against the Dodgers. He hit .450 with five homers and a double. He hit four home runs in a row in two games. He hit three in a row in the final game on three consecutive pitches off three different pitchers, a feat as unlikely to be matched as Lou Gehrig's astonishing feat of 2,130 consecutive games played.

Gehrig died in 1941 of a crippling nerve and muscle disease known as amyotrophic lateral sclerosis. The ALS Society was looking for a celebrated honorary national chairman in 1977. It selected Reggie Jackson, who would serve admirably and honorably in fund-raising, public relations, and publicity events for what is now commonly called Lou Gehrig's disease.

After his five Series homers, Jackson was undeniably the most famous athlete in America.

The Standard Brands Company even recognized the fact. It named a candy bar after him. It was called the Reggie bar.

"One's a Born Liar, the Other's Convicted"

HOME RUN HITTERS ARE HEROES, TO KIDS, TO FANS, to teammates, to sportswriters. Babe Ruth was loved. Hank Aaron was held in awe. Ted Williams was admired for his magnificent skills. Mickey Mantle destroyed his body by partying and playing, yet received undying devotion for both. Willie Mays was Leo Durocher's pet, his Say Hey, Kid, as well as a nation's joy. Frank Robinson, Harmon Killebrew, Ernie Banks, Ralph Kiner, all of them home run hitters, received constant acclaim. It is why so many hitters sacrifice singles for the attempt at home runs.

Only Roger Maris, who broke the Babe's one-season homer record, was vilified. He just wasn't the Babe. He wasn't lovable. Morose, laconic, stubborn, he didn't fit the role. He still hit more home runs in one baseball season than any man in the history of the game. You could look it up, as Casey Stengel loved to say.

And then there was Reggie. Arrogant, proud to a fault,

vain, sensitive, craving love, but always denied it. A home run hitter strangely booed in his own home park.

The Yankees had a new team president in the spring of 1978. George Steinbrenner had hired Al Rosen, the former Cleveland Indian third baseman, away from his job as a public relations man for Billy Weinberger's Caesars Palace. Rosen and Steinbrenner had worked together in Cleveland for the betterment of the city as members of Group 66, a collection of successful local businessmen interested in improving the image of that beleaguered town.

"I missed baseball," Rosen says. "Every minute I was out of the game I never stopped thinking about getting back in it."

Gabe Paul had left the Yankees to return to Cleveland. He was now a part owner of that club. He was also free of the pressures imposed on him by Steinbrenner.

Rosen would now handle those pressures. He was a hero to Steinbrenner, a former Cleveland great when Steinbrenner was growing up there, and he was intelligent, personable, handsome, articulate. He was a good fellow who didn't have to fall down drunk to be fun at a party. Billy Martin quickly decided Rosen would be his ally against Steinbrenner and Reggie Jackson.

"Al played the game. He understands what it is like," Martin said. "Gabe got in the way. He didn't know the game."

Gabe Paul had been in baseball since 1928, when he started as a batboy in his hometown of Rochester, New York. He had built several franchises in Cincinnati, Houston, and Cleveland. He had built the Yankees into a winner in four years. Now he was attempting to do the same thing in Cleveland. Gabe also seemed impervious to criticism. "I try not to worry about things I can't control," he says. "I don't worry about rain. It will stop. It always has."

*   *   *

Minutes after the Yankees gathered for spring training at Fort Lauderdale's Yankee Stadium in 1978, it was clear nothing had changed. Reggie Jackson was absent, and Billy Martin was enraged. George Steinbrenner was inflammatory, first siding with Billy, angry at Reggie's absence, then siding with Reggie, announcing he had given Jackson permission to be late. Intrigue was everywhere.

"It got so," says Lou Piniella, "that I hated everything about playing for the Yankees except the games. I used to love baseball, everything, the game, the clubhouse, the fans, the fun, the talk, the friendships. Now that was all bitter to me. The squabbles, the back-and-forth backbiting disgusted me. I wished I could quit. I just wasn't rich enough. So I swallowed it."

Jackson drove the Rolls-Royce through the players' gate. He signed a few autographs. He waved to some fans already in the stands. He kidded the gate attendant on his added winter girth. He marched to his locker. No player greeted him. He didn't need them. The press was there. He put his foot up on his locker stool and talked for twenty minutes.

"George understands me. He's a businessman. I had business to take care of," Reggie was saying. "Billy doesn't understand that. He's only a baseball manager."

"Some guys don't need spring training," Billy was snarling to his favorite reporters. His neck muscles were taut. His skin was pinched tight. His stomach was churning. It was obvious that the big guy was getting to him again.

Reggie Jackson hit a home run in the opening game of the 1978 season much to Billy Martin's displeasure. The home run almost caused a riot. Standard Brands had presented its new Reggie bars, a chocolaty, gooey, stick-to-the-roof-of-your-mouth candy to each fan. When Reggie's homer cleared the wall, a few Reggie bars floated down from the second deck of the stadium. Then more and more and more. Soon thousands of Reggie bars inundated the field. The game was held up for fifteen minutes as grounds keepers picked up Reggie bars one by one. Would the candy company start the barrage itself by throwing the bars on the field?

"Oh, my, no," Reggie said. "I just think it was an honest expression of appreciation for what I've done to help this ball club."

The Red Sox surged ahead quickly in the pennant race. Jim Rice was having a sensational season. Except for Ron Guidry, the skinny left-hander saved from the minors a year earlier by Gabe Paul, none of the Yankees was. The Yankees went to Boston for a June series and were crushed. A young, tall, college-educated pitcher named Jim Beattie was beaten, 9–2. Steinbrenner was at the game. He left the park enraged but not before he said to New York sportswriters, "Beattie was scared stiff. What the hell was he doing out there?" When reporters reached the clubhouse, Beattie was gone. He had been sent to the minors by Steinbrenner's abrasive phone call. "Get rid of him," he shouted to coach Gene Michael.

"Who?" innocently asked Michael, not knowing if Steinbrenner wanted Beattie or Billy fired on the spot.

"What about Billy?" reporters asked Steinbrenner.

"That's Al Rosen's decision."

Billy Martin drank heavily that night. He was drinking heavily almost every night in the summer of 1978. His buddy and pitching coach, Art Fowler, kept pace with him drink for drink. Fowler had been with Billy everywhere he managed. When Billy took over in New York, he wanted Fowler again. Gabe Paul would have none of that. "He's a drunk," Paul said.

Then the Yankees hired Bob Lemon as the pitching coach in 1976. "What a joke that was," Billy later said. "They wouldn't let me have Fowler, but they let me have Lemon, who drinks more." It would be impossible to measure who drinks more or less, but Lemon once said, "I never take the game home with me. I always leave it in some bar."

Bob Lemon had been fired as manager early in 1978 at

Chicago by his old pal Bill Veeck. He had gone home to California, where he received a phone call from another ex-Cleveland teammate, Al Rosen. "Stay loose, meat, we'll want you in the Yankee organization sooner or later."

Rosen wanted Lemon to manage the Yankees. A plot had been hatched before Lemon's firing to trade Martin for Lemon. The deal fell through. Then Lemon went home. Martin stayed in purgatory, managing the Yankees as they fell farther back, distrusting Al Rosen, whispering sarcastic remarks about his lack of baseball knowledge, complaining about Steinbrenner's interference. Martin saw enemies everywhere, feuded with the press, fought with umpires, confronted always with the presence of Reggie Jackson. Jackson was the salt on his open wounds. Martin was bitterly jealous of the man, frustrated he couldn't bend him, determined that he would humiliate him any way he could.

A leading Bellevue psychiatrist was once asked to explain the relationship between Billy Martin and Reggie Jackson. Promised anonymity since he had never met either man but only read of them, he said, "I'm fascinated by Reggie. I must admit that. He is a very special human being. He is intuitively brilliant. Reggie has the aura of success Billy seeks and can't reach. Reggie would be successful in any endeavor he tries. If he were a brain surgeon, he'd be the best. If he were a janitor, he'd be the best. Some people just have that aura. Race is also an important factor here, very important. Billy's background of poverty, lower-class Italian working people, and financial struggle—all suggests prejudice. Hardly a man from that background does not have prejudice built into him. Some fight it. I believe Billy has controlled it. I think he deals with players on their abilities. But blacks are different. Blacks test him, test his abilities, his beginnings, his background, his insecurities. The most prejudiced are generally the least successful, the ones who have little and guard it fanatically. Billy is comfortable with blacks who know their place. Reggie doesn't know his place. Reggie makes Billy uncomfortable."

There was one other element in Billy Martin's life that seemed significant. The fans. What of the fans?

"People identify with his aggression," the doctor says. "He represents the American way, the gunfighter from the West, the hero outlaw. He is Jesse James robbing a train or Bonnie and Clyde robbing a bank. He acts on his own anger. The athlete in America is a hero figure because we can sublimate our anger through his action. It wouldn't be socially acceptable conduct to slug someone at a bar. It would be socially acceptable conduct to sit in the stands and egg Billy Martin on against an umpire, an authority figure. He fights our battles for us at no loss of status and no pain."

In the public mind, the battle among Steinbrenner, Jackson, and Martin was no contest. Steinbrenner was rich. There weren't that many millionaires sitting in the stands at baseball games. As a result, he could not receive the fans' sympathy. Reggie was snooty, arrogant, and vain. Fans like their heroes to be humble. No one ever accused Reggie Jackson of being humble. But there was a much larger factor, less spoken, more obvious to those who cared to face the truth—the matter of race. Reggie Jackson was a black star who lacked even a trace of servility.

Baseball fans are overwhelmingly white, and many found Jackson's attitude offensive. Jackson could never gain the sympathy of the fans pitted against the skinny, downtrodden, aggressive, Italian American from the Depression era poverty of Berkeley. Reggie Jackson and George Steinbrenner were the villains, while Billy Martin was the hero. Reggie could "hot dog" it all he liked and Billy Martin would still be a bigger hero to the guys in the torn T-shirts, beer cups in hand, sitting in the top rows of the grandstands.

The Yankees slipped farther back in the pennant race, six games, eight games, ten games. Steinbrenner was restless. He constantly harangued Martin on the phone, about not playing Reggie enough, about not batting him higher in the batting order, about Munson's hitting too low in the order or too high, about his not using Guidry enough or using Gossage too much. Would Billy be fired? Steinbrenner pushed the press to Rosen. "Billy Martin is the manager of this ball club," said Rosen.

By late June Steinbrenner decided some drastic action was necessary. Instead of firing Billy, who he still begrudgingly conceded was a good field manager, he tried firing pitching coach Art Fowler. When he met with Martin to tell him, Billy begged him to change his mind. They argued about it for more than an hour. Steinbrenner, still thinking Billy could pull off a miracle and get the Yankees back in the race, compromised. Fowler could stay, mostly as Billy's drinking buddy. Clyde King, the minor-league pitching instructor, would serve as the pitching coach, in fact, especially with Beattie and the younger pitchers.

By the middle of the season reasonable hopes for a Yankee pennant seemed lost. On July 17 the Yankees lost to Kansas City and fell fourteen games out of first place. Boston was blazing. It seemed the Red Sox could win by as many as twenty games. Even that unhappy possibility was lost in New York because of a new fuss, one of the most celebrated episodes in recent baseball history.

Reggie Jackson had forced Billy Martin's hand.

With relief pitcher Al Hrabowsky pitching for Kansas City on Monday night, July 17, and the score tied in the tenth inning, Munson singled to right. Jackson, batting fourth, was ordered to bunt. It was a public humiliation. Big sluggers batting fourth go for home runs in tie games, not bunts. Jackson was incensed. He made a halfhearted attempt to get into bunt position and then drew back on the pitch. The Kansas City infield, believing that Reggie might really bunt, had moved in. Martin switched signs. He flashed the hit sign to third base coach Dick Howser. Howser moved down from the line toward Jackson. "Billy took the bunt sign off," Howser said.

"I'm going to bunt," Jackson said.

"He wants you to swing the bat," Howser said.

Jackson bunted and missed for a strike. Martin was incredulous, livid with rage. Howser flashed the hit sign once, twice, three times. Jackson looked straight ahead. Hrabowsky threw a fastball. Jackson bunted it foul. Martin was livid on the bench. "What the fuck is he doing, trying to show me up? He can't do this to me. He can't do this to me." The next pitch was a straight fastball. Jackson bunted foul again. He was struck out. He walked past Martin into the clubhouse. Kansas City scored two runs in the top of the eleventh to win, 9–7. Jackson, who had finished his day as the designated hitter, was standing in front of his locker as his losing teammates came in. Martin paraded around the clubhouse like a wild man. He threw a clock radio to the floor. He flung a drinking glass against a door. He ducked and dodged reporters. "No interviews, no fucking interviews," he screamed.

Reggie, as always, was gladly giving interviews. He spoke softly, carefully, measuring every word, explaining his position. "Why did you bunt, why did you bunt?" a reporter screamed.

"I was trying to advance the runner," he said.

"Did you miss the hit sign?"

Jackson looked straight ahead. "I don't miss signs. My job was to advance the runner. I tried to do that. How can they say I'm a threat if I swing the bat? I'm not even an every-day player. I'm a part-time player."

Executive vice-president Cedric Tallis was in Martin's office now. They were on the phone to Steinbrenner, who was at his Tampa home. They were on the phone after that with Al Rosen, who was upstairs in the Yankee offices. Rosen would not enter the clubhouse. Tallis faced the press. "Reggie Jackson is suspended immediately without pay."

Jackson flew home to Oakland that night, while the Yankees flew on to Minnesota. They were scheduled for eight games on the road in Minnesota, Chicago, and Kansas City. Jackson flew to Chicago on Saturday night to rejoin the club. The Yankees had won five in a row in his absence. Boston was slumping. Injuries were cutting the Sox down. Nobody noticed. The team bus left for the park in Chicago. Jackson took a cab with Fran Healy.

"Reggie was tense," says Healy, "as tense as I had ever seen him. This was a hot situation. Even Reggie had never gone through anything like this before."

There were more than thirty reporters near his locker, crowding a small clubhouse. "Fucking reporters," Martin bellowed as he entered the clubhouse.

A dozen red roses, with a card reading, "Love, from Andrea and Diane," sat on Reggie's locker stool. More than a dozen telegrams were piled in his locker. Letters were neatly tied in a bundle. His uniform shirt was on a hook. He faced the press.

Dick Schaap of NBC had flown in from New York the previous evening to be on hand. "How do you feel?" Schaap asked.

"Nervous," Reggie answered. "This is a bitch. This is a motherfucker to have to go through this."

Now the cameras were on. "I'm here to do my job," Reggie told Schaap quietly. "I'll play as hard as I can as I always have, if the manager plays me."

The manager did not, yet the Yankees won again. Jackson sat in uniform at the end of the dugout. None of his teammates noticed he was there. Jackson went into the clubhouse after the game, quietly talked to the press again, and dressed for the trip to Kansas City. Martin showered quickly and rushed upstairs to the Bard's Room, the press lounge in Comiskey Park. He drank four quick scotches as he stood at the bar. He ate nothing. Steinbrenner told the press Billy's drinking was out of control. He said Billy had been examined, had been discovered to have a spot on his liver, and ordered to quit. He continued to drink. "I made a vow in church when I was a kid that I would not drink until I was eighteen," he once said. "I've made up for it since."

Now the New York writers gathered around Martin in

the press room. He had been told by Veeck that he and Steinbrenner had contemplated a trade of managers. That upset him. He wanted the press to tell him if Reggie seemed apologetic for disobeying his orders. He was told Reggie did not. Martin became more agitated, the tension in his face more visible, the anger growing more evident, less controllable. Now the Yankees were on the team bus to O'Hare Airport for the flight to Kansas City. Billy Martin looked ill. He leaned over to sportswriter Murray Chass of *The New York Times.* "When we get to the airport, can I see you for a few minutes?"

Martin and Chass walked through the passageway toward the gate. Martin said, "I'm saying, shut up, Reggie Jackson. If he doesn't shut up, he won't play. I don't care what George says. He can replace me right now."

Managing the Yankees was Billy Martin's life. He had no other. His second marriage was in a shambles. Players whispered about his liaisons with women. He often arrived at the park late, sometimes with the smell of alcohol on his breath, hardly the picture of the Yankee image Steinbrenner struggled fiercely to protect and defend. Now he was willing to relinquish the Yankee job, he was saying, if he could not get total control over Jackson.

Martin's words were called in to the *Times* by Chass. He returned to Billy and was walking with the manager and sportswriter Henry Hecht of the *New York Post,* while Martin continued to criticize Jackson bitterly. Venom poured forth, spilling over from all the months of anguish he had suffered. He hated listening to Reggie, being upstaged by him, watching him win George over. Reggie and George dined at "21" together. Reggie and George had a couple of drinks together at Jimmy Weston's or P. J. Clarke's. Reggie sat in George's office. Reggie was George's boy, his pal, his equal. He hated George, and he hated Reggie. He imagined they always lied about him. Billy Martin became swallowed up by his anguish.

"The two of them deserve each other. One's a born liar, the other's convicted," he blurted out.

It was out of his mouth now. It would soon be in print. Steinbrenner would hear it and become almost speechless. Rosen would be shocked and saddened for the Yankees. Yankee players snickered. When a reporter told Jackson what Martin had said, Reggie shook his head and said, "The man's sick."

Soon Steinbrenner was on the phone with Rosen. He wanted him to fly to Kansas City. After he got there and talked with Billy, asking him if he had really said it, the decision would be made. Rosen knew George wanted him fired. He phoned pal Bob Lemon at his Long Beach, California, home. "Keep yourself in cold storage, meat. I just wanted to know if you were home. We might be making a change."

* * *

At 3:22 P.M. the next afternoon, Monday, July 24, 1978, Billy Martin announced his resignation at a televised press conference from the balcony level of the Crown Center Hotel in Kansas City. Bob Lemon would be the new Yankee manager. Dick Howser would serve that night until Lemon arrived. Lemon, not one for press conferences or announcements, simply said, "We'll go back to the lineup that won it last year and see what happens."

That meant Thurman Munson, who had been playing right field because of ailing knees, would go back to catching. Rookie Mike Heath would go to the bench. Bucky Dent would play nine innings of shortstop and not be pinch-hit for. Mickey Rivers would be free to run. Ed Figueroa would pitch every fourth day. And Reggie Jackson, back from his one-week vacation, would play right field and bat fourth.

"We'll see how far we can go," said Lemon.

Bob Lemon, a Hall of Fame pitcher, was as comfortable as an old slipper. His genius lay in nonconfrontation. After nearly three tumultuous years of Billy Martin's rantings the Yankees were allowed to play baseball.

"You can't imagine what that was like," Reggie Jackson

says. "You come to the park, and there are no reporters around your locker, waiting to get your reaction to the latest story in the papers. You can dress in peace. You can pick your game bat out, think of the opposing pitcher, clear your mind. You can breathe free. The art of hitting is combining physical skill with mental discipline, concentration, seeing that baseball in the pitcher's hand, studying it, watching it, flailing at it with your mind totally on that mission. I could breathe free again."

The Yankee locker room had been heavy with intrigue. Thurman Munson would be in one corner whispering to Graig Nettles. Reggie Jackson would be whispering to a reporter or to Fran Healy. Lou Piniella and Sparky Lyle would be straddling the training table. The deafening silence after a loss would be broken only by the opening of a beer can or the sound of a shower shoe squeaking on the carpeted floor.

Bucky Dent, a gentle, tightly wound shortstop, remembers that transitional period with clarity.

"My stomach stopped churning," he says. "I was under such enormous pressure playing for Billy, worried about mistakes, afraid to make a move, wanting the games to be over sometimes even before they began. Then Lemon came. All I had to do was play baseball as best I could. All of a sudden I could walk into that room and think only of the game."

There were a couple of hard-core supporters of Martin. Graig Nettles, a brilliant third baseman, a witty man ("Some kids want to grow up and be in the circus. Some kids want to play for the Yankees. I've done both," he said of his team), but an agitator, had played for Billy in 1968 at Denver as a Minnesota farmhand. He supported Billy strongly and defended him against the press, which found Martin difficult to deal with. Sparky Lyle liked Billy. Munson liked Billy. The others were neutral or in opposition.

"I played for Billy in Texas and in New York," says first baseman Jim Spencer. "In Texas all he seemed to talk about were the glory days with the Yankees as a player.

'I'll be managing them someday,' he would say. A strange thing for the manager of the Texas Rangers to say. Then he came here, and all he was worried about was losing his job. He was hard to play for because he caused so much commotion on a team. Sometimes you almost lost track of the real job of hitting and catching the ball because of the turmoil."

The Yankees quickly rallied both in terms of morale and on-the-field play.

They were hitting and catching the ball. Boston started losing. Jim Rice slowed down. Fred Lynn was injured. Carl Yastrzemski was showing his advancing age. Catcher Carlton Fisk, the lifeblood of the team, couldn't throw. Pitcher Bill Lee, the freest spirit among baseball men, described his chubby, bald, tobacco-chewing manager, Don Zimmer, as a "gerbil" and was banished to the bullpen. The ten-game lead was reduced to eight, then six, then four. The Yankees were coming to town for a September series, four games at Fenway. A split would probably give the Red Sox the pennant; even one victory would keep Boston two games ahead with three weeks to go.

New York hadn't swept a four-game series at Fenway in thirty years. They swept this one in an astonishing weekend of play. Ken Clay beat Mike Torrez, the ex-Yankee, 15–3. Jim Beattie, who had failed miserably in June, came back on September 8 to win, 13–2. This time he showed no signs of fright. Ron Guidry, who had missed pitching there in June and was now having as marvelous a pitching season as anyone had ever recorded in baseball, beat Dennis Eckersley, 7–0. Then Ed Figueroa beat Bob Sprowl, 7–4, and the Yankees had tied the Red Sox after 142 games. There were supposed to be 20 games to go, but it turned out to be 21.

*   *   *

On October 2, 1978, handsome Boston right-hander Mike Torrez suffered a cruel blow. Torrez was pitching brilliantly that sunny afternoon against Ron Guidry. He led, 2–0, into the seventh. The hitter was Bucky Dent, the soft-voiced Yankee shortstop. Two men were on base. George Steinbrenner sat quietly in a front-row box seat. Al Rosen sat next to him. Bob Lemon sat serenely, his hands folded, at the end of the Yankee dugout. Billy Martin, away from it all, wearing a red hunting jacket and hip boots, a 30.07 hunting rifle in hand, sat down next to a tree deep in the woods outside Boulder, Colorado. Dent swung and fouled a pitch off his leg. Trainer Gene Monahan administered some pain-killing spray. Mickey Rivers offered Dent his own bat in exchange for the bad-luck bat Dent had just hurt himself with. Torrez stood on the mound waiting. "I lost my concentration," he would say later. "I lost my good groove."

Torrez now held the baseball against his belt buckle. He sucked in a breath of clean October air. He moved his arms upward and threw the baseball, a slider that was to cut sharply across the letters on Dent's uniform. Steinbrenner wet his lips with his tongue. Rosen had a flash of his own youth, the chilling joy of hitting a baseball hard. Lemon rubbed his huge hands across his mouth.

In a crash Dent's fly ball raced for that maddening screen. In less than two seconds the ball had landed softly on the lower left-handed corner of the screen, Yankee players were leaping from their dugout seats, two runners were scoring, and Dent was coming around to home. A small grin escaped from the corner of his mouth, his eyes searching out the stands for his wife, Stormy. Oppressive silence filled the ball park at Jersey Street in the Fenway Back Bay section of Boston. "BuckyFuckingDent" became the name of a hated enemy of Boston. "BuckyFuckingDent," repeated many citizens in many Boston bars that night.

* * *

Billy Martin moved forward in the woods, unaware of the actions of the team he had left behind. He could think ahead now only to 1980, when George Steinbrenner had promised him he would manage the Yankees again. After his resignation Steinbrenner had been pressured by heavy mail and traumatic guilt to rehire Martin. Nothing had been signed despite the emotional outpouring of affection for Martin in the shocking rehiring on Old Timers' Day. Nobody believed it. Some thought it was Steinbrenner's final kindness to a dying man.

* * *

The game still had to be won because Boston would not quit. Honor was still important. Thurman Munson drove in another run in the seventh inning after a walk with a long double. Reggie Jackson drove in the fifth Yankee run with a huge homer. Boston rallied for two runs in the eighth. The score was 5–4 in the ninth, with runners on first and second, Jim Rice at bat, and Goose Gossage pitching. Gossage threw as hard as he could, and Rice flied deep to right. Two out. Yastrzemski, the captain of the Red Sox, was at the plate. "All I wanted to do," he said later, "was hit the ball hard someplace." He hit it softly, straight up into the air, twisting just in front of the third base coaching box, coming down now to third baseman Graig Nettles. Nettles squeezed the ball, leaped into the air, and moved toward Gossage. The race was over.

Reporters were around Dent, the homer hero, surging on Lemon, the incredible manager, and moving on Gossage for an emotional description of the final out. Off to one side, Reggie Jackson surveyed the scene. He seemed calm as his teammates howled.

"We never would have won it with Billy," he said quietly. "Too much furor. We were too far behind to deal with furor."

Dent had hit the surprising homer. Guidry had pitched brilliantly again. Gossage had survived incredible pressure. Munson had knocked in an important run. The final score was 5–4. Jackson had accounted for the lead run, the run that won the division title in the second play-off in

American League history. (Cleveland, with Bob Lemon and a rookie named Al Rosen sitting on the bench, had beaten Boston in 1948.) Lemon was being doused in champagne, and Rosen and Steinbrenner were offering congratulations. Jackson suddenly presented a reality.

"We ain't done nothing yet," he said. "This is only the start. We gotta beat Kansas City. We gotta get to the Series and beat the National League. If you ain't done that, you ain't done nothin' at all. I wanna get it all, every bit of it, I wanna fill these fingers with World Series rings, man, I want every bit of it, the whole loaf, not just a taste. Reggie Jackson does not settle for a taste. A taste is for losers. Second best is for losers. Reggie Jackson is a winner."

* * *

The American League championship series against Kansas City seems a blur. The emotions of the Boston play-off win still rang from every steeple. For the third time in three years the Yankees beat Kansas City out of the pennant. This time it was easy. Jim Beattie, living his fantasy now, won the first game, 7–1, Larry Gura halted the Yankees for a day with a 10–4 Kansas City win, Thurman Munson hit the longest homer of his life for a 6–5 third-game win, and Ron Guidry won, 2–1, in the fourth game. The Yankees, who had not won a pennant until Babe Ruth joined them, had won thirty-two pennants in fifty-seven years. The Yankees would meet the Dodgers again in the World Series.

Los Angeles, riding high on the emotional fallout after the death of coach Jim Gilliam, was a winner in the opening game. The Dodgers also won the second game, but not before one of the most thrilling baseball confrontations brought about an end to the game.

There is an emotional hold power hitters have on baseball fans: Ruth, Gehrig, Mantle, DiMaggio—the power of the Yankees, now represented by Reggie Jackson. And there is also the appeal of the power pitchers: Sandy Koufax, Don Drysdale, Don Newcombe. The name this time was Bob Welch, a twenty-one-year-old right-hander, later to announce he was an alcoholic. Two out, two on, 3–2 count on Reggie Jackson, power hitter, power pitcher, high fastballs, all crashing in on Jackson from sixty feet six inches away. The crowds screamed, the players stared, the peanut vendors stopped, and 50,000 people breathed silently. The pitcher lunged forward; Jackson swung violently; three times, four times, five times, the baseball trickled off to the side or back into the stands or down a line or against a seat. Another high, explosive fastball, turning over and over, rising with a hop at the last instant as it came forward. Jackson started his swing, slightly upward; the ball moved at nearly 100 miles an hour; the bat moved after it at about the same speed; the crowd paused to study the result. Finally, the roar, huge, loud, complete outpourings of sounds, as mighty Reggie Jackson has struck out. There was much joy in Los Angeles.

Jackson stood at the plate unconvinced. He moved slowly toward the dugout, his helmet flying against the back wall, his bat stabbing the dirt, all eyes in Dodger Stadium watching his performance. Bob Lemon moved up to the top step of the dugout, and Jackson shoved him back down. He wanted no consolation. He had failed. He had been challenged, and he had been beaten. It was October, it was his time of the year, and this kid pitcher had flamed a baseball past his swing.

In the clubhouse Lemon was gentle. "No fuss, Reggie didn't swing at me, we collided as we were walking down the stairs, no problems."

Reggie had recovered. The fires were burning out. "We'll meet again before this is over," he said.

Ron Guidry won the third game at Yankee Stadium. Graig Nettles was marvelous at third. The Dodgers fell apart. The Yankees won the Series with four straight victories, the last on October 17, 1978. Catfish Hunter pitched and won his last Series game. Reggie Jackson even singled off Bob Welch the next time they met.

* * *

Reggie Jackson spent a great deal of time in New York that winter. He worked for ABC, did several television shows, traveled to Hawaii to host ABC's *Superstars,* signed contracts to represent several more companies. He also spent time in Oakland, traveled often to Tempe, hatched a few more land projects with Gary Walker, enjoyed some loud social evenings at Studio 54 in New York or at Xenon or at other popular, public spots for Beautiful People. Few were as Beautiful as Jackson, serene now with the absence of Martin, piling one business success upon another, still at his peak as a player, looking forward to a chance to win again in 1979 and acquire his sixth World Series ring.

On October 27, 1978, Jerry Lemon, the twenty-six-year-old son of manager Bob Lemon, was killed in an automobile crash thirty miles outside Phoenix on Interstate 10. At the young man's funeral in Long Beach, California, where he had set out several days earlier by jeep to visit his older brother, a bouquet of flowers stood near the casket. It was addressed to Mr. and Mrs. Bob Lemon and signed with affection from "Number 44."

The death of Jerry Lemon profoundly changed Bob Lemon, the New York Yankees, and all who played for the team, including Reggie Jackson. It was the first tragedy in a fateful set of three that made 1979 one of the most agonizing years of Reggie Jackson's life.

14

The Longest Season

THE TRIPLE TRAGEDIES AFFECTING THE YANKEES IN the 1979 season made for a melancholy summer.

Manager Bob Lemon arrived at Fort Lauderdale for spring training with weakened spirit and heavy heart. His young son was gone now, and the triumphs in Boston and in Kansas City and Los Angeles bore no importance to the weary man, suddenly grown old, sitting aimlessly on the Yankee bench each day watching the team go through its drills. Lemon had always been a heavy, convivial drinker. He enjoyed the fraternalism of a drinking bout, telling tall tales, laughing at himself, spreading joy among his companions. This spring he was a serious drinker, unable to see much joy in the sport, closing the hotel bar each night, feeling numbed instead of lightened by the alcohol. "We tried everything," said his pal Al Rosen. "We went to dinner and tried to laugh. We talked of the club. We spent hours discussing personnel. We tried to interest him in the old gang. Nothing worked. The hurt was too deep."

The players sensed that Lemon had lost his heart for the job. Baseball players, being people, started cheating on him, first in little ways—skipping an exercise, skipping a few laps, missing a cutoff man in a squad game without undue concern. George Steinbrenner was nervous about the team's spring performance. He warned Al Rosen that Lemon had to shake his lethargy or the club would get away from him. Rosen, calm, poised, intelligent, soothed Steinbrenner's emotions and suggested the season still had not started. "You watch," Steinbrenner shouted at him one day, "when the season starts, we won't be ready."

There was an air of arrogance that hung over the Yankees. They had beaten Boston in one of the most dramatic baseball games ever played. They had waltzed through Kansas City and Los Angeles to another World Series triumph. There was no need to grow agitated about a bad spring. They were the best. They knew it. They could turn it on anytime they wanted. They had so many experienced players in Graig Nettles, Thurman Munson, Lou Piniella, Willie Randolph, Bucky Dent, and Ron Guidry that they knew they would win when they had to. Confidence, arrogance, poise under pressure, respect for their status—the Yankees had them in abundance. The Yankees knew the rest of the league was frightened of their pinstripes. In a tough pennant race, tradition was as much a factor in their winning as their bats, balls, and gloves. Reggie Jackson understood the importance of that respect. "If they respect you," he says, "it makes it tougher for them to beat you."

Jackson always carried that credo of respect with him. The word "respect" came up over and over, when he played, when he negotiated contracts, when he made appearances, when he was setting a tone for a relationship. On the night before he was to sign his first Yankee contract, they almost lost him because he thought they failed to show him respect.

Jackson had quietly slipped into town with his blonde

girlfriend. The limousine ordered by the Yankees was waiting at the airport. The driver was instructed to take Jackson and his friend to the Americana Hotel. A suite would be waiting there for him, the same suite reserved only weeks earlier for the newly elected President of the United States, Jimmy Carter. Jackson arrived at the hotel, the bellboys took his bags, the preregistration form needed only to be signed, and Jackson was on his way up to the suite. The doors to the huge rooms were opened, Jackson and his friend entered, the bellboy put down the bags—and Jackson exploded.

"What is this shit?" he screamed.

The bedroom of the suite had two twin beds. Jackson was enraged. What kind of hotel was this anyway? He demanded a change to a suite with king-sized double beds. No such thing existed in the Americana. He demanded to see the hotel manager. He was not available at this late hour. He called George Steinbrenner. He complained bitterly about his accommodations. Steinbrenner got on the phone to his public relations director, Marty Appel, who had made the arrangements.

"You're fired," screamed Steinbrenner.

"What is it?" asked a sleepy Appel at 2:00 A.M.

"Reggie doesn't like his room. No double beds," Steinbrenner said. "I thought you said everything has been taken care of."

Before Appel could explain that he assumed what was good enough for Jimmy Carter would be good enough for Reggie Jackson, Steinbrenner hung up. Appel checked with the Americana. He found out the hotel had no king-sized beds. He called the Plaza and was informed it had king-sized beds. Jackson and his friend could be quickly transported over there. The move was made, and Jackson was finally comfortable. He signed the next day with the Yankees. He had earned respect by standing firm on his demands. It was his way of doing things.

The Yankees started out slowly in 1979. The respect was still there. They had won in 1978. The same players were back. A few early losses were no reason to panic. Then came the second blow to the Yankee season of '79.

The Yankees had lost a game on Thursday afternoon, April 19, to the Baltimore Orioles. They were 3-6 in the early season, listless, playing uninspired baseball, still enjoying the afterglow of the wonders of 1978. Rich Gossage, the huge, hard-throwing relief pitcher, sat across the clubhouse from Cliff Johnson, a hulking, jocular utility catcher. Johnson had not played that day, and it galled him that manager Lemon had skipped over him. He was in no mood for teasing.

Reggie Jackson was undressing a few feet away from Johnson. Jackson has always enjoyed teasing teammates, engaging them in clubhouse dialogue. In contrast with the early sullen days of 1977, Jackson now found it easy to engage in conversation with his teammates. They still didn't particularly like him, but they understood him. They knew they needed his bat to win. They respected his play. So they tolerated his teasing. They felt that Reggie Jackson was like a *yenta,* a Jewish gossip or washerwoman, who had to be in every conversation within earshot. He enjoyed talking. He was a "people" person. It hardly mattered if a conversation was his business or not. Gossage and Johnson were talking about Goose's pitching speed. Jackson, looking for a rise out of the discouraged Johnson, asked, "How did you hit Goose when you were in the National League?"

"He couldn't hit what he couldn't see," said Gossage.

Johnson fired a rolled-up piece of tape at Gossage. Jackson laughed. A few more kidding words followed. Gossage went into the sauna to bake his big body. As he emerged, Johnson was coming from the shower. "Did you really mean that?" Johnson asked the pitcher. "Do you think I couldn't hit you?"

Gossage laughed.

The large black utility catcher threw a punch at the huge relief pitcher. Soon these two very big people were rolling on the floor, the noise awakening the quiet clubhouse, the turmoil taking everyone's mind off another defeat.

Goose Gossage suffered a torn right thumb. He would not pitch again until July. The Yankees would be lost without him. He was probably the one irreplaceable player on the team. Lemon tried Dick Tidrow, a solid, steady pitcher, in short relief. Tidrow could not make the adjustment. He was soon traded by Al Rosen because Steinbrenner wanted him out of his sight. It was a major loss for the Yankees. Tidrow was an important, well-liked member of the team and a very valuable pitcher who could start, pitch long relief, and pitch short relief if given time to make the adjustment. Ray Burris, a quiet pitcher with a history of arm trouble, was obtained in exchange. He proved to be a bust.

The Yankees staggered through May and into June. Reggie Jackson had a pulled hamstring muscle and hadn't played since June 2. It was now June 15. The Yankees were in Texas. They had just blown two games in Minnesota. They lost again that night in Texas. George Steinbrenner decided to make a move. He wanted Billy Martin back to manage his team. Lemon had provided calm in 1978 and won the pennant. Now George wanted fire. He knew of only one man who could provide him with it. Rumors quickly floated around the Yankees. Jackson heard them. He was shocked that Martin might actually be coming back. He didn't think the Yankees, after all that had transpired between him and Billy, were big enough for both of them. He picked up the phone and called Steinbrenner.

"Is it true you are planning to bring Billy back?" Reggie asked.

"It's none of your goddamn business," Steinbrenner said. "This is my club. You're only a goddamn player here. I'll do what I want."

"I won't play for him," Jackson said.

"You've got a contract," Steinbrenner shouted.

"George, don't do it. You'll be making a terrible mistake."

Steinbrenner hung up the phone. Jackson seethed. The special relationship between the owner and the right fielder was over. Steinbrenner couldn't live with Billy, and he couldn't live without him.

Early Monday morning, after the club returned from Texas, the announcement was made. Bob Lemon was out, and Billy Martin was in. Rosen had to tell Lemon, his best friend, he was fired. Al broke down and cried. "Sometimes," Rosen said later, "it is just better never to hire friends in baseball. Then you don't have to fire them."

A month later, harassed by Steinbrenner, ignored by Martin, ashamed of what he had to do to his old Cleveland pal Lemon, Al Rosen resigned as Yankee president. He soon moved into an executive position with Bally Manufacturing, makers of gambling equipment for casinos. He waited for a return to baseball.

"I had nothing to do with Al Rosen leaving," Martin insisted.

Rosen would say nothing publicly. Privately he assured friends the situation had become intolerable. He simply could not work with Martin. George had sided with Billy in every conflict since he had rehired him, and Rosen's authority was being destroyed. The Yankees were one big unhappy family.

The night Billy Martin returned, Jackson hid from the press, a rather untypical act for this open, honest, and garrulous man. He wanted to avoid confrontation. He chose to meet with Al Rosen in his upstairs office, slip back into the clubhouse as the game started, undergo some treatment on his leg, and slip back out before the press could corner him.

On June 29, his leg recovered, he returned to action under Billy Martin again. He struck out four times in his first game back. Two days later he hit his first home run in more than a month. Soon he was playing regularly and well under Martin. There was no conflict with him. Martin played him, and Jackson kept quiet about him.

"I was probably helped by Billy's return," he says. "I didn't want any more fuss. I wanted to do well. I concentrated harder, so there would be no excuses for not playing me. It helped make me a better hitter. I owe Billy that."

Martin was pleased with his play. He avoided any discussions about Jackson. As the Yankees slipped out of the pennant race, he seemed distracted by other things. He was working hard on his plans for a comeback in 1980.

As Reggie continued to have another fine season, there was only one more public outburst. On July 19 Rosen resigned. Reggie defended him. "Al was a good man who tried to be a good president of the club," he said. "He was. He just couldn't take being subservient to the man [Steinbrenner]. He had pride. He had done things in this game. What George has done to him is terrible. George just thinks he can buy everybody. Some guys have pride. You can't buy them."

"What will happen after George reads this?" a reporter asked Reggie.

"Nothing can happen to me because I can hit the ball over the wall," he said. "When I can't hit the ball over the wall, they'll get me, too. I know that. George will get me someday."

While the rest of the Yankees seemed to be sauntering through the summer in search of a paycheck, Jackson continued playing well. On August 1 his average was at .299, he had 19 homers, he had 58 RBIs, and he had scored 52 runs. The Yankees were in fourth place, fourteen games out, with the interest centering on which players would be back in 1980.

August 2 was an off day. The Yankees had flown home from Chicago the night before and scattered to their homes for a day of rest. The Yankees had seen the captain of the team, Thurman Munson, moving to a different area of Chicago's O'Hare Airport that night in order to fly his

Cessna Citation twin-engine jet home to Canton. He arrived home at 3:00 A.M.

Munson had been having trouble with his knees. He was thirty-two years old, and the grind of catching every day was wearing his body out. Martin had been using him at first base and as the designated hitter to rest his knees. On that Wednesday game he had started at first, twisted a knee, and was removed from the game in pain. His baseball future was clouded.

Few baseball observers had ever seen a player relationship as fraught with tension as the one between Jackson and Munson. The 1977 magazine article—"I'm the straw that stirs the drink"—had left a deep wound in Munson's psyche. By late 1978 and early in 1979 the relationship between Jackson and Munson changed slightly. Each respected the other's ability. Jackson often said, "Thurman is the best hitter on this team." Thurman often said, "We can't win unless Reggie knocks in the runs." They spoke casually in the clubhouse about baseball. They talked some about business. They lounged together before games in the trainer's room. They rarely socialized after games, though Jackson would sometimes join a group of Yankees, including Munson, for a postgame drink on the road in the team's hotel.

Munson seemed concerned with accumulating great wealth. He fought hard for increased salary from the Yankees. He invested heavily in real estate, shopping centers, and industrial properties around his hometown of Canton, Ohio.

"I once visited out there," says George Steinbrenner, "and I saw the wonderful investments Thurman had. I could see how wisely he used his money. I could appreciate his financial interests."

The three wealthiest Yankees were George Steinbrenner, Reggie Jackson, and Thurman Munson. Steinbrenner and Jackson each lived high, enjoyed their wealth, spread a lot of it around with gifts and charity work. Munson accumulated his.

He purchased his $1.5 million jet to use for transportation home to see his wife and three children whenever he could. He also used it to get back to Canton to consummate the business deals he always seemed to have working. That was the twofold purpose of his flying trip home on August 2—family and business.

"The plane had been giving him some trouble," teammate Lou Piniella remembers. "He wanted to get home to have it checked out."

At 3:02 P.M., 1,000 feet shy of runway 19 of the Canton-Akron Airport, with Munson at the controls of the powerful jet and two friends along, David Hall, thirty-two, and Jerry Anderson, thirty-one, both licensed pilots, as instructors while he practiced touch-and-go landings, the plane crashed. It was soon engulfed in flames. Anderson and Hall escaped the fiery plane. Munson, strapped into his seat, could not get out. He had broken his neck in the crash. An autopsy later revealed that he had died of smoke inhalation. Federal Aviation Administration investigators later listed "pilot error" as the contributory cause of the crash.

The phone soon rang in George Steinbrenner's Yankee offices. An official of the FAA called Steinbrenner and said, "Your player Thurman Munson, he's been killed."

Steinbrenner gasped. "Are you sure?" He was told two friends were with Munson. They had survived, and they had identified him. Steinbrenner immediately called his public relations assistant, Mickey Morabito, into his office and told him the news. Then they set out calling the players. "I'll call Reggie," George said. "You call Billy."

Jackson was not at his Fifth Avenue apartment. He had gone to visit friends in Connecticut for the day. He would hear the news on the radio, stiffen, and weep. Billy Martin was called off a fishing boat, where he had gone with his fifteen-year-old son, Billy Joe. He was told the news and broke down.

Bobby Murcer, who had only recently rejoined the Yankees for a second time, and his wife flew to Canton to be with Diane Munson and the children. Condolence calls, letters, telegrams, and flowers poured into the Munson home. Players expressed their sadness in their own way. Lou Piniella talked of a fishing trip planned with Thurman. Graig Nettles said, "I expected to be a friend of his all my life." Murcer, a small man as players go, seemed decreased in size by the loss. Reggie Jackson would not say much. It would be a sham to say how close he was to the man. He talked of Munson, the player, how much he admired him, how much he was impressed by him, how much he respected him. After all the turmoil, all the pettiness, all the vindictiveness on the part of both these men, it had come down to respect. Each finally learned to respect the skills of the other. They were not friends; they could never have been friends; they could only have learned to appreciate the accomplishments each had achieved in the game, the different routes they had taken to get there, the talents they brought to the field each day.

Now it was too late.

On Monday, August 6, the Yankees flew by chartered plane to the Canton-Akron Airport, where Thurman Munson had been killed, to attend his funeral. Most of them had gotten up at 5:00 A.M. to make the early flight. The funeral services took place at the Canton Memorial Civic Center. More than 500 people were invited inside. More than 1,000 listened outside. The casket was covered with an American flag. A huge portrait of a smiling Munson in his Yankee uniform hung on the wall. There were several dozen floral displays, one in the shape of a baseball, another in the Yankee insignia, another with his huge number 15 on it. The Reverend J. Robert Coleman, pastor of St. Paul's Roman Catholic Church in Canton, who had married Thurman and Diane eleven years earlier, delivered the eulogy. "He was hard to know," said the Reverend Coleman, "but once you did, he was a great friend." Reggie Jackson listened intently. Billy Martin sat in the front row with tears running down his cheeks. Bobby Murcer, a close friend, spoke. "He lived, he led, he loved.

Whatever he was to each of us—catcher, captain, competitor, husband, father, friend—he should be remembered as a man who valued and followed the basic principles of life."

Sudden youthful death makes all men martyrs. No one would remind a funeral audience that Lou Gehrig had been stingy, that John F. Kennedy was an adulterer, that Robert F. Kennedy was ruthless in his political conduct, that Thurman Lee Munson, to many men, was unlovable, a complainer, a man who could be loving to friends and family, nasty to press and public. Thurman Munson's death did not change his life.

The Yankees flew back to New York after the funeral. They gathered again for a day of work at Yankee Stadium. They trailed the Orioles, 4–0, into the seventh. Bobby Murcer hit his first Yankee Stadium homer since September 28, 1973, with two men on to cut the lead to 4–3. In the ninth inning Murcer singled two runners home as the Yankees won a dramatic game, 5–4.

The long day ended with the Yankees slowly leaving the clubhouse at the stadium. It was quiet now, except for the soft sound of Pete Sheehy, the aging clubhouse man (he had been with the Yankees since 1926) sweeping up the last piles of dust. He soon left the clubhouse for the night, and before he did, he turned to gaze once more at the empty locker on the far left side of the large room. A pinstriped shirt hung over a hanger, the "NY" facing out; a pair of pinstriped pants hung loosely on a hook, a Yankee cap on the top shelf, a catcher's mask on another hook. Atop the locker was a metal plate bearing simply the number 15. It would always be the locker of the captain.

*   *   *

Reggie Jackson continued to excel in a losing cause as the 1979 season wound down. The death of Bob Lemon's son, the eventual firing of Lemon, the return of Billy Martin, the early loss of Goose Gossage, the shocking death of

Thurman Munson—all had tended to diminish his season. There was little attention paid to on-field performance. But Jackson had batted .297 for his career high, just missing a .300 season by a couple of hits in a long summer. He had smashed 29 home runs and knocked in 89 runs. In the confusion of 1979 Jackson had one of his finest seasons ever.

When the season ended on September 30, there could be no baseball for Mr. October in his favorite month this year. Jackson cleaned some things up in his New York apartment, flew to California, picked up his girlfriend, and flew to Hawaii for a vacation. He felt satisfied by his season's work. He had played hard for Billy Martin, the manager seemed to appreciate it, and Reggie viewed the 1980 season with calm. Much of the anger between the two seemed to have disappeared. Reggie could not ever feel warm toward Martin, just respectful. The man knew how to manage, knew how to motivate, knew how to win. Now Reggie's anger seemed aimed at Steinbrenner for not considering him more important in the Yankee scheme of things.

As he sunned himself in Hawaii and waited to fly back to California to film a couple of television programs, Jackson felt content. He would be thirty-four in 1980. It was time he concentrated on adding to his impressive statistics in a Hall of Fame bid, time to help the Yankees win again, so he could put on another display, time to drive hard for a new 1982 contract. When there were no television commitments, no endorsements, no sponsors to deal with, no commercials to film, Jackson worked out hard in the gymnasium he had built in his Oakland home. He knew he had to be physically in shape if he was to continue in the style he had grown accustomed to.

But first he would get a huge surprise.

The Yankees had finished fourth in the 1979 American League East pennant race some thirteen and a half games behind Baltimore. They had been eight and a half games back when Billy Martin had taken over the team on June

19. Martin's presence had added nothing to their season. The loss of Gossage, the negative ebb and flow of the early days, the loss of Tidrow, the decreased efficiency of Mickey Rivers, Catfish Hunter, and Thurman Munson, and, finally, the last crushing blow, the August 2 death of the captain, had ruined the summer. Except for an occasional showpiece outburst, Martin had seemed under control. He seemed less nervous than he had been the year before, less testy with the press, more ebullient as he talked of the Yankee future in 1980, less inclined to make every issue into a major episode. The impossible seemed to have happened: George Steinbrenner, Billy Martin, and Reggie Jackson were working in harmony for the betterment of the Yankees.

Of course, this was no easy trick for any of the three. For Steinbrenner, his energies turned toward improving the Yankees in 1980, studying and possibly signing free agent players, promotion of his longtime disciple Gene Michael, the former Yankee shortstop and Columbus manager, to the post of Yankee general manager. Even in the dying days of the 1979 season these interests kept Steinbrenner out front, where he yearned to be.

Jackson had always been out front. As he played hard for Martin, Jackson remained the most important player on the team. "He was that way, out front, as far back as junior high school and high school," says Bill Goff, a New York art gallery owner who was graduated from Cheltenham High in Jackson's 1964 class. "We once had a car-lifting contest as kids, three of us trying to lift a car. We couldn't do it. Reggie lifted the car by himself and enjoyed the glory. In football he was a natural. I once saw him pick up a golf club for the first time in his life and drive a ball two hundred fifty yards straight down the fairway. He loved the fuss made over him. One time we were at a party. Reggie was bored. Some kid came over to him, recognized this, and said, 'Goff wants to fight you.' Reggie thought it would turn the attention of the party to him. He came over. I said I never was interested in fighting him. I wasn't crazy."

So much of what Reggie did separated him from the crowd, made him stand out, made him unique. In school he was a black kid who went out with a pretty white girl named Sandra Hench. That made him special. He was a black who lived in Wyncote, a white neighborhood, instead of Lamotte, the neighboring black community. That made him special.

"Reggie always had to be the center of attention," says Goff. "One time a kid named Michael Simon, a football player, got a new pair of cleats, size sixteen, and everybody else on the team studied those huge shoes. You can't imagine what a fuss people made over the size of those shoes. Suddenly Reggie grabbed one of the shoes, ran down the locker room, and filled it with water. I think he hated that shoe because it took attention from him."

This drive for attention seemed diminished in the last days of 1979. The season had been a downer, and Jackson, like all of the players, was glad it was ending. He simply wanted to get out of New York.

Billy Martin felt the same way. He stayed around his New Jersey apartment as the Orioles and Pirates played the World Series, enjoyed some quiet golf days with his pal Phil Rizzuto, put in a couple of appearances at his western wear store on New York's Madison Avenue, and finally flew to Minneapolis. There he met his pal Howard Wong, owner of a local Chinese restaurant. They drove together to South Dakota for some pheasant hunting. Martin then returned to Minneapolis with Wong to fly to Dallas for a visit with Mickey Mantle. Martin's marriage was over, so he needed something to occupy his time until spring training.

After returning by pickup truck to the Minneapolis area, Martin decided he would spend the night at the Hotel de France before flying out the next morning to Dallas and his visit with Mickey. It was Tuesday, October 23.

A large, husky marshmallow salesman from Lincolnshire, Illinois, named Joseph W. Cooper came up to Martin while he was sitting with Wong in the hotel bar. They began talking baseball. Cooper suddenly offered the opinion that Dick Williams, the manager at Montreal, and Earl Weaver, Billy's bitter Baltimore rival, were marvelous managers, better than Billy.

"They're both assholes," said Martin, "and so are you for saying it."

Soon the marshmallow man and the mighty manager were baiting each other, moving closer and closer to confrontation. When Cooper suggested that Billy wasn't so tough and that he, Cooper, could lay him out in a minute, Martin pulled $300 from his pocket. "Put a penny there, and we'll bet that you can't whip me," Martin said.

Cooper pulled the penny from his pocket. Billy moved outside. Cooper followed. They walked through an archway to the lobby. Martin quickly turned and knocked Cooper down with a right hand to the jaw.

"I heard this thud," said bellboy Steve Holland. "I was in the lobby. I heard this guy hit the ground real hard."

Cooper was taken to Fairview Southdale Hospital, where he had his lip stitched with fourteen sutures. Martin went up to his hotel room. Another man in the bar called the St. Paul *Dispatch*. "There's been a fight," a breathless voice said to reporter Doug Hennes. "Billy Martin coldcocked a guy. The cops are there. The Hotel de France." Then he hung up.

Soon the news was in the local paper, on the wires, and being expanded into a front-page story in the *New York Post*. Martin called Yankee publicity director Mickey Morabito, was told the *Post* was playing the incident up. Martin dictated a statement. He tried to lie his way out of the jam by saying the salesman fell down.

"I immediately made a few calls on my own," Steinbrenner said. "I learned what happened. When I found out Billy hit the guy, I knew he was gone. The guy could have gotten killed when he fell. Wouldn't that be something? The manager of the Yankees would be on trial for murder."

While Martin awaited his fate, he called the soon-to-be general manager Gene Michael.

"How's George taking it?" he asked.

"He's pissed," Michael said.

"Will he get over it?"

"I don't think so," Michael said.

On Sunday night, October 28, 1979, Mickey Morabito read George Steinbrenner's statement to the press: "Billy Martin has been relieved of his duties as manager of the New York Yankees and Dick Howser has been named to succeed him effective immediately."

The news came to Reggie Jackson in a Los Angeles hotel room, where he had gone from his Oakland home on a television assignment. He was asked his opinion of Martin's firing. "Too bad," he said, "I was getting along fine with Billy at the end. I can't say I'm real surprised. Billy seemed in better control of himself. Maybe not."

Publicly Jackson reacted with calm. He made sure to say the right things, the dignified statement, avoiding any inflammatory comment. Privately he told friends this was one of the best things ever to happen to him. He knew Howser well. He had been a Yankee coach and a tough player. They respected each other. Howser had a high degree of tolerance. He had a small ego. There would be no personality conflict here.

* * *

The Yankees traded for a catcher to replace Thurman Munson: Rick Cerone, a tough, young, aggressive receiver out of Seton Hall College in New Jersey. They obtained a fleet center fielder from Seattle named Ruppert Jones to replace the departed Mickey Rivers. They signed free agents Bob Watson, a large right-handed hitting first baseman, and Rudy May, a dashing left-handed pitcher from Montreal.

Manager Dick Howser and general manager Gene Michael were rebuilding the 1980 Yankees out of the ruins of 1979. Under George Steinbrenner's aggressive hand and because of his open wallet, they reconstructed the team with the best players available to them. Steinbrenner signed shortstop Bucky Dent and first baseman Jim Spencer, neither of whom would have returned if Martin had remained. He also signed third baseman Graig Nettles to a new long-term contract. The core of a marvelous pitching staff, built around starters Tommy John and Ron Guidry and relief pitcher Goose Gossage, remained. The Yankees were certain to be a serious contender in 1980 if they could keep away from injuries. There was one other thing. They needed production out of the big guy in right field, the man they all depended on, the man called Mr. October for his postseason exploits in the toughest days of a long baseball season.

"I won't have any problems with Reggie," said Dick Howser. "I'll just put him out there and let him play."

Jackson glowed when he heard that.

"Reggie knows the young players on this team will be looking to him for leadership," said George Steinbrenner.

That brought a grin to Reggie's face. They had finally come to recognize his qualities. He would now be the legitimate leader of this team. Indeed, he would be the main man, this generation's Babe Ruth, Lou Gehrig, Joe DiMaggio, Mickey Mantle.

As Reggie Jackson walked out of his Fifth Avenue apartment and stood on the patio overlooking a barren Central Park one bitter cold winter day in February 1980, just before spring training, he knew he was at peace with his world. He knew he had persevered over everything. He knew, finally, that 1980 was destined to be one sweet summer.

A Touch of Class

LATE ON A SUMMER AFTERNOON IN 1980, AN HOUR OR so before the Yankees were to take batting practice, a well-dressed young man, in his middle thirties, walked toward the Yankee clubhouse. He pulled out his business card, scribbled a few words on the back of it, and handed it to the usher.

"Tell Reggie Jackson I'd like to see him," the man said. "I'm an old friend."

The guard walked inside, turned the card over, read the handwritten words "Cheltenham High, 1964," and went to Jackson. He was sitting alone at his locker, reading an automotive magazine. He was in his shorts, and half a dozen dark bats leaned against the front of his locker.

"There's a guy out there, says he knows you, wants you to come out," the usher said. He handed Reggie the card. Jackson turned it over, read the name, and then read the scribbled identification of his high school on the back side.

"Tell him I knew him then," he said with a smile, "but I don't know him now."

Then he went back to his magazine, and the guard went back to his post to get rid of the 1964 classmate of Jackson's.

By 1980 Reggie Jackson had learned to dispatch people without pain. He had learned how to slide gracefully from one controversy to another without anger. He had learned to live with the torturous pressure of the fans, as they had learned to love him. It was finally a season without boos, a season without much furor about him. It was also a season of much satisfaction, high numbers on the field, a .300 batting average at last, 41 home runs for a career total of 410 (changed daily on a huge Panasonic advertisement high above the New Jersey side of the Lincoln Tunnel), and 111 RBIs. Finally, it was a season with another division title.

"I think he finally became comfortable here," says Lou Piniella, the handsome, bright Yankee outfielder. "When Reggie came here, he expected to take this team and this town by storm. It didn't work that way. For three years he fought it. This year he accepted it. He learned that other players have egos and pride. He learned to be one of the guys."

Piniella is one of the most decent of men, and his antagonism was no different from that of all other Yankees in the tumultuous summer of 1977. It eased in time as the two players grew accustomed to each other. One of their bonds, at first obscured by the controversies, was their command of Spanish. Piniella is of Spanish parentage.

"Reggie's comfortable in Spanish. If he was walking down a street in San Juan, he wouldn't go hungry," Piniella said.

"I still don't think this city really understands me," Reggie says. "I think they want too much of me. Sometimes I am amazed at the magnitude of me. There is so much demanded of me, so much of my life pulled away from me by the people. It is not easy being me."

Reggie Jackson enjoys talking about Reggie Jackson as "Reggie Jackson." It is as if he, too, were in awe of his own incredible presence.

"You know," he said one day before the Muhammad Ali fight in Las Vegas against Larry Holmes, "they spend a lot of time interviewing Ali now. Next week it's forgotten. But Reggie Jackson gets interviewed every day everywhere, at all hours. Nobody gives more interviews than Reggie Jackson."

It may well be true because he has the patience for long interviews, enjoys bantering with sportswriters, commands attention anywhere he goes, and always seems to be opinionated on all aspects of baseball, on and off the field.

In 1977 his endless interviews angered most of his teammates. In 1980 his interviews were accepted by his teammates, many of whom were not around in 1977.

"I haven't changed," Reggie says, "but they have."

"He's mellower," says shortstop Fred Stanley. "Thurman is gone. Billy isn't around. George stays away most of the time. There is nobody sticking pins in his hide."

One of the changes in the Yankee clubhouse in 1979 and 1980 was the presence of the wise old pitcher Luis Tiant.

"I tell you about Reggie," says the Cuban-born Tiant as he sits at his Yankee Stadium locker only dressed in his cigar. "He comes to the park to do business. He's a good kid. I like him. Sure, he's a lotta bullshit, but we all lotta bullshit sometime. They say he is a troublemaker on the club. I know a lot of troublemakers on a lotta clubs, and they can't play. He no perfect. Lotta people no perfect. People sometimes look at him funny. Maybe they should look at themselves."

The absence of Munson, the absence of Martin's abrasive tone, the absence of more than a little harassment from Steinbrenner made things easy in 1980 for Reggie. It really all began on October 28, 1979. Dick Howser was named the manager of the Yankees that day.

"He's my right fielder," Howser told a jammed press conference at the Tavern on the Green.

No designated hitter talk, no talk about his poor defense, no conversations whispered to sportswriters with a wink and a leer.

"Dick Howser respects me," says Jackson.

The test came early. Jackson was in New York in late February. He was posing for advertising pictures for one of his newest clients, Murjani jeans. There was a jeans speech for a couple of minutes, and then Reggie got down to business.

"I just bought this property in Carmel for a new house, five hundred thousand dollars, but I don't want the price in the papers because somebody might try to kidnap me, but I have to close on it Saturday."

Saturday happened to be the opening day of spring training for Yankee regulars.

"But Saturday is . . ." a reporter said.

"George knows I'll be late. He's helped me put the financing together. I told him I would be late. He wants me there on time for the new manager, but he understands."

For the next two days the sports pages of the New York papers were filled with speculation about Jackson's tardiness at the camp. He finally arrived to a fully orchestrated press conference, getting off a San Francisco-to-Fort Lauderdale plane in cowboy boots, cowboy hat, blue jeans, and a full beard. He arrived at the ball park at 7:30 A.M. He knew a beard was against Yankee regulations. He quickly shaved it. "I flushed it down the drain," he kidded. "It's on its way to the Atlantic Ocean. Now will they make me write a composition for being late?"

Jackson met with new general manager Gene Michael, new manager Dick Howser, and the steady vice-president Cedric Tallis. He was fined $2,000, made out a check to the Public Schools Athletic League of New York, and went to work.

"I want to have a good year," he said. "I want to run in the grass and sit in the sun."

The Yankees of 1980 had some new players and a serious no-nonsense attitude in spring training. They had been losers in 1979. Nobody worked harder than Reggie in March 1980 under the grueling Florida sun. There was one other major addition in the camp, a defensive outfield coach named Paul Blair, the former Oriole defensive whiz and a former Yankee teammate. He spent endless hours working with Reggie on his fielding.

"He's too tense in the outfield," said Blair. "He's got to learn to relax the way he does at bat. He also runs flat-footed; he jiggles; he isn't smooth. We have to get him smooth."

After each workout ended, Jackson stayed in right field, caught fly balls, watched Blair catch them, moved his feet, changed his running style, finally regained the confidence he once had as an Oakland outfielder before Billy Martin removed him often for a defensive replacement.

The season began in Texas and Chicago. Then the Yankees returned home to open against Milwaukee on April 18. It was the first anniversary of the infamous Goose Gossage-Cliff Johnson fight, a major factor in the lost season of '79. It all seemed remote. Gossage was pitching well again; Johnson was gone; Jackson was spirited as he got off well. There seemed to be another dramatic change in the Yankee season in the early days of 1980. It came about one April evening against Baltimore, the hated rival, the defending champions, managed by feisty Earl Weaver. Jackson struck out twice.

There was silence each time he struck out, resignation, some gasping sounds of disappointment, but not one discernible boo. First Jackson seemed not to notice, but after the second strikeout he jogged back toward the dugout and peeked at the stands. Some people were standing and applauding, thanking him for a thrilling swing, albeit a miss, applauding his efforts.

"I knew then," he says, "they had changed toward me."

The animosity, centered on Munson, Martin, and Steinbrenner, had disappeared. The fans no longer were forced to choose among Munson, Martin, George, and Reggie. Billy was in Oakland. George was quietly observing most of it in Tampa. An opening-day appearance by Mrs. Thurman Munson left few dry eyes, but the captain was gone. The fans seemed to sense that Reggie needed their support. He was the big guy, uncontested, the player they had to encourage if they cared about another pennant in Yankee Stadium.

Soon this acceptance of Jackson, this understanding of his dynamics, this realization that he owed the fans nothing but baseball excellence eased the pressures. Jackson enjoyed the fans, tipped his cap often, threw foul balls into the stands, waved at the greetings he got from the right-field seat holders after long home runs.

"I think I finally won them over," he said one night after one of his long home runs won a game. "I think they love me. I really think they do."

Jackson was hitting well, fielding with a degree of confidence he had not recently exhibited, sliding as hard as ever—the hardest in the league according to Boston shortstop Rick Burleson—and driving on 400 career home runs.

There was only one thing that seemed upsetting to him as the Yankees moved into the second month of the season. He had been hit by pitches seven times and knocked down maybe seventy times.

"I believe I get knocked down more than any other hitter in the league," Reggie said. "I'm sure I've got a lot of guys who do hate me. I hear from other players. It's bitterness and jealousy. I have friends, players who tell me." Then Reggie paused and thought carefully before he continued. "I'm a target, sure. It seems they knock down black players more than they do white players. It's hard for me to make that statement. I won't get any sympathy for saying that."

Luis Tiant was asked if he agreed with Reggie's assessment. "Sure he gets knocked down. When I pitch against him, I knock him on his ass. Sometimes he take me downtown. I have to show him I don't like it. Is it because he is a black player? It is because he is a big player."

In spite of these dustings and bearings, Jackson showed his tough and aggressive side at the plate. But he can be soft, quiet, shy, and extremely sensitive. In June he revealed the other side of his crazy quilt personality.

An eight-year-old boy named Christopher Paust, a cute blond youngster from Yonkers, was in the Sloan-Kettering cancer center in New York, suffering from a terminal bone cancer. Christopher was a baseball fan, a Yankee fan, a Reggie Jackson fan. He told his parents that he wished he could see Reggie. "I think he'd could help me get well," the lad said.

The parents called the local newspaper. Its sports reporter was asked if it was at all possible that Reggie might break away for a short while to visit with the boy. "All I can do is ask," the reporter said.

He asked, and Reggie answered, "What time does he want me?"

Reggie Jackson walked into Sloan-Kettering the next afternoon. He carried a couple of autographed baseballs, a picture button of himself, an autographed bat, and a half dozen photographs. He sat with the boy for nearly thirty minutes. He talked to the parents and kidded with the nurses. He told the boy as he was leaving, "My next home run will be for you, Christopher."

The following night, on June 19, Jackson hit a home run against the California Angels. The story had appeared in the local papers, and the fans recognized that Reggie was giving that one to Christopher as he held up one finger.

One week later, on June 26, 1980, Christopher Paust, aged eight, died in his mother's arms.

"I'm shocked and saddened about Christopher's death," said Jackson. "But I'm happy I could have brought some joy into Christopher's life."

As always, there were some players, some members of

the press, some baseball officials who saw Jackson's relationship with the youngster as nothing more than an artifi-
cial attempt at "winning one for the Gipper" or re-creat-
ing the old legend about the Babe's hitting one for a dying
kid.

There were people who seemed to react negatively to
anything Reggie did, anything anyone else did to him,
regardless of the merits of the case. The attitude of many
people toward Reggie was put to the test in two separate
incidents that season.

The Yankees had played a Friday night game against
the Toronto Blue Jays, and Jackson's homer had won the
contest for the Yankees. After the game Jackson, as was his
habit, drove up to Oren & Aretsky's Restaurant at Third
Avenue and Eighty-fourth Street. He was often alone
there late at night, after a game, eating his favorite salmon
dish. "There aren't too many places you can eat a good
meal at two in the morning," he says. Unless Fran Healy,
a teammate, a business associate, or a friend joins him, he
eats alone. His housekeeper at his Fifth Avenue apartment works days and leaves at sundown after the apartment is cleaned and the breakfast dishes are put away.

Jackson drove his Rolls-Royce up Third Avenue, looking
for a parking place. He pulled behind a car which was
blocking the intersection. The car didn't move. Jackson
honked his horn. The car still didn't move. Suddenly a
passenger in the car, a man later identified by police as
Angel Viera, a twenty-five-year-old unemployed Manhat-
tanite, jumped out and began cursing Jackson. Reggie,
never one to duck a confrontation, jumped out of his car
and screamed back. Jackson got back in his car after the
verbal assault, the other car moved, and he drove a block
to a red light. Here the car pulled alongside his again,
Viera came alongside with two broken bottles in his hand
and threw them at Jackson. By now two passersby who
had seen the fuss recognized Reggie and joined in the
fray, finally chasing Viera down a street.

Viera disappeared into a darkened alley. Jackson, who

had been serving as the Yankees' designated hitter because of a calf muscle injury, couldn't run well and returned to his car. He was talking to his newly found friends when Viera returned, this time with a gun, and fired three shots from across the street. Jackson heard the bang of the shots and ran into Oren & Aretsky's. Police were called, and Viera was picked up and charged with attempted murder, reckless endangerment, and possession of a deadly weapon.

Dick Howser rested Reggie against the Blue Jays the following afternoon. When sportswriters gathered in front of his locker, Jackson attempted to minimize the situation.

"When I get involved," he said, "everything gets distorted."

Reggie later admitted he may have helped cause the incident by screaming back at Viera. "That's the way I am. I can't let anybody get away with calling me names and insulting my mother. I forgot this was New York. I forgot a lot of people walk around with guns."

Six weeks later, on the night he hit his four hundredth homer, he was involved in another life crisis. Somebody put a gun to his head.

Jackson had been dining quietly in Jim McMullen's at Seventy-seventh Street and Third Avenue with his agent, Matt Merola. They finished dinner at 2:00 A.M., and Jackson walked to his car, the ever-present Rolls. He stepped into his car. As he prepared to turn the key, a black teenager put a .45 caliber pistol to his head and ordered him out of the car. He told Jackson to turn over everything he had to him.

As Jackson turned toward him, the young man seemed, finally, to recognize the man he was mugging.

"A look of horror came over his face," Jackson remembers, "and he slowly dropped his hand. As he stood there, I just turned and ran away. When I did that, the kid ran into my car and attempted to start it. He was unable to do it, finally jumped out, and ran down the street."

Jackson still seemed uneasy when he described the incident to reporters at his locker the next evening.

"My life didn't flash in front of me, nothing like that, but I was damn scared. When I saw that gun at my head, I just cringed. I could almost feel the pain as if I had already been shot."

When a reporter suggested that maybe the June incident and this latest one were related, both being created by Baltimore manager Earl Weaver in an attempt to neutralize Jackson in the pennant race, Reggie bristled.

"You think this is a damn joke," he said with some anger. "I don't like guys standing over me with guns. If a guy wants to fight me, I'll fight him. But a gun? That's something else. I'm just tired of all this, tired of being made a target for all these nuts on the street."

The attempted robbery stole much of the attention from Jackson's performance that night. It was the kind of drama no star could handle with as much excitement as Reggie. Eighteen players have hit 400 career homers. Jackson had started the season 31 homers short of that mark. As he got closer to that figure, the tensions built. He became nervous. His chats with reporters were strained. His father, up from Philadelphia, waited each day in the stands for the historic event. "I hope he gets it soon," Martínez Jackson said after three games without a homer. "The clothes are piling up in the shop." Jackson was angered that the reports of each game suggested he had "failed" before he finally "succeeded" in hitting the home run. "See that rash around his mouth," his father said. "Now maybe it can go away as he relaxes a little."

Everything Jackson does on a baseball field is done under a magnifying glass. His home runs are bigger; his strikeouts are bigger; his reactions are bigger. The four hundredth homer, on August 11, 1980, was a long shot into the right-field seats. A ten-year-old girl from Congers, New York, by the name of Cheryl Hanchar, had outrun some bigger boys in retrieving the baseball. When the game was over, she was brought to the ramp outside the

Yankee clubhouse, given a Yankee cap and a different baseball, sat on Reggie's lap, and posed for pictures.

"I've always been a Reggie Jackson fan," the youngster said. "Isn't everybody?"

Jackson talked with some degree of strain as photographers fired pictures of him, their light bulbs making him squint. Television camera lights heated up the entire area, and more than forty reporters closed in tight on Reggie and the sweet-looking little girl on his lap.

"I'm glad it's over," he said. "Maybe now people will stop writing how I failed. It took me a week to get it. So what? It took me thirteen years to get the other three hundred ninety-nine."

He had his say, got his point across, and now seemed to again enjoy the attention, the genuine awe, and the publicity. He laughed when somebody asked if he could catch Hank Aaron, who had retired with 755 homers.

"Aaron is a career away," said Reggie. "Nobody will catch him."

Finally, the press had enough. The reporters allowed Reggie to return to the Yankee locker room, to take a long, quiet shower, to sit in front of his locker, to let the impact of his achievement settle in.

"I remember the first home run and the tenth and the one hundredth and all of them," he was saying now. "I always knew I could hit homers. I don't even think about that anymore. That's not important. Winning is where it's at. See these fingers. I want them covered with World Series rings."

Jackson had been on three Oakland world champions and two more in New York. He had given World Series rings to his father and to his mother, to a sister and to a brother. He had kept only one, the first one, the 1972 Oakland A's, and even though he had missed that Series with an injury, it was his fondest championship. That was the year the baseball world had noticed that Jackson was a winner.

"Individual achievements are important, sure, but you

have to win. You have to get into October still going for it," he was saying. "October. That's when they pay off for playing ball."

The rain was coming down hard outside the stadium now as Jackson finished dressing. He wore blue jeans, a thin polo shirt, and alligator shoes. His body was muscular and trim. The locker room was empty now except for clubhouse man Pete Sheehy, and Jackson looked back before he left for the night and aimlessly said, "I don't know if I really belong here."

Reggie Jackson had been a Yankee for nearly four seasons. The Yankees had won two World Series in his first two seasons, slipped to fourth in 1979, and now seemed certain of another championship. They were two and a half games ahead of Baltimore, playing well and getting their fans anxious for another New York World Series. Jackson still sensed he was not as loved and admired as he wanted to be. Perhaps no player ever could be. Four hundred homers were a notable achievement. But it meant that fans had come to hundreds of games and not seen him hit a homer. To them, on any given night, he could be a disappointment. They had finally stopped booing, but they still felt cheated when they had driven long distances to see him play and he had not hit a home run.

"I guess no matter what I do," he said that night, "it will not change some people's mind about me."

There had been some significant changes in attitude about him inside the clubhouse. Jackson could finally feel as much a part of the Yankees as any player. The cliques were gone.

"When Billy was here, the ego clash was so heavy it carried over to all of us," says shortstop Bucky Dent. "I hated that tension. I think everybody did. Reggie always played hard, but he knew everybody was looking at him. Now we look at him only when he does something significant in the game. He can have a bad night like anybody else, and it won't be a life-or-death matter. I think he created a lot of problems for himself, but I like the guy. He helps us win; he helps make money for me. He is a proud and confident man. I admire that in him."

In 1976 left-handed pitcher Rudy May had played with Jackson in Baltimore, and in 1980, after signing a free agent contract, he was reunited with him in New York. May is a black man married to an attractive blonde woman. He has undergone psychiatric therapy and is now one of the most self-contained baseball players around.

"I had some tough times," says May, "but I learned what was really important, love and family and home, not strikeouts, not well-pitched games. Baseball is my profession; it isn't my entire life."

May says that he spent many evenings with Jackson in Baltimore, many more in New York with him in 1980, discussing values and philosophy and life.

"Reggie is an extremely sensitive guy, easily hurt, one of the most sincere guys I ever met," May says. "I think the public doesn't know him. I think he doesn't allow them to know him. He likes to put on this hard exterior, this combative, ego-oriented personality. I don't think that's his true self. I think Reggie's true self is soft, a little afraid sometimes, sensitive of being hurt, like all the rest of us."

A former teammate of Reggie's at Oakland, Mike Hegan, now a Milwaukee broadcaster, once said of him, "He is the most complex man I ever met. Is there anybody who really knows him? Does he really know himself?"

As his mercurial personality took its twists and turns, one thing seemed to remain constant: Reggie Jackson was one of the best hitters in the game. He was also improving at the age of thirty-four.

"I think he is a much better hitter today than he was when I was here in 1978," says Dick Howser. "He is smarter, more difficult to fool. His bat control is excellent. He knows when to go for a home run and he knows when to go for a single."

Late in the 1980 season he also seemed to demonstrate a poise, a restraint, a touch of class that he had not exhibited in his three earlier Yankee seasons.

In September the Yankees moved ahead of Baltimore by five games and then saw their lead slip away. Jackson had his first slump at the worst time. Baltimore was driving and the Yankees were slipping as the season drained away.

Yankee owner George Steinbrenner, frightened that his club would not survive the race with the Orioles, told reporters he was disappointed in the play of Reggie Jackson.

"Reggie isn't doing the job," Steinbrenner said after Jackson was hitless against Baltimore as the lead shrank to half a game. "I don't know what's wrong with him."

What was wrong with him was that his body was weary from carrying the burden of the Yankee offense for five months. He finally had a slump, a universal baseball disease which had befallen Babe Ruth, Ty Cobb, Ted Williams, Stan Musial, and once in a while Reggie Jackson.

Jackson had always before reacted to Steinbrenner's tirades with sarcasm. He had answered his boss back in the press when George had attacked him in the press. Steinbrenner never considered it important to praise Reggie, only to bury him when he was struggling. Steinbrenner's motivation had always been a desire to win. He cared little for the sensitivities or human reactions of his players. He drove himself, and he drove all those around him.

"Let George say what he wants," Jackson said. "I'm not going to get into a dispute with him. I'm trying to win. I'm trying the best I know how. If we don't win, we don't win."

Jackson had cornered his boss. Reggie wouldn't take the bait anymore. Quiet determination, a touch of class had replaced confrontation management. At thirty-four, with his 400 home runs and a chance, finally, to hit .300, Jackson concentrated on the chore at hand.

It all ended happily for Reggie Jackson and the Yankees on Saturday, October 4, 1980. The Yankees beat the Detroit Tigers, 5–2, to clinch the Eastern Division title. Earl Weaver had tried to agitate the Yankees by suggesting they would choke as their lead dwindled and needled George by saying, "George is the guy with the boats. One of them is the *Titanic.*" The Yankees did not choke. They did not sink from first place in the East. On that October day Jackson hit his forty-first homer of the season, a three-run shot into the third deck at Yankee Stadium, for the runs needed for the victory. The next day he got his hit to finish at .300 for the first time in his career.

"It's been a struggle all along, and Reggie did it for us," said manager Dick Howser. "It couldn't happen to a better guy. October looks like it will be a very good month for him."

Reggie Jackson would display his wares again in baseball's most significant time. He was going into the play-offs against the Kansas City Royals in a marvelous frame of mind. He had enjoyed the season, had enjoyed playing for Dick Howser, and was thrilled by Howser's kind words. Big guy or not, he needed a pat on the back once in a while, too, a thought which had never occurred to Billy Martin.

A Life on Hold

A BASEBALL LOCKER GENERALLY PROVIDES AN AC-
curate reflection of the man who uses the locker.
There are gloves and bats and baseballs, of course,
in Reggie Jackson's locker, a few automotive magazines to
be read leisurely, a pile of letters, a Bible, and stacks of
autographed pictures. At the bottom of his locker, where
other players generally stash their pinup magazines, Jackson has a small plaque. On the plaque is a picture of Jackie
Robinson, a few words inscribed under the picture—"A
LIFE IS NOT IMPORTANT EXCEPT IN THE IMPACT IT HAS
ON OTHER LIVES"—and Robinson's signature.

After the August night when Reggie Jackson hit his four
hundredth home run, he received a phone call from
Miami, Arizona, from Jennie Campos, the former Mrs.
Reggie Jackson. She was in the final days of her summer
vacation on leave from teaching school in Japan. She had
read of Reggie's heroic homer and his unhappy experience in the streets of New York later that night.

"It was some four years since we had last talked," Jennie Campos says, "and something moved me to call him and congratulate him. I was no longer part of his life, but I still felt some warmth toward him. I wanted him to know I was happy for him and to wish him continued success."

The phone rang in Reggie's Fifth Avenue apartment, Jackson answered, and Jennie identified herself.

"Wait a minute, Jennie," he said. "I have a business call on the other line. I'll have to put you on hold."

The suspicion lingers that Reggie Jackson has put his personal life on hold, that he is anxious to finish out in a blaze of glory, that he is anxious—and certain now—to enter the Hall of Fame, that he is secure and comfortable in his on-field performance. Yet the future is vague beyond the confines of the ball parks.

"See, he's going to own a team someday," says his dad, Martínez Jackson, "and I'm going to scout for him. We've talked about that a lot. He almost bought a basketball team from Charlie Finley. He could buy a baseball team. He has the money. He has his baseball job and those outside companies, and he gets paid seven hundred fifty thousand dollars a year from ABC. I think he would really like to have a team of his own."

Jackson has done a great deal of television work. He has his own production company, likes the management end of the television industry, and feels his future might lie in some production involvement. "I want to hire and fire," he says, "like George."

Jackson has the instant identification, the intelligence, the drive, the ambition to do whatever he chooses. He has also learned to live in peace with his teammates, his employer, and his fans. Not even a play-off loss could disturb his equilibrium.

For the first October of his life Jackson was less than inspiring in three big games. He failed to hit in the first game of the championship series at Kansas City. Steinbrenner reacted as most expected he would, berating pitcher Ron Guidry and nonhitter Reggie Jackson. He suggested Reggie had better start earning his money or else. Cartoonist Paul Rigby drew a picture in the *New York Post* showing an angry Steinbrenner leaning over Reggie with a whip, imploring him to greater heights. Reggie seemed bemused by it all, saying, "I guess George wants me to read about him in the papers."

The Yankees lost the second game of the play-offs when third base coach Mike Ferraro made the correct play in sending speedy Willie Randolph toward home on Bob Watson's long ball. Randolph was out on a close play when the Royals connected on a lucky relay from Willie Wilson to George Brett to catcher Darrell Porter. Steinbrenner attacked Ferraro. Jackson laughed. "Anything to take the heat off me," he said.

After three straight play-off losses to the Yankees, the Royals finally got even by sweeping the Yankees to go into the World Series and a four-games-to-two loss against Philadelphia. The last play-off game was a thriller before 56,588 screaming fans.

Kansas City had scored first in the fifth inning off Tommy John. Then New York went ahead, 2–1, in the sixth. The big hit was Reggie Jackson's double. In the top of the seventh New York led, 2–1, with two out, two on for Kansas City, and George Brett at the plate. Brett had batted .390 after flirting with .400 for most of the last part of the season.

Rich Gossage was on the mound for New York, and Brett, who had once hit three homers in a single play-off game against the Yankees, unloaded on Gossage's ninety-eight-mile-per-hour fastball. The ball landed in the third deck, and Kansas City led, 4–2.

Now it was the eighth inning. Watson tripled to the left-center-field wall. Jackson, the man the Royals feared the most, was walked by reliever Dan Quisenberry. Oscar Gamble followed with a walk. The Yankees had loaded the bases with nobody out, were two runs back, and seemed certain to tie the game. Catcher Rick Cerone was at the plate. He caught one of Quisenberry's sinkers and drilled it toward left field. Jackson, taking a good lead as the tying run, took two more steps toward third as the ball was flying on a straight line. But Kansas City shortstop U. L. Washington was in the direct path of the baseball. He caught the ball easily, flipped to second baseman Frank White, and Jackson was out.

He stood at the base for a moment, staring out at the center-field stands, wondering if there could have been some mistake, some reprieve from this solitary hell of jogging back to the bench after being picked off. The crowd was silent. Again, there were no boos for Jackson. It was an instantaneous error. It had happened to Ruth and Cobb and all the others. The human brain simply cannot always react fast enough to avoid a line drive double play.

Jackson was jogging toward the Yankee bench now, his head down, his arms close to his side, his eyes watching the lush stadium grass disappear under his feet. He turned around without a word as he sat on the bench and watched the last out of the inning. Then he picked up his glove and ran toward right field. Three Kansas City outs in the ninth and three quick Yankee outs in the bottom of the ninth, and the 1980 season was over in New York.

Jackson made no excuses when the press collected around him. He told the truth as he saw it, as he always had.

"I wanted to get a good lead, so I could score on a hit," he said. "I probably shouldn't have been that far off. I know that now. I didn't know it then. I didn't know Cerone would hit a line drive at the shortstop."

Soon the press was gone. Jackson gathered up a few things and put them in his bag. He was satisfied with his summer even if there was not much to the play-offs for him and the Yankees. He had smashed 41 homers, crossed the 400-homer mark, knocked in 111 runs, helped his team win a division title, and batted .300 for the first time in his life. He had developed, finally, a rapport with the fans and an easy, comfortable style with his teammates. He had

worked smoothly with his manager, and he had contributed handsomely to the success of some of the
younger players on the team.

He would remain for a few days in New York, resting
up, thinking of his coming contract negotiations with
George Steinbrenner because his pact was to run out after
the 1981 season, planning his winter business tours to Hawaii to do *Superstars* for ABC, to Los Angeles for more
television appearances, back to New York to make appearances for Murjani and Panasonic and Getty and Standard Brands.

"His winter schedule is a lot worse than his summer
schedule," says Ray Negron, the bright young man who
handles much of Jackson's off-field business commitments.
"The production company is growing. That might be a
full-time thing someday."

It would be impossible to forecast the future for such a
dynamic man. He could buy that baseball team, maybe
this one, the New York Yankees, from George Steinbrenner, or he could become a television management executive, or he could settle for sports broadcasting and travel
the earth in search of other Reggie Jacksons. It would be
unlikely he would find a similar human being.

"I have so many things I could do after I quit," he says.
"All I know is it will have something to do with business.
I want to make sure my financial future is secure."

He helps out his mother and his father financially, but
they are aging and need very little now.

"You know," his father said one day, "he's got all that
money, but I don't think that's so important. You know
what's important, a Reggie Jackson, Junior, that's what
important, that's what I'd like to see."

Jackson talks of playing for four or five more years,
hitting another 150 home runs or so, seeing his records
lead him to the Hall of Fame, leaving behind some sweet
memories for the thousands who were thrilled by his
magic.

"I'd like some kids," he says. "Right now I'm not interested in being married, but I'll get married when I get out of baseball. When I don't have these restrictions I have now, I'll build a family and teach them the good things of life."

There were still pennants to win and home runs to drive into distant seats and hidden mountains to climb. Jennie Campos said of him, "I hope when he gets to that mountaintop, it is what he hopes it to be."

At last, after many years of turmoil, a career filled with drama and excitement, he seems to have found peace. Undoubtedly there will still be more heroic moments, new controversies, endless attention paid to this complex man.

But in the end, when the bat finally slows and the timing goes and the reflexes can no longer challenge those young fastball pitchers, there will be the memories—of balls racing off that dark bat, baseballs crashing into distant seats, home runs hit to win so many games. And the picture of the man will remain—the bat at his feet, his hands at his side, his eyes on the outfield fence, the large man with the huge 44 on his back jogging all the way home. It will be October.